WHAT'S THAT SMELL?

Norden & Tuscher f.

Profil de la tête co[

Frederic Louis Norden's depiction of the Great Sphinx of Giza from *Voyage d'Égypte et de Nubie* (1755).

le du Sphinx.

SHORT CIRCUITS
Mladen Dolar, Alenka Zupančič, and Slavoj Žižek, editors

WHAT'S THAT SMELL?

A PHILOSOPHY OF THE OLFACTORY

Simon Hajdini

THE MIT PRESS   CAMBRIDGE, MASSACHUSETTS   LONDON, ENGLAND

The MIT Press would like to thank the anonymous peer reviewers who provided comments on drafts of this book. The generous work of academic experts is essential for establishing the authority and quality of our publications. We acknowledge with gratitude the contributions of these otherwise uncredited readers.

This book was set in Copperplate Gothic Std and Joanna MT Pro by New Best-set Typesetters Ltd. Printed and bound in the United States of America.

Library of Congress Cataloging-in-Publication Data is available.

ISBN: 978-0-262-54756-7

10   9   8   7   6   5   4   3   2   1

For Lidija, for sure

They haven't got no noses,
The fallen sons of Eve;
Even the smell of roses
Is not what they supposes;
But more than mind discloses
And more than men believe.

. . .

And Quoodle here discloses
All things that Quoodle can,
They haven't got no noses,
They haven't got no noses,
And goodness only knowses
The Noselessness of Man.
—G. K. Chesterton, "The Song of Quoodle"

CONTENTS

A short circuit occurs when there is a faulty connection in the network—faulty, of course, from the standpoint of the network's smooth functioning. Is not the shock of short-circuiting, therefore, one of the best metaphors for a critical reading? Is not one of the most effective critical procedures to cross wires that do not usually touch: to take a major classic (text, author, notion) and read it in a short-circuiting way, through the lens of a "minor" author, text, or conceptual apparatus ("minor" should be understood here in Deleuze's sense: not "of lesser quality," but marginalized, disavowed by the hegemonic ideology, or dealing with a "lower," less dignified topic)? If the minor reference is well chosen, such a procedure can lead to insights that completely shatter and undermine our common perceptions. This is what Marx, among others, did with philosophy and religion (short-circuiting philosophical speculation through the lens of political economy, that is to say, economic speculation); this is what Freud and Nietzsche did with morality (short-circuiting the highest ethical notions through the lens of the unconscious libidinal economy). What such a reading achieves is not a simple "desublimation," a reduction of the higher intellectual content to its lower economic or libidinal cause; the aim of such an approach is, rather, the inherent decentering of the interpreted text, which brings to light its "unthought," its disavowed presuppositions and consequences.

And this is what "Short Circuits" wants to do, again and again. The underlying premise of the series is that Lacanian psychoanalysis is a privileged instrument of such an approach, whose purpose is to illuminate a standard text or ideological formation, making it readable in a totally new way—the long history of Lacanian interventions in philosophy, religion, the arts (from the visual arts to the cinema, music, and literature), ideology, and politics justifies this premise. This, then, is not a new series of books on psychoanalysis, but a series of "connections in the Freudian field"—of short Lacanian interventions in art, philosophy, theology, and ideology.

"Short Circuits" intends to revive a practice of reading that confronts a classic text, author, or notion with its own hidden presuppositions, and thus reveals its disavowed truth. The basic criterion for the texts that will be published is that they effectuate such a theoretical short circuit. After reading a book in this series, the reader should not simply have learned something new: the point is, rather, to make him or her aware of another—disturbing—side of something he or she knew all the time.

Slavoj Žižek

NAMES AT THE TIP OF THE NOSE

What's in a name? That which we call a rose By any other word would smell as sweet.
—Shakespeare, *Romeo and Juliet*

A SIGNIFYING STRESS

It is no coincidence that Juliet expands on her initial question by relating names to the anomic realm of smells. In Indo-European languages at least, smells notoriously lack proper names, in turn acquiring roundabout names such as "smell of rose."[1] Smells keep the tongue on its toes. To name them is to relate them to their sources, to the names of objects that emit them, rather than naming the objects, or qualities, that they themselves are. There appears to be an unavoidable, compulsory choice between smelling and spelling: smells cast spells on us, rendering us essentially speechless. The essential being of smells eludes signification such that we can only ever speak of them without spelling them out. To name them is to speak of them as if they were unwanted guests at our dinner table whom we could only address in the third person, slandering them in their presence. Metonymically named, smells strike us as essentially euphemistic. But unlike euphemisms proper that—in providing indirect expressions substituted for those considered too disagreeable—make up the vast and ever-shifting sociocultural lexicon of embarrassment, smells are reflexively euphemistic and therefore indicative of the embarrassment of language itself. In her adage, Juliet moves, in a single speculative stroke, from a name to a smell—that is, from *naming to a void of naming*.[2]

Two typical instances of this metonymicity of smell, singular among the physical senses, are found in Juliet's passage. First, there's "a rose," "the smell of rose," uttering a smell's missing proper name as its descriptive source-name. Here, the smell-name is voiced with a reference to an object ("a rose") with which the particular subjective sensation of smell (the unnamable "X") is correlated. And second, there's "sweetness," "the sweet smell," where the unnamed "X" is named not in relation to its source, or objective correlate, but by being step-named, that is, by borrowing its name from the register of taste as the other of the two chemical senses. In the absence of first names, smells only have second names. However, they only acquire these *nomina impropria* either as *orphans*, structurally abandoned by their linguistic parents who are always already dead and unknowable, or as sensuous *bastards*, as illegitimate children of a foreign household of sense. Every scent is the second scent. But contrary to Simone de Beauvoir's notion of "the second sex" as the Other in relation to the first sex, there is no first scent, no default expression that could be related to or substituted for another. Altogether lacking their proper place in the Other as the locus of speech, smells are always called "by any word other" than their own. Rendering us essentially speechless, *smells induce a signifying stress* as the flipside of the impossibility of their linguistic containment.[3]

When step-named, smells typically borrow their names from the vocabulary of gustatory perception. However, one also speaks of smell "faces" and scent "palettes," relating smells to visual perception; of smells as "compositions" containing "notes" and "sub-tones," relating them to the sense of hearing; and one even relates smells to the sense of touch by calling them "pungent." Such synesthetic borrowing, as well as source-naming, are common among the senses ("sweet voice," "sharp taste," "warm color," among others), however, with smells such source- and step-naming take place in the absence of *nomina propria* that would be distinctive of them.[4] Imagine a case of color anomia in which, when referring to the color "white," the subject would be obliged to use a source-name and say, for instance, "(the appearance of) snow," or a step-name such as "(it looks) cold." That is precisely what we do with smells each and every time we name them.[5]

For sake of clarity and to avoid a possible misunderstanding, let's add that all sense perceptions can be spoken of—using either the verb or the noun—objectively (with reference to the object) and subjectively (with reference to the perceiving subject). But in the case of all other sense perceptions, with the singular exception of smell, we possess the names for qualities referred either to the object perceived or to the perceiving subject. In English, such qualities include *sight* ("shine," "bright," "color," "light," "dark"), *taste* ("sweet," "sour," "salty," "bitter," "acid"), and *touch* ("hard," "soft," "rough," "smooth," "wet," "dry," "hot"). *Hearing* comes closest to smell in the sense of its nearly exclusive borrowing of names for its perceptual qualities from other senses ("sharp noise," "soft voice"); however, with hearing there is at least one adjective that is a deafening exception to this rule: "loud."[6]

What's in a smell? Pausing to consider synesthetic borrowing, Aristotle mentions the lack of generic names for smells while adding that "because smells are much less easy to discriminate than flavours, the names of these varieties are applied to smells in virtue of similarity."[7] But such an application of step-names to smells "in virtue of similarity" is underpinned, and necessitated, by a blatant "similarity disorder," to deploy Roman Jakobson's famous term.[8] Smells stand for lexical voids and represent the singular site of a universal linguistic disturbance, a *universal olfactory anomia*. We are capable, for the most part, of naming smells in a roundabout, metonymical way, typically relating them to the names of their sources, but are materially barred from directly metaphorically grasping them: the signifying function of, say, "smell of" . . . "rose" is congruent with the elision of meaning. To paraphrase the Duchess's famous line from *Alice's Adventures in Wonderland*: If only we could take care of the sense, the scents would take care of themselves. With reference to Jakobson's analysis of the twofold character of language, Jacques Lacan's formula of metonymy emphasizes this resistance to signification, where the signifying function (f S) of the linking of the signifier to the signifier (S . . . S′) is congruent with ($\cong$) the maintenance of the bar (−) that separates the signifier from the signified so that no new meaning (s) can be produced: f (S . . . S′) S $\cong$ S (−) s.[9] The sense of smell, however, does not merely exemplify this resistance to signification, but rather embodies the signifying stress, thus figuring as the topograph of the unconscious.

Jakobson illustrates the similarity disorder as it effects the elision of meaning, and as relating to the impossibility of metaphorical selection or substitution, with the following prototypically Beckettian utterance of an aphasic patient: "But I am here below, well if I have been I know not, who that, now if I, if that now but, still, yes. What you here, if I, oh I know not, who that here was yes." "Thus only the framework," Jakobson comments, "the connecting links of communication, is spared by this type of aphasia at its critical stage."[10] In another example cited from Fritz Lotmar, upon being shown the picture of a "compass," the patient experiences the tip-of-the-tongue phenomenon. When asked to name the pictorial sign of the "compass," he replies: "Yes, it's a . . . I know what it belongs to, but I cannot recall the technical expression . . . Yes . . . direction . . . to show direction . . . a magnet points to the north."[11]

The prime example of this uncanny proximity between the similarity disorder, as conceived of by Jakobson, and universal olfactory anomia, as proposed here, is provided by the famous case of H.M. In 1953, in an attempt at surgically alleviating his severe epileptic seizures, Henry Molaison, sometimes considered neuropsychology's most famous patient, underwent a bilateral temporal lobe resection that resulted in anterograde amnesia, that is, a nearly complete loss of the capacity to form new memories.[12] In 1983, a study of H.M.'s olfactory capacities yielded salient results.[13] H.M. exhibited an olfactory impairment that related neither to detection nor to adaptation and intensity discrimination, but rather exclusively to recognizing and naming the qualities of his olfactory perceptions.[14] A brief glance at the results of testing

H.M.'s ability to name common odorants reveals that, in attempting to name them, he is displaying standard symptoms of similarity disorder. Much like Lotmar's patient who, unable to identify the presented object as "compass," names the object metonymically by using descriptors such as "direction" and "a magnet points to the north," instead of qualifying the presented odorant as "cloves," "mint," "raspberry," or "rose," H.M. would qualify them as "dead fish, washed ashore," "an acid," "carrion, a squirrel," and "bad water," respectively. Does that which we call "rose" by the words "bad water" smell as sweet?

NAMING OF COMMON ODORANTS BY H.M.[15]

Odour	Test 1	Test 2
Coconut	"Soap"	"Flowers"
Mint	"Flowers"	"An acid"
Almond	"A wild flower"	"An acid"
Lemon	"Flowers"	"An acid"
Vanilla	"Weak roses"	"Newly made paper"
Orange	"An acid"	"Weak perfume"
Cloves	"Fresh woodwork"	"Dead fish, washed ashore"
Raspberry	"Flowers"	"Carrion, a squirrel"
Rose	"A rose flower"	"Bad water"
Water	"I can't smell anything"	"I can't smell anything"

To be clear: what is at issue here is not H.M.'s anomia, but our own. The point is not merely that H.M. exhibits a similarity disorder that results from brain damage that he suffered. The point is rather that our own normal ability of naming smells already qualifies as a universal similarity disorder. This becomes clear the moment we cease focusing on columns 2 and 3 (*Tests 1 and 2*), instead looking at the "veridical labels" indicated in column 1 (*Odour*) and listing the generic names of odorant objects that H.M. is unable to retrieve and convey. These labels testify to the fact that when it comes to naming odors all of us are aphasics, unable to name the qualities of smells, instead having to rely on stand-ins in the form of names of the odors' most representative referents ("coconut," "mint"). Paradoxically, all generic names for smells are nongeneric and hence specific; moreover, they are specific to something other than smells.

This universal olfactory anomia is further redoubled by a partial olfactory agnosia that, in effecting an inability of source-naming familiar smells, further mirrors H.M.'s condition. As it turns out, the antinomy of names and smells, seemingly resolved by source-naming ("smell of rose"), step-naming ("sweet smell"), or a combination of the two ("sweet smell of rose"), in fact stubbornly persists as a pronounced and striking human inability of odor identification. Experiments suggest that although

> humans detect odors quite well and can discriminate between hundreds of odors, their ability to identify an odor is extremely limited. In an unaided identification task, a person with a normal sense of smell is seldom able to identify familiar odors in >50% of the cases. . . . One recognizes an odor as familiar and belonging to a general category, but is unable to recall its specific name. When given the name of the odor, it is recognized immediately and one is puzzled why one could not retrieve it before.[16]

Even with source-names and step-names readily available and at hand, half the time we are still unable to retrieve and relate them to everyday olfactory impressions. Our immediate physical ability to detect and interpret olfactory sensations is unimpaired—we are anomic, not anosmic. We can detect smells, that is, their presence or absence; distinguish between their intensities, that is, discriminate, in Kantian terms, between "stronger" or "weaker" realities of smells as they affect our sense; and recognize them instantly as familiar qualities. We are, however, curiously unable to recognize and name the objects that emit them and that provide them with their common names.

But unlike normosmic subjects, who—once the odor name was given to them—could recognize it immediately, H.M.'s "performance was not improved when odour names were given. . . . Once, having correctly identified a lemon by sight, he sniffed it and remarked, 'Funny, it doesn't smell like a lemon!'"[17] H.M.'s remark could be read along the lines of the famous Marx Brothers joke: "You're Emanuel Ravelli?—I am Emanuel Ravelli.—Well, no wonder you look like him." H.M. seems to be saying: "This is a lemon?—This is a lemon.—Well, no wonder it doesn't smell like one!" Consider in this regard the following example of an aphasic patient with a similarity disorder who, when asked to simply repeat back a word, cannot bring himself to do it: "Told to repeat the word *no*, Head's patient replied 'No, I don't know how to do it.' . . . he could not produce the purest form of equational predication, the tautology $a = a$: /no/ is /no/."[18]

FUNNY, IT DOESN'T SMELL LIKE A LEMON!

A chimeric encounter: a lemon that doesn't smell like a lemon; a word that can't be substituted for itself. Here is the rose, so here we must dance.[19] Incapable of calling odors presented to him by their correct names, H.M. is also unable to distinguish between them, their differences steadily collapsing into indifference: coconut and mint, lemon and raspberry are all equated with "flower"; mint, almond, lemon, and orange all smell like "an acid." But while he erratically discovers precarious identities where there are only differences, he also discerns difference where there is only identity: vanilla, for instance, is made to differ from itself by equaling both "weak roses" and "newly made paper." In none of the individual cases are the two smell-names H.M. provides in linguistic agreement, nor are they in agreement with the smells' veridical labels or their generic names.[20] Each time H.M. catches a whiff of something, this something is subjected to incessant "self-othering," *Sichanderswerden*, to use Hegel's term.[21] If he is unable to identify identical odors as the same, and different odors as different, it is precisely because a smell is never identical with itself. The defect in substitution, characteristic of the similarity disorder generally and of the universal olfactory anomia specifically, does not merely affect the subject's ability to substitute one name for another, but encompasses substitution at its purest, that is, the substitution of a name for itself.

The impossibility of directly naming olfactory impressions as sensuous qualities of objects extends beyond their perceptual emergence in the relation between a perceiving subject and the object of their perception to encompass an inability to name these objects themselves. When no assistance is required in conjuring up a source-name with which to identify a given smell, the "veridical label" or "correct odor name" given and related to an olfactory impression still remains intrinsically unstable and precarious. *Orthos logos*, the correct or proper name, can only improperly capture the smell. Hence, we should pause here to reflect on the term "veridical label" itself. The latter defines a "correct" smell-name as the one considered to coincide with the reality of its respective odorant. The veridical labels are hence taken to correspond to the reality of the odorant object they name. Such correspondence lies at the core of the traditional philosophical notion of truth as *adequatio* or correspondence between knowledge and being, intellect and thing, or proposition and reality. Therefore, the problem of naming is not just any philosophical problem, but rather one that is central to classical ontology, with the latter depending on the notion of names (*onomata*) as latching onto things (*pragmata*) in their essential being.

Since the beginnings of Western philosophy, the problems of truth and naming were considered principally interdependent. And Plato—in his *Cratylus*, explicitly concerned with "correctness of names"—was in fact the first to systematically broach the issue of "veridical labels." Since the concept of truth as *adequatio* ultimately hinges on the relation of reflexive identity ($A = A$), the correct name is not simply the one that succeeds in latching onto the thing, but the one that succeeds in adequately (truthfully) designating the object in its identity-with-itself, thus revealing its *nominata*'s essential being. Ultimately, it is such use of names that distinguishes philosophical discourse from that of the sophist, who at best is concerned with "correct diction," *orthoepeia*, disregarding the correctness of names, *orthotes onomaton*. As we have seen, H.M.'s anomia, taken here as revealing of the very essence of smells, subverts the relation of equality by undermining its reflexivity, that is, it subverts the principle that things "are by themselves, in relation to their own being or essence, which is theirs by nature."[22] According to Plato, (correct) names are imitations of things in their essential being, their truthful copies; however, the moment the copies lose their grip on their models or things, things themselves seem to run amok, losing their essential being.

Names are seen as latching onto self-identical objects. By Plato's lights, they do so in a way that is itself revealing of the self-identical essence. Used correctly, signifiers are taken to be meaningful in themselves; they inhabit the true sense of what they express. They are in possession of meaning, or—better still—are entirely possessed by it. This true sense can be revealed by etymological examination, itself etymologically revealing of its own essence as *logía*, "study of," *étumon*, "true sense." The etymological section of the *Cratylus* makes out the bulk of the dialogue and is perhaps the lengthiest digression in the history of philosophy. To pick only one example out of the myriad etymologies proposed by Plato, that of *anthrōpoi*, "humans":

> The name "human" signifies that the other animals do not investigate or reason about anything they see, nor do they observe anything closely. But a human being, no sooner sees something—that is to say, "*opōpe*"—than he observes it closely and reasons about it. Hence human beings alone among the animals are correctly named "*anthrōpos*"—one who observes closely what he has seen (*anathrōn ha opōpe*). (Crat. 399c)

The true sense of "human" is revelatory of a capacity essential to humans, which makes "human" a correct name. Not to dwell on the dubiousness of Plato's etymological endeavors, it is nevertheless important to note that these attempts are entirely oriented by meaning that—with great virtuosity and substantial efforts—is made to fit the names, bringing metonymic deferral to a standstill. Plato's etymologies are an exorcism in reverse; their function is to charge signifiers with meaning so as to reveal how meaning always already takes charge of them. If one makes the effort to "observe closely what one has seen," the name will reveal itself as what it is: an anagram of the thing. Accordingly, every correct name is in fact a source-name and all names are eponymous, that is, named after the essential being of the things they name.[23]

Words have a hard time latching onto smells in their essential being. In the smellscape, nothing smells like itself because nothing is itself. It is no surprise that Cratylus of Athens, Plato's teacher, should have felicitously captured the self-othering dissolution of reflexive identity by reproaching his own teacher, Heraclitus, "for saying that it is impossible to step twice into the same river; for he [Cratylus] thought one could not do it even once" (Met. 1010a10). H.M.'s olfactory anomia recaps Cratylus's hypercritique of Heraclitus. For H.M., it is not only impossible to catch a whiff of the same smell twice, the later having already been transformed in the process; he cannot do it even once. Hence, the partial olfactory agnosia, as considered here, is not a cognitive disorder that would result from brain damage, but rather stands for the "brain damage" of cognition itself, that is, for the inherent deadlock of the cognitive process. And while anomia typically stands for a form of aphasic disturbance that is considered a pathological deviation from the subject's normal ability to use language, universal olfactory anomia points not to a pathological deviation from the norm but rather to an intrinsic pathology of the norm itself: as inherently deodorized, language is permeated with lexical voids. These lexical voids are not mere, and merely abstract, structural absences. Rather, they are coextensive with the emergence of the subject as the name for the deadlock of naming. I will return to this.

THE MOST EXTREME OF THE VIEWS

If sensible nature in all its parts is caught in incessant flux, continually moving and changing, such that no true statement can be uttered about it, we may be inclined to give up on language altogether and resort to merely moving our finger. "It was this belief," Aristotle reports, "that blossomed into the most extreme of the views . . . of the professed Heracliteans, such as was held by Cratylus, who finally did not think it right to say anything but only moved his finger" (Met. 1010a10). Since following Cratylus's example would be a self-defeating and contradictory endeavor (for how could one sample a river, in which it is impossible to step even once?), let us ask instead: is pointing a finger the same as moving it? Does indication necessarily entail motion? A lot is at stake in how we choose to answer this question. For by amending Heraclitus's thesis, Søren Kierkegaard believed, Cratylus played right into the opponent's hand, assisting in the Eleatic denial of motion. If going back can sometimes take us further, going further can sometimes set us back:

> "One must go further, one must go further." This urge to go further is an old story in the world. . . . Heraclitus the obscure said: One cannot walk through the same river twice. Heraclitus the obscure had a disciple who did not remain standing there but went further—and added: One cannot do it even once. Poor Heraclitus, to have a disciple like that! By this improvement, the Heraclitean thesis was amended into an Eleatic thesis that denies motion, and yet that disciple wished only to be a disciple of Heraclitus who went further, not back to what Heraclitus had abandoned.[24]

In *Seminar II* (1954–1955), Lacan makes the same point about Hegel, no doubt tacitly referencing this passage from Kierkegaard: "As I have often pointed out, I don't much like hearing that we have *gone beyond* Hegel. . . . We go beyond everything and always end up in the same place."[25] Attempting to move beyond something, we end up compulsively repeating it. Yet we end up compulsively repeating it in the strict Kierkegaardian sense of the term (adopted by Lacan) of failing to reproduce it in its identity. For Kierkegaard, repetition is impossible, yet when repeating, it is this impossibility of repeating that we repeat, in turn overturning the self-identical nature of what is being repeated. For Kierkegaard, repetition is central to modern philosophy, yet at the same time something we are yet to discover by going back to the dispute between the Eleatics and Heraclitus: "Repetition is the new category that must be discovered. If one knows something about modern philosophy, and is conversant with Greek philosophy, one will easily see that precisely this category explains the relation between the Eleatics and Heraclitus."[26] Contrary to Kierkegaard's reading, Cratylus's radicalization of Heraclitus's dictum effectively articulates the very gist of Kierkegaardian repetition: saying that it is impossible to step in the same river even once, implies that the river we step into did not simply cease to be what it was, but rather wasn't what it was to begin with (and never is what it is). From this point of view, the moving of the finger can very well come to Cratylus's rescue, and perhaps he resorted to it to avoid the consequence mentioned by Kierkegaard. Couldn't the moving of the finger be read as a flipping of the finger to the Eleatic opponents in a gesture anticipating Galileo's *Eppur si muove*, "And yet it moves"? And doesn't Cratylus's thesis, rather than adhering to the Eleatic conception of a universal Unity of Being, spell out its critique? Saying that it is impossible to step in the same river even once neither implies that everything is sheer multiplicity, forever in flux, nor does it suggest that "All is One" (*hen kai pan*). Rather, it asserts a splitting of the One, the impossibility of the One to be one with itself, thus affirming its inherent opposition to itself without reducing it to a pure multiple.[27]

What is the point of Cratylus's pointing? Is the abandoning of signs for gestures a surrender of *logos*? And is gesturing the same as abandoning language? Is the pointing, as Louis Althusser would have had it, an index of "the primacy of the gesture over the word, of the material trace over the sign"?[28] Is it an iconic index that would testify to "the hegemony exerted by perceptual and sensorimotor experience over verbal utterances," as Paolo Virno would perhaps claim?[29] Does smell's troubled relationship with language ultimately bring us closer to singular essences of all things, to the immediacy of extralinguistic experience?

Certain ethnologists have made a striking observation: that in the most primitive of observable societies, those of the Australian Aborigines or African Pygmies, nominalist philosophy seems to hold sway in person— not only at the level of thought, that is, of language, but also in practice, in reality. Conclusive recent studies have shown that, for these societies, there exist only singular entities, and each singularity, each particularity, is designated by a word that is equally singular. Thus the world consists exclusively of singular, unique objects, each with its own specific name and singular properties. "Here and now," which, ultimately, cannot be named, but only pointed to, because words themselves are abstractions—we would have to be able to speak without words, that is, to show. This indicates the primacy of the gesture over the word, of the material trace over the sign.[30]

Is the gesture of pointing intended to point out the essential thread of linguistic naturalism that Cratylus, in Plato's eponymous dialogue, so sedulously defends against Hermogenes's conventionalism? Is Cratylus's index finger a *natural sign*? In this reading, Cratylus would not abandon language at all but rather reduce it to what in his view accounts for its bare essentials, that is, to indication as a gesture of originary designation.[31] This has important, and paradoxical, implications. Contrary to Althusser's interpretation of indices, the indexical bypassing of the name does not lead to a primordial fusion with the prelinguistic natural essence of all things, but rather effects the opposite: by merging the name with its object, *it naturalizes the name*.

We must practice caution so as not to risk succumbing to conceptual vulgarities. Such a reading is supported both by Plato's accounts of Cratylus's linguistic naturalism and by twentieth-century theories of indexicality that go back to Charles Sanders Peirce. The first thing to note is that the two types of indices mentioned by Althusser—gestures and traces—entail important differences. A gesture, say the gesture of pointing a finger, only "exists" in the "here and now," that is, in the temporally unlocalizable interval in between two successive moments. As such, the gesture touches ground without leaving a trace, its appearance is an appearance in disappearance. It "exists" without existing, since for anything to exist it must first persist or endure for an interval of time, however brief. Mary Ann Doane best captures this duality:

> The index as Peirce describes it has what often appear to be two contradictory, or at least incompatible, definitions. First, when the index is exemplified by the footprint or the photograph, it is a sign that can be described as a trace or imprint of its object. Something of the object leaves a legible residue through the medium of touch. The index as trace implies a material connection between sign and object as well as an insistent temporality—the reproducibility of a past moment. The trace does not evaporate in the moment of its production, but remains as the witness of an anteriority. Hence, this understanding of the index necessarily aligns it with historicity, the "that has been" of Barthes's photographic image. The second definition of the index, on the other hand, often seems to harbor a resistance to the first. The index as deixis—the pointing finger, the "this" of language—does exhaust itself in the moment of its implementation and is ineluctably linked to presence. There is always a gap between sign and object, and touch here is only figurative. Of these two dimensions of the index emphasized by Peirce, the latter is frequently forgotten in the drive to ground the photochemical image as trace.[32]

Unlike the gesture, the trace persists and endures as an imprint of the indexical touching of the ground of reality. However, it only persists as anterior, as an imprint of a past existence, of something persistently past, as a hollowed-out monument to a "(once) here and now (gone)." Unlike a gesture that has a grip on the object in the "here and now," a footprint is not a foothold. As material indices of material existence, which can be reconstructed following causality as the basic law of natural change, traces are footloose, indicative of objects on the loose. However, is it not once again obvious that this material existence ultimately "exists" without existing, and that it is no less of an abstraction than words? To slightly, though importantly, alter Doane's point, it is not "something of the object," but rather nothing (itself) of the object that "leaves a legible residue through the medium of touch."

My critical reading of indexicality proceeds against the backdrop of Peirce's famous positing of an existential relationship between indices and objects: "The index is physically connected to its object; they make an organic pair."[33] Despite the precariousness of their pairing, there exists an organic link between gestures and their objects that makes them inseparable (in the "here and now"). Because of this organic relation, or due to their association by contiguity, indices are the true chimeras of language: natural signs. However, Lacan emphasizes a key difference between the two classes of natural signs. The trace does not seem to adhere to the same organic association by contiguity: "in its negative aspect, [the trace] draws the natural sign to a limit at which it becomes evanescent."[34] In the case of the trace, the organic pairing of the pointing finger and its material reference point is impaired by the unpairing of the foot and its footprint. A footprint is indicative of a foot no longer "here and now": "the trace is precisely what the object leaves behind once it has gone off somewhere else."[35] But "something" is nevertheless found by being left behind, namely the sign as signifying an absence of a sign. How is the foot present in the footprint, if not by way of its absence, that is, as nothing? There is no sign of the foot in the footprint, yet the footprint is the sign of the absence of the foot.

Traces cannot escape the negativity of language and hence fail to capture the immediacy of the "here and now." In the *Phenomenology of Spirit*, Hegel famously addresses the issue of indexicality, highlighting the impasses encountered by the natural consciousness in attempting to reach for what is immediately given. Hegel demonstrates the illusory nature of natural signs, of their supposed capacity for an organic unity of subject and object. Importantly, he shows that, like traces, gestures too are not immune to the germ of linguistic abstraction:

The Here pointed out, to which I hold fast, is similarly a this Here which, in fact, is not this Here, but a Before and Behind, an Above and Below, a Right and

Left. The Above is itself similarly this manifold otherness of above, below, etc. The Here, which was supposed to have been pointed out, vanishes in other Heres, but these likewise vanish. What is pointed out, held fast, and abides, is a *negative* This, which is negative only when the Heres are taken as they should be, but, in being so taken, they supersede themselves; what abides is a simple complex of many Heres. The Here that is *meant* would be the point; but it is not: on the contrary, when it is pointed out as something that is, the pointing-out shows itself to be not an immediate knowing [of the point], but a movement from the Here that is *meant* through many Heres into the universal Here which is a simple plurality of Heres, just as the day is a simple plurality of Nows.[36]

The indexical "speaking without words," as Althusser calls it, always already carries with it the germ of linguistic abstraction. Paradoxically, that which "cannot be named" can only be named. The pointing points out the pointlessness of the notion of speaking without words. An index, be it a gesture or a trace, does not preexist in a space unoccupied by our clumsy linguistic devices. Strictly speaking, it is language that *unoccupies* the space subsequently squatted by gestures and traces whose existence relies entirely upon the voids of language (in the possessive sense of the term). Althusser's positing of the opposition between indices and signs therefore remains untenable. There is no such thing as a natural sign: the indices's emergence is correlative with the loss of their objects. Furthermore, and to add insult to injury, not only are indices signs, but they are also representational signs par excellence. A pointed finger is an accusation, and hence a representational sign of (the idea of) "blame." Smoke rising in the distance or a footprint on a country path are representational signs of (the idea of) "fire" or of (the idea of) "a foot." Far from testifying to a "primacy" of indexicality over signs, gestures and traces seem to be entirely absorbed by them. In attempting to move beyond the abstractions of language in this way, we appear to be left with the crudest and sketchiest of materialisms.

HERE IS THE ROSE, DANCE HERE

We can hardly dispute the basic indexicality of smells. Smells are essentially smell-traces of objects wasting away. Paraphrasing Lacan, we could say that the smell-trace draws the natural sign to a limit at which it becomes evanescent. Due to their troubled relationship with language, smells seem exemplary of the ability to "speak without words" and hence revealing of "the primacy of the gesture over the word, of the material trace over the sign." However, it is precisely as indices that smells hand down the most persuasive indictment against extra-linguistic materialism.[37]

In addressing this claim, let us take another look at Plato's *Cratylus*. A good portion of the dialogue revolves around the question of the name-giver, an expert dialectician assigning names to things. As maker of veridical labels (*veridicus* deriving from *verus*, "true," and *dicere*, "say"), the name-giver figures as the guarantor of the truthfulness of speech, or, to use Lacan's term, the subject supposed to know (the correct names). In olfactory identification tests, veridical labels rely on just such a supposition; they amount to replies expected by the examiner, with the latter standing in for the dialectician, determining the correctness of names provided by the examinees. Here, two interrelated meanings of Lacan's phrase *sujet supposé savoir* come to the fore. For the examinee, the examiner is the subject supposed to know. The examinee supposes that the examiner knows, that is, that they have knowledge of them as subjects. But there is an interesting flip side to this relation. For the examinee, the examiner is the subject supposed to know (the correct names), while for the examiner, the examinee is the supposed subject of knowledge. The examiner, in possession of veridical labels, supposes there exist subjects of knowledge, such that the examiner finds their supposed knowledge affirmed only when knowledge finds its subject in the examinee. From the examiner's point of view, the correct names, or veridical labels, are not a matter of mere convention. If anything, the convention is a mere by-product of the subject's capacity to recognize and spell out the existential relation between the (smell-)trace and its (source-)object characteristic of natural signs.

Unlike other sensuous qualities, however, smells not only lack proper names that would be reflective of their essential being, in turn forcing us to rely on metonymical stand-ins; these stand-ins themselves are adopted haphazardly, lacking consensus, and verging on idiolects.[38] By making this point, we are, for the time being, bidding farewell to the register of adequation as guarantor and measure of objectivity, instead focusing on the register of intersubjectivity as the basis of experimental, scientific truth.[39] But here, too, smell-naming poses a problem akin to the one posed for the regime of adequation. Rather than relying on the scientific consensus of an expert community of dialecticians, smell-naming appears to lack agreement and depend on the flimsy expertise of an *idiolectician*. Suffice it to recall the problems associated with the University of Pennsylvania Smell Identification Test (UPSIT), perhaps the most used commercially available tool for testing the functioning of the olfactory system. Using scratch-and-sniff strips embedded with microencapsulated odorants, the test has been criticized for its limited cross-cultural applicability. To amend these shortcomings, the so-called twelve-item cross-cultural smell identification test (CC-SIT) was developed, excluding odorants considered unfamiliar to subjects outside of the North American cultural context, while essentially attempting to free names of their cultural bias:

> In a few cases, we substituted words that may not be culture-free for the response alternatives. For example, we substituted "dog" for "skunk,"

"garlic" for "pumpkin pie," "woody" for "pine," "fruit" for "cola,"
"apple" for "dill pickle," "strawberry" for "root beer," and "chocolate"
for "licorice."[40]

Do "pumpkin pie" and "dill pickle" by the names "garlic" and "apple"
smell the same? What is at issue here is not so much the problem of cultural
translatability and universal familiarity; rather, the issue lies with the inherent instability of linguistic agreements between sign and referent, on the one
hand, and signifier and meaning, on the other, that account for the structural
ambiguity of language. In terms of our discussion, these odor-identification
tests paradoxically rely on the assumption that language can be deodorized,
that is, that names can be made to fully match the sample stimuli, establishing
a fixed, "culture-free" biunivocal relation. They presuppose that the cultural
charge, supposedly standing in the way of univocal sense, can be discharged
in a way that would free language of its ambiguities. And it is precisely such
a biunivocal agreement between sign and object that lies at the core of the
untenable concept of natural signs.

Smells flesh out the deadlocks of such a conception of signs as natural and
representational, impeaching extra-linguistic materialism in the process. So
let's return to the two ways of metonymically capturing smells. Step-naming
clearly disputes the supposed immediacy of the subject-object relation: in
step-naming, a smell's relation to its object is moved to another sensory register and hence denaturalized; it is transposed onto a foreign perceptual territory and hence deterritorialized. Smell-names lack an organic connection
to the objects: a particular smell is not deemed "sweet" due to the immediate
presence of the "sweet" object, but rather in the absence of any material or
physical "sweetness" (for nothing is tasted). As indices, smells are supposed to
immediately assure us of the existence of objects, their "thereness." Yet, to use
Hegel's formulation, the "here" that smell-names point to (say, "sweetness"),
is only here by not being here; in other words, it is here only as an abstraction. The supposed naturalness is a flimsy convention; nature is sheer mimicry.

Source-names only further solidify such a conclusion. Source-naming
spells out the essential structure of indication by highlighting smell's organic,
existential relation to the object ("smell of rose"). However, this seemingly
organic bond is immediately unbound, and the smell is abstracted from its
organic object. The affirmation of the object coincides with its negation, the
appearance of the organic contiguity with its immediate abstract dissolution—
its birth with its linguistic abortion. A smell ("rose") is tied to the concrete
("a rose") in ways that are abstract, inorganic, and unnatural. The archetypal
is the mimetic. The association by contiguity, characteristic of indices, is
essentially an interrupted contiguity, the existential relation is a non-relation.
With the naming of a smell, its object is not *presented to*, but rather *absented*

(better still: abscented) from us. Smell-names are death sentences declared in abscentia.

So much for the *naturalness* of olfactory signs. What about their *representational* character? Where does following the indexical smell-trail lead us? As representational signs, smells trigger ideas of things that are empirically misnamed and ontologically unnamable. We can express this yet another way: smells trigger memories that we cannot remember. Upon sniffing, we are left wondering what exactly it is that we remember.[41] Smells flesh out, *excarnate* memories that no re-membering can reincarnate: "To remember, to re-member, is to give back a body to one's memories."[42] We cannot avoid pausing for a moment to make two, perhaps obvious, references. Smells are known to elicit memories, and their capacity to cue recollections is sometimes referred to as "the Proust phenomenon." In Proust's *In Search of Lost Time*, we find the infamous passage, in which Marcel sips a spoonful of tea mixed with madeleine cake. The smell[43] of a few tiny crumbs is enough to trigger an outpour of vivid childhood memories, ultimately resulting in a book of more than a million words. The muteness and minuteness of a smell, "the tiny and almost impalpable drop," triggers unparalleled eloquence, like a snowflake unleashing an avalanche, a drop giving rise to a flood.[44] Not a Proust scholar, I am reluctant to dwell on this, but would nonetheless like to point out one significant detail that is of direct relevance to our discussion. Until that fatal whiff, Marcel had a hard time remembering anything of Combray, "except what lay in the theatre and the drama of my going to bed there."[45] In sharp contrast to his unmemorable existence as a creature of habit, the smell of *petites madeleines* managed to trigger the splendidly evocative orgy of meticulously detailed memories, catapulting him into the living presence of "lost time." But in this duality between memories and the unmemorable, another sharp contrast is revealed, namely the one between memories and the immemorable as that which never ceases not being remembered.

The orgy of remembrance stems from a failure to remember. Beckett was perhaps the first to have taken note of this failure so central to Proust's writing by outrageously asserting against all common sense that "Proust has a bad memory."[46] Yet empirical findings have proved Beckett right: the first versions of the novel make no mention of *petites madeleines*. Instead, they mention "honey-mixed toast," thereby indicating Proust's genuine difficulties linking the smell to its natural object.[47] Reportedly, it took him at least three drafts to nose ahead and to finally sniff out the *nomen proprium*.[48] Or did he perhaps settle on it as the best stand-in for the ultimately missing proper name? Proust's novel was triggered and haunted by the million-word question: *What's that smell?*

My second brief interjection is perhaps even more obvious: the invention of psychoanalysis hinges on names that can't be recalled. Like Marcel, Freud's hysterical patients, too, were haunted by memories they failed to remember, whereby these failures took fascinatingly troubling indexical forms. Instead of a flood of words, they took on the form of somatic symptoms or bodily inner-vations as displaced, converted expressions of psychic trauma. Like Proust, the hysterics, as Freud and Breuer first believed, "*suffer mainly from reminiscences*"[49] that cannot be retold and recalled. Unlike Proust, Freud would initially treat these symptoms with the help of suggestion, until finally adopting the so-called talking cure. Although dreams may very well be the *via regia*, or "*the royal road to a knowledge of the unconscious activities of the mind*,"[50] Freud's discovery of psychoanalytic interpretation and its ground-rule of free association had to do not with a dream but with a name Freud failed to remember, a name he misremembered and which lingered at the tip of his tongue: Signorelli.[51] This missing proper name, first appearing as an ellipsis, a falling short of Freud's memory, subsequently reappears in the guise of the metonymical stand-ins of Botticeli and Boltrafio that unfittingly inhabit its void, much like source-names and step-names inhabit the olfactory void of naming. Nevertheless, such a comparison seems to fall short: the *nomen proprium* Signorelli, briefly withdrawn and replaced by the *nomina impropria* of Botticeli and Boltrafio, is eventually recalled and remembered, whereas the proper name of a given smell is forgotten without being memorized in the first place—as if in a case of an all too successful repression, that is, a repression without a return of the repressed. This seeming shortcoming, however, results from a misunderstand-ing of psychoanalytic interpretation, during which the missing name (e.g., Signorelli) is itself revealed as a metonymical stand-in for the subject's insist-ing and forever displaced unconscious desire, that is, for the unconscious as the inner gap of reflexivity.[52] A successful psychoanalytic interpretation there-fore does not end with a proper name, the *nomen proprium*, unearthed from under the "million-word" rubble of its deceptive stand-ins that make out the talking cure, but ends with the coming to terms with the hedonic "aroma" of the enjoyment attached to it. Moreover, the *nomen proprium* is not recollected, but rather intervenes as if from the future, illuminating the subject's predica-ment and organizing the mode of the subject's enjoyment. In this sense, the psychoanalytic search for the *nomen proprium*, like Proust's search, consists not in digging up the past but in digging up the future.[53]

THE PAST IS YET TO COME

Following these brief interjections, let's return to Jakobson and his example of the similarity disorder:

> The same difficulty arises when the patient is asked to name an object pointed to or handled by the examiner. The aphasic with a defect in substitution will not supplement the pointing or handling gesture of the

examiner with the name of the object pointed to. Instead of saying, "This is [called] a pencil," he will merely add an elliptical note about its use: "To write." If one of the synonymic signs is present . . . then the other sign . . . becomes redundant and consequently superfluous. . . . Likewise, the picture of an object will cause suppression of its name: a verbal sign is supplanted by a pictorial sign. When the picture of a compass was presented to a patient of Lotmar's, he responded: "Yes, it's a . . . I know what it belongs to, but I cannot recall the technical expression . . . Yes . . . direction . . . to show direction . . . a magnet points to the north" . . . Such patients fail to shift, as Peirce would say, from an index or icon to a corresponding verbal symbol.[54]

Following Jakobson's text on aphasia, we are once again chasing Cratylus's shadow. In the olfactory experiments, the familiar smell presented to the subjects can be said to function analogously to the pictorial sign of the object ("compass") in causing "suppression of its name," which the subjects are only able to utter in a roundabout way ("Yes . . . direction . . . to show direction . . . a magnet points to the north"). The odor presented to the subjects by the examiner is itself an olfactory index (finger) pointing at an object that the subjects are required to name. It is this olfactory sign that effects the suppression of the verbal sign, that is, the name of the odor as it is commonly source-named. Just like Lotmar's aphasic was unable to recall the object's name once its pictorial sign was presented to him, in more than 50 percent of the cases we seem to forget the names of smells at the exact moment when we smell (and recognize) them.

However, in the case of olfactory anomia, what is suppressed is not merely a name, but a source-name, not the *nomen proprium* but the *nomen improprium*, that is, a name standing in for the structurally missing proper name. In Freudian terms, we can say that the suppression of the name is a *Nachdrängen* of the source-name (its "after-pressure" or "after-repression"), further conditioned by an *Urverdrängung* (or "primal repression") of the irreducibly missing proper name. By Freud's lights, repression proper is merely an "after-pressure" that derives its weight from the gravitational force pulling it to the primordially repressed "X."[55]

This line of thought prompts us to pose a naive question: Why do we spontaneously assume that source-names are secondary mimetic stand-ins for the primary and archetypal *nomen proprium*? Might not the proper name come second? Referencing Wilfrid Sellars, Andrew Cutrofello addressed this precise challenge in one of our private communications: "I take it that for him [Sellars] our ability to isolate all sense data originated out of the use of step-names and source-names. Olfactory sensations may have lagged behind others, but even now-salient features of color-space like 'green' would originally have been called things like 'grass-colored.' I take it this is consonant with your analysis." Yet there is nothing standing in the way of us moving from "grass-colored" to "green," but there is something structurally in the way of us proceeding from "grass-smelling" to the repressed "X." What is truly valuable about Cutrofello's challenge is the newly proposed succession of the terms. If we posit that the *nomen proprium* comes after the *nomen improprium*, and if the olfactory *nomen improprium* is the stand-in for the primordially repressed *nomen proprium*, then repression must be oriented toward the future instead of toward the past. *Nachdrängen*, "after-repression," precedes *Urverdrängung*, "primal repression," chasing *after* it into the future. *Nachdrängen* is a pushing forward, a propelling. Its temporal vector points forward into the immemorial future of *das Urverdrängte*, instead of backward into the immemorial past. Repression is prospective rather than retrospective, like remembrance in Proust and repetition in Kierkegaard.[56] The past, we could say, is yet to come. It only comes first in the sense of being irreducible. Lacan is very clear about this. Consider, for instance, his use of the terms "unary" and "binary" signifier. Paradoxically, it is the binary and not the unary signifier that is *urverdrängt*, primordially repressed, once again indicating a reversal of the succession of the terms. As primordially repressed, the binary signifier operates from the future, repetitively pulling, *anziehen*, the subject toward his or her fate.[57]

How does all of this relate to Cratylus's radicalized Heracliteanism, to his proto-Kierkegaardian concept of repetition? In my reading, Cratylus's gesture would not be a representational sign at all, but rather an index of the inner gap of reflexivity, that is, the difference or negativity separating an entity from itself. That is why Cratylus can say to Hermogenes that "Hermogenes" is not his real name. The indexical gesture is not an act of assigning an identity to a concept under which an object is subsumed. Quite the contrary: Cratylus's gesture captures the point of impossibility of such a subsumption and assignation, thus providing a metaphor of the subject as the nameless void of naming.[58] Contrary to Kierkegaard's criticism of Cratylus, who supposedly surpassed his teacher by playing right into the opponent's hand, Cratylus's gesture of pointing should be viewed as pinpointing exactly where Heraclitus failed to radically undermine Eleatic principles. Hence, Cratylus did not go beyond his teacher, ending up in the same place of Eleatic Sameness and Unity of Being. His critique is strictly internal to his teacher's philosophical doctrines in the sense of pushing the inner premise of Heraclitean principles to their logical extreme (without abandoning them), unfolding their true inner potential for thought. To say that it's impossible to step into the same river even once, is to affirm difference in a radicalized way that remained dormant in Heraclitus's account, bringing the concept of difference to its excessive dialectical extreme, to the verge of its disappearance. Affirming Heraclitean difference, Cratylus zeroes in on the self-different, undermining the self-identical. That is what is at stake in his rephrasing of the Heraclitean motto: Heraclitus didn't go far enough in undermining the Unity of Being. By affirming external difference, he has left the reflective core of identity fully intact.

To unpack this, I want to follow the basic tenets of Lacanian hyperstructuralism proposed by Jacques-Alain Miller in his classical text "Matrix."[59] The river into which we cannot step even once: each step equals the next with nothing between them. However, this Nothing between them counts and accounts for the river's distance from itself, its inherent self-splitting. With Miller, we must say that each step is at once a separation and an absorption: it is a division separating the river from itself by leaving Nothing between the river and itself.[60] The difference of the same, better still: same difference. The river stays the same with each step, yet the two rivers we stepped into are not undistinguished, and hence are un-undistinguished by Nothing distinguishing the river from itself. Hegel's formulation best encapsulates the gist of this self-splitting:

> Pure being and pure nothing are, therefore, the same. What is the truth is neither being nor nothing, but that being—does not pass over but has passed over—into nothing, and nothing into being. But it is equally true that they are not undistinguished from each other, that, on the contrary, they are not the same, that they are absolutely distinct, and yet that they are unseparated and inseparable and that each immediately vanishes in its opposite. Their truth is, therefore, this movement of the immediate vanishing of the one in the other: becoming, a movement in which both are distinguished, but by a difference which has equally immediately resolved itself.[61]

By means of Eric Santner's quip, we can say that Nothing "unties things together."[62] Things are at odds with themselves, they are reflexively oppositional due to Nothing separating them from within. If their self-identity is to be made possible, it is only made possible by Nothing being impossible. "Reflexive opposition" signifies the property of reflexivity, first grasped by Hegel, and central to Lacan's notion of the relation of opposition.[63] This centrality was articulated by Jean-Claude Milner in Le périple structural (2002) as the basic tenet of what he terms Lacan's "hyperstructuralism." Milner pinpoints the scandalous reasoning behind it:

> In classical ontology, the fundamental relation of equivalence is that of identity. Reflexivity, in other words: identity-with-itself, $A = A$, here is the decisive point. In Saussurean ontology, founding the structural procedures, the function which was based on the principle of identity is replaced by the principle of opposition; we can no longer say $A = A$, but rather: A is in distinctive opposition to A, or, formulated in the traditional language of identity: A exists in the structure only to the strict extent that A is not identical to A. A strange supposition, and we understand why it was

impossible to proclaim it without restraint, for nothing could be more alien to the philosophical tradition, even to thought itself.[64]

In Plato's *Cratylus*, naming is tasked with organizing things in accordance with their essential nature or true being. This organizational effort proceeds by way of a "dividing of being": "So," Socrates comments, "just as a shuttle is a tool for dividing warp and woof, a name is a tool for giving instruction, that is to say, for dividing being" (Cra. 388b). Things that differ essentially (that is: in nature) have nothing in common. Only by way of having nothing (essential to their being) in common do they differ from each other. When their essences are substitutable for one another, when there is an essential symmetry between them, they are the same rather than different. But they are only different in nature if they have a self-identical nature in the first place, which implies that the dividing of being is predicated upon there being self-identical beings. I said that the dividing of being is only made possible by Nothing (non-being) being impossible. Yet, that which makes the dividing of being possible, that is, the impossibility of Nothing, is precisely what makes it impossible: differing beings are self-identical—with Nothing between them and themselves.

Hence, it is certainly possible to step into the same river twice; we just cannot do it once. Recall once again the case of H.M. Where smells were concerned, H.M. had a hard time "dividing being," organizing smells according to their nature. Things of different natures collapsed into indifference, while identical things were perceived as opposed to themselves, as subject to incessant self-othering. In the smellscape, we witness not the dividing of being but the division of the subject as the symptom of the division of being. And while Being allows for divisions by being self-identical, the subject is divided by being self-different. Not a reflection-into-self of external differences, the subject is the division-into-self of all things self-identical. Unlike other instances of Being, the subject is different not only from other things but also from itself. And since, minimally speaking, a thing is only a thing if it is identical with itself, the subject is no-thing at all.

It is interesting to note that the two statements Cratylus is known for entail the two elementary forms of indication: the gesture (of the pointed finger) and the trace (of the stepping into the river). A closer look at the latter allows us to once again address the key feature of Kierkegaard's criticism: Does denying the possibility of stepping into the same river once also eliminate movement? The footprint is the absence of the foot, yet this absence is a fundamental part of the entity lacking it. Rather than eliminating movement, this dynamic of being and nothing is the primoradial movement of an entity's passing from itself to itself, that is, passing from emergence to passing, between being and nothing. Even at the moment of absolute contiguity between gesture and surface, or between foot and footprint—that is, even when there is nothing separating them—there is Nothing between them, interrupting their contiguity, marking their organic relation with a non-relation, untying the two together. Following Miller, we can say that the river has the topological structure of the Möbius strip. There is only a single side of Being, such that the threshold or the point of passing from one state to the next is at once nowhere and everywhere and therefore can at once only and never be crossed. The point of passage can only be localized by a cut. And is Cratylus's finger pointing not just such a gesture of introducing a cut? And rather than pointing out something, is it not intended to point out Nothing, that is, the unlocalizable twist, the impossible point of passage between a surface and itself? This cut can only be self-sabotaging in the sense of doing away with the twisted surface and hence immediately losing the twist it purported to be reaching for. In this regard, the pointing is literally a pointing out, an expulsion of Being, effecting the precarious appearance (of Nothing) in disappearance (of Being). Contrary to Peirce's point, indices are formative of an inexistential relation—the word is the murder of the thing.[65]

Let's return to our chimeric encounter between a word that cannot be substituted for itself and an object not smelling like itself. What emerges in the first of these two entities reflexively opposed to themselves, is the subject as the Nothingness of signification, the inner gap of reflexivity, or the subject as the division in Being (rather than the dividing of Being), the point of Being's inherent impossibility. In this regard, the olfactory subject is the paradigm of Lacanian subjectivity. As divided, the subject is formed in relation to the indivisible remainder, to use Schelling's term adopted by Žižek.[66] As we have seen, smell-objects are paradigmatically indivisible, escaping the linguistic containment and the "dividing of being." The divided subject and the indivisible objet petit a form the two sides of this chimeric encounter. Their relation (if they in fact form a relation) is clearly not one of existence and referentiality. Instead of forming an existential relation, their relation is revealing of the fundamental fantasy of referentiality. Unsurprisingly, for Lacan the structure untying them together is precisely that of fantasy: $\$ \lozenge a$. Relating a word that can't be substituted for itself ($\$$) to an object that escapes the dividing of being (a), the fantasy unties together the void and the excess of naming. Reflexive oppositivity underlying the emergence of the subject undermines referentiality (and consciousness): it hinges on words not substitutable for themselves, words uncorrelated to anything, considering that any-thing reflexively opposed to itself is no-thing at all. In turn, the indivisible remainder of no-thing is nothing the subject is, or could become, conscious of. Rather, the fantasy-structure depicts the divided subject's becoming unconscious of itself.[67] The indivisible remainder figures as a trace of subjectivity, inhabiting its division. This trace does not prefigure the subject; as an index of the subject, object a is not the figure but the disfigure of subjectivity, a stain of subjectivity beyond figuration. Contrary to, and symptomatic of, indices proper and their forging of a privileged relation to the reality of existing objects, instead of indicating the *reality* of the subject, object *a* is indicative of subjectivity as emphatically *unrealized*.[68] Neither being nor non-being, the subject is simultaneously unborn and undead, its death is anterior to its birth, its birth posthumous.

The ultimately meaningless and unsymbolizable nature of the stain fuels a drive for its hermeneutical containment, sprouting the subject's imagination, configuring that which eludes figuration. In his discussion of the iconic stain on the shroud of Turin, Georges Didi-Huberman notes how, paradoxically, the very "empty" referentiality of the stain is taken as a mark and guarantor of an authentic existential relation: "The effacement of all figuration in this trace is itself the guarantee of a link, of authenticity; if there is no figuration it is because contact has taken place. The noniconic, nonmimetic nature of this stain guarantees its indexical value."[69] As a stain, object *a* is not a witness to the reality of the subject's anteriority, its anterior "thereness," but rather of the unreality of its fate, forever split between almost being and almost not being, between the unborn and the undead. Insisting in pulsating flashes without existing (and hence without persisting), the unreal and reflexively opposed subject is "represented" by the unsymbolizable abject. Cratylus understood this very well. For what is the absolute limit of the "dividing of being"; that which cannot be divided any further? It is certainly not the self-identical, the *eidos*, the substance of a thing, but rather division itself in its conceptual extreme of self-difference. It comes as no surprise then that, first, that which cannot be divided any further—division as such—can only be captured by the indivisible, and that, second, that which eludes imaginary and symbolic figuration can only be captured by the Real of a disfigured stain.

FOLLOW YOUR NOSE (TO THE LETTER)

One last point concerning the referentiality of smells. Apart from being unable to name smells themselves as qualities, in turn literally having to *outsource them*, we are—to a surprising extent—also unable to name these sources themselves. With the linguistic umbilical cord tying smells to names irreducibly cut, smells not only lose a firm footing in their objective correlate or primary referent, but are indicative of the fantasy of referentiality. The difficulty of identifying familiar odors by relating them to source-objects (or rather to the names of these objects considered to be representative olfactory referents) is further accentuated in the case of complex mixtures that we encounter in perfumery. These olfactory "compositions," consisting of a number of "notes," be they synthetic or natural, altogether lack identifiable referents in the world, such that they cannot be referenced to in relation to an object-source and hence also cannot be source-named. They present us with pure nameless sensory qualities of essentially unidentifiable odorant objects.[70]

We have seen that when it comes to odor identification, odor-names cannot be made to fully match the sample stimuli and thus establish a fixed, "culture-free" biunivocal relation. Though such a universalization can be accomplished neither by speech nor by supposedly extra-linguistic indexation, it can certainly be accomplished by stringent scientific formalization. If language falls short of grasping olfactory qualities, through mathematical formulae the latter can no doubt be grasped by and to the letter. If smells are *abscented* from us as speaking beings, they can only be grasped from the outside of language, that is, as *absensed* (to use Lacan's term from "L'étourdit"). And this is precisely the wager of formalization: its letters capture the object by bypassing the linguistic bypass, in turn securing the integral transmissibility of knowledge impossible to accomplish with our clumsy linguistic devices.

If language fails to denote even the most common of odorants, how can we expect it to capture complex synthetic odor-compositions that altogether lack a linguistically identifiable referent in the objective world? Unlike language, formalization can capture the very objectal materiality of such a compound, the support vehicle of the "perfume," as an extant object that the sensuous subject encounters in the world and perceives as emitting an odor. Although such odors have no identifiable objective referents, they do have identifiable odorants as entities in the world that are distinct from identifiable empirically existing objects. Odorants are conceptually akin to "value" as distinct from "worth." For Marx, the latter refers to the aspect of a commodity immediately embodied in the material properties of the "actual thing," while the former only "exists" as an element within a network of differential relations, that is, only on account of a commodity differing from other commodities. Likening odorants to value, we can say there is nothing "positively" material about them. That which can be perceived as their empirical actuality, is merely their accidental support-vehicle. The materiality of odorants relies entirely on distinctive combination of letters. Like the "phantom-like objectivity" of value,[71] odorants, too, can only be grasped by way of scientific literalization. An odorant (as distinct from the object) is the active material "stuff" of objects qualified as odorous, a "substance" that is often extracted from these objects and isolated as a stand-alone chemical compound. Thus, 2-phenylethanol, or $C_8H_{10}O$, is found in and often (though not exclusively) extracted from the empirically existing object we call "a rose."

Source-naming was indicative of the "stuffiness" of odors, structurally attached to things. Here, a new distinction was introduced. When source-naming smells, we are in fact referring them not to the source-object but to the odorant object, to *stuff* rather than *things*—a distinction indicated in our use of language: we say, "smell of rose" and not "smell of a rose."[72] However, the odorant as the object-source, the "real stuff" of smells, is reducible not to some empiricist-vitalist materiality of matter, but rather to the "phantom-like" materiality of the letter, or to scientific "literalization."[73] The letter is the "real stuff" of odors: $C_8H_{10}O$ stands for the pure and purely literal materiality of the odorant object colloquially called "rose." In other words: an object either contains or is itself the odorant, that is, the "stuff" of the quality in virtue of which the object is qualified as odorous.

However, there is a whopping "however" here: instead of solving the problem of odor identification, formalization merely transposes it. Let us not forget that the crux of the issue with smells lies in the impossibility of equational predication. With formalization, universal knowledge is gained, but can only be spelled out without being spoken. Jacques-Alain Miller cites § 206 of Pascal's *Pensées* as indicative of the "gag order" instituted by modern science and its reliance on formalization:

> "The eternal silence of these infinite spaces frightens me." . . . It is precisely the discourse of science, since the emergence of mathematical physics, that makes the world become silent. Lacan sums up this proposition, which I believe is unquestionable, by saying that science assumes that there exists in the world the signifier which means nothing—and for nobody.[74]

Knowledge is spelled out without being spoken and without speaking to anyone. The truth of the smell's relation to its object cannot be repeated back. "Told to repeat the word *no*, Head's patient replied 'No, I don't know how to do it.'" The emphasis should be placed on the patient's choice of words. Jakobson interprets this as a sign of the patient's impotence ("he could not"). However, the patient does not say that he cannot do it. He says that he doesn't know, is ignorant as to how to go about it ("I don't know how . . ."). Moreover, he says he doesn't know how to do it, while doing it, while speaking it, thereby signaling that "it," in being spoken, cannot be spoken. In saying that he doesn't know how to do it while doing it, he is implying that it cannot be done, that it is impossible. And this is precisely the knowledge formulated and hence formalized by Jakobson: at its core, the patient's ignorance ("I don't know how . . .") is an impotence to know ("he could not"): "he could not produce the purest form of equational predication, the tautology $a = a$: /no/ is /no/." That which cannot be repeated back can be written as the formula of reflexive identity: $a = a$.

Yet the problem persists. The formalization, too, cannot be repeated back: the patient's ignorance is an *impotence* that signals an *impossibility*. Therefore, the example is symptomatic of modern science: modern science produces formulas that cannot be repeated back. $a = a$ can be formalized but it cannot be spoken. The patient's anomia therefore mirrors the anomia of the Universe as conceived by modern science, of a world deodorized. Formalization solves the problem by substituting knowledge for ignorance but creates another problem by substituting impossibility for impotence. The moment we repeat back $a = a$, the moment we speak it, $a \neq a$ applies. The patient's response spells out the impossibility of equational predication: /no/ $\neq$ /no/. Scientific knowledge is spelled out without being spoken and *without speaking to anyone*. The later part of this claim can now be amended to *without addressing the subject* in the literal sense of failing to come to terms with the subject's reflexive oppositivity.

A ROSE IS A ROSE IS A ROSE IS A ROSE . . .

Aristotle defines the category of quality as an abstract property pertaining to concrete things. In conceptualizing the relation between quality and the qualified, Aristotle also considers the problem of naming: the concrete thing qualified is named after, or in relation to, its abstract quality, or: qualifieds are paronyms of qualities (Cat. 10a 27–30). This is true, Aristotle continues, "in practically all" cases, meaning that "in most cases . . . things are called paronymously, as the pale man from paleness." There are exceptions to this observation, however, which Aristotle pauses to consider. First, there are qualifieds, such as "boxer," the names of which are not paronymously derived from any quality that would signify the "skill of boxing," "for there are no names for the capacities in virtue of which these men are said to be qualified" (Cat. 10a 32–10b 6). However, even though the names of such qualifieds are not derived paronymously from the names of qualities in virtue of which they are qualified, their names are nevertheless paronymously derived from another identifiable name. In other cases, which are equally rare, the quality itself has a name, but the paronym of the qualified is derived from a name other than that of the quality of which it is the qualified (Cat. 10b 6–10).

Consider this logic from the perspective of the problem of naming and smells. In the case of step-naming, the name of the qualified ("sweet") is a paronym of a quality ("sweetness"); however, as such it is not derived from the name of a quality in virtue of which it is qualified (for such a quality has no name) and is thus a paronym of an essentially non-olfactory quality. This quality, pertaining to gustatory sensation, is used to the effect of relating an olfactory quality to an olfactorily qualified thing in the absence of the quality's proper name. In the case of source-naming, the relation of derivation is not merely translated into another sensory register and thus kept intact. Here, the name of the qualified ("smell of rose" or "rosy") is derived from the name of the quality ("smell of rose-ness" or "rosiness"), which refers to the name of the odorant ("rose"), which derives from the name of the object ("a rose") that is said to be representative of the missing quality (the unnamed "X"). But derivations such as these (e.g., "rose," "rosy" and "rosiness," or "mint,"

"minty" and "mintiness") are deployed rarely and perhaps for the sole purpose of linguistically marking the conceptual difference between what are in
fact not three but four interrelated terms. Commonly, we would use a single
word ("rose") for an empirical object ("a rose"), an odorant ("rose"), an
olfactory quality ("rose") and its qualified ("rose"): *A rose is a rose is a rose is
a rose* . . .

In olfactory source-naming, the name of the qualified (a thing "smelling of
rose") is a paronym not of a quality ("X") but of an object ("a rose") standing in for the lacking quality (now called "rose"). "Whiteness" is a quality
of an object qualified as "white." But the qualified is not to be equated with
the object: "whiteness" is that in virtue of which, for instance, "snow" (as an
object) is qualified as "white," meaning that the quality of "whiteness" does
not correspond to the object "snow" but rather to the color "white" as its
qualified. Unlike sensuous qualities such as "whiteness" that can be related
to the qualified ("white") without a reference to a particular referent (say,
"snow"), source-named olfactory qualities ("rose") are linguistically undistinguished from the names of their corresponding qualifieds ("rose"), as well
as linguistically undistinguishable from their odorant ("rose") or referent ("a
rose"). The one crucial consequence of this undistinguishability that tends
to hide in plain sight is that the moment we pose the problem of naming
and smells, we find ourselves caught in a loop of classification where a given
quality is the common attribute of a certain number of objects, *which include
among them this quality itself*. It is as if a set of objects qualified as "white" would
include the quality of "whiteness" as one of its qualified members. Unlike the
smell we call "rose" that qualifies objects, including "a rose," as smelling of
"rose," "whiteness" qualifies objects (e.g., "snow," "milk") as "white," but is
itself not an object qualified by itself as "white." The olfactory quality we call
"rose" is that in virtue of which, apart from several other objects ("soap," for
instance), "a rose" is qualified as "smelling of rose," that is, as *smelling of itself*.
There is one such self-referentially qualified referent for every olfactory quality expressed by source-naming. This implies that any olfactory set of qualified
members is a set that includes itself as its member. Or put differently: for any
set of objects qualified in virtue of a given olfactory quality, there is One that
qualifies all other objects—and itself.

Another way of capturing this loop of classification is provided by the
genera–species distinction introduced by Aristotle to spell out a key difference
between qualities and their qualifieds. Whereas qualities as genera "are spoken
of in relation to something, . . . none of the particular cases [or qualifieds] is"
(Cat. 11a 20–25). Aristotle takes "knowledge" to be the example of a genus; as
such, the quality of "knowledge" is always spoken of in relation to something,
while its species, for instance "grammar," are not. Genera or qualities are rela-
tives, but species or qualifieds are not. Species only enter the relative form as

species of their genera: "grammar" is not "grammar of something," but rather "knowledge of something." Or take the example of the quality of color. Color is a genus and hence is spoken of in relation to something: we speak of the "whiteness of snow" but not of "snow of something." And just like "grammar" is a particular species of the genus "knowledge" and hence the "knowledge of something," "snow" is a particular qualified species of the genus "whiteness" and hence stands for the "whiteness of something." Now, Aristotle goes on to add, "there is nothing absurd" about a thing being both a qualification and a relative (Cat. 11a 35); for instance, "music" is a form of "knowledge" and hence a "knowledge of music," but "music" can also be spoken of in relation to something like, say, "film" ("film music"). The moment we consider our example of smell, an instance of redoubling becomes obvious: "'smell of rose' of a rose." "A rose" as a particular case of the genus "smell of rose" is in fact spoken of in relation to something, but unlike "music" it is not simply spoken of in relation to something *other than itself* ("film") but in relation to *itself*. The genus is spoken of in relation to its species, which, generally, are not themselves spoken of in relation to anything; however, for each genus of smell, there is one species (in relation to which the genus is spoken of) that is itself spoken of in relation to the genus, that is, to itself.

The biblical story of the formation of Adam is a story of the making of "man" and of "mankind" (with the two referred to indiscriminately as "the man") and hence the perhaps ultimate example of the redoubling at stake here. It is noteworthy that Adam's formation from fine particles of solid matter, the dust of the earth would have remained unfinished, had God not administered a bit of CPR, infusing his lifeless dusty formation with the breath of life. It is rather striking that God administered his artificial ventilation through the nose rather than the mouth: "Then the LORD God formed a man from the dust of the ground and breathed into his nostrils the breath of life, and the man became a living being" (Gen. 2:7). It is curious that *logos*, the Word, would be tasked with the creation, but not with the formation of life and therefore of man. But this second curious detail sheds light on the first one. Since God does not create man with the aid of *logos*, he does not breathe life into him through the mouth as the seat and instrument of language, but rather through the nose as the locus of the primordial linguistic void. The nose is to smell what the mouth is to language. These two body orifices, two ins and outs of the body, have a crucial thing in common. They both provide entry to the respiratory system and hence enable breathing, this vital sign of life. Breathing represents their shared territoriality, one subsequently deterritorialized in divergent ways and split between speaking and smelling, that is, between naming, or *logos*, and its olfactory voids.

This should remind us of the alternative so dear to Deleuze: "to eat or to speak," either "bits of things" or "bits of Shakespeare."[75] With the emergence of speech, the mouth is deterritorialized, stripped of its natural function and robbed of its natural object, so that to speak is to hunger.[76] Smell complicates this schema. Can the nose be deterritorialized, detached from its biological function? Or does it stand for an irreducible territoriality, immune to linguistic deterritorialization of sensibility? The choice between breathing and smelling, between bits of air or bits of odor, can effectively never be made. And since it is impossible to breathe (through the nose) without smelling, one must wonder what the breath of life smelled like. And was it the smell rather than the air that brought Adam into being? This would certainly further explain God's unusual choice of CPR. Did God have bad breath? Was it the stuffy and pungent sting rather than the influx of oxygen that animated the lifeless dusty matter, perhaps prompting the first man to speak his first words: "Bad air! Bad air!"[77]

Back to our Aristotelian exercise: Man is formed from dust and infused with God's breath. However, it is only from the moment when Eve is formed from Adam's rib (and formed as a "woman") that the name "Adam" begins to signify both the species of "man" and the genus of "man(kind)." "Man" (as in "male human") can only enter a relation of distinctive opposition with "woman" (as his "female" counterpart) on condition of entering an opposition with himself as "man(kind)." The genus and species of "man" emerge at the same point in logical time, in the immediate aftermath of the emergence of the "woman." In the biblical story, this redoubling, or splitting, whereby the genus "man" as standing for "mankind" appears as one of its own species ("male human") and therefore as different not merely from its other ("woman") but also from itself, coincides precisely with the introduction of the lack: "woman" is made out of "man's" rib, literally standing in for what "man" henceforth is lacking.

It is interesting to note that Eve comes into being—triggering this self-split of "man"—as an immediate consequence of Adam's encounter with the void of naming: God was looking to make "a helper fit for him," for it "is not good that the man should be alone," so he "formed every beast of the field and every bird of the heavens" and "brought them to the man to see what he would call them. And whatever the man called every living creature, that was its name" (Gen. 2:18–23). The making of the "helpers" is God's work, the making sense of them is the work of man. But the moment Adam made sense of the "helpers" by calling them by their names, he realized that he has "not found a helper fit for him." Among all these names he had just uttered, one name was missing. And as a good Freudian, God looked for the missing name in Adam's "deep sleep": "So the LORD God caused a deep sleep to fall upon the man, and while he slept took one of his ribs and closed up its place with flesh. And the rib that the LORD God had taken from the man he made into a woman and brought her to the man." The man exclaimed: "This at last is bone of my bones / and flesh of my flesh; / she shall be called Woman, / because she was taken out of Man." Thus, "woman" quite literally emerges from "man's" lack. As a stand-in for the missing name, she emerges from a void of naming. But the emergence of "woman" in the place of the lacking name does not result in the totalization of the universe of names, henceforth neatly ordered and complete. Rather, with this name ("woman") "man" himself is split into two, with a part of him appearing outside of himself ("she was taken out of Man"). For this reason, "woman" is not merely a symmetrical opposite of "man" but rather (as Lacan claims) his symptom, that is, the symptom of "man's" thwarted relation to himself as "man," just as smell is the generic symptom of naming's thwarted relation to itself. Take again the genus of "whiteness" and, for instance, the difference between two qualified species of "snow" and "milk." The difference between the two is the difference between two species as species of the genus "whiteness." However, with "a rose" and, for instance, "soap" (as qualified by the same quality of "smell of rose"), or between "man" and "woman," the difference between the two species ("rose" and "soap," "man" and "woman") coincides with a difference between a species ("soap," "woman") and its genus ("rose," "man[kind]").

An olfactory source-name simultaneously stands for an "ordinary" quality qualifying its qualifieds ("soap" smells of "rose") and for an "empty" quality qualifying itself ("a rose" smells of "rose," which smells of "a rose"). An olfactory quality qualifies not only something other than itself but also itself as an other; its qualification coincides with and is indistinguishable from its self-othering. In marking sensuous objects with a distinctive qualitative difference, it simultaneously marks itself as split and as differing from itself. With each source-name the externality of the nameless void of naming that characterizes the realm of smells is not simply named, linguistically integrated, contained, and aborted, but is rather transposed and emerges as the inner-heterogeneous void splitting source-names from within. Apart from being an ordinary name for a number of qualifieds, every source-name is an empty name for itself, and as such it is the name for the lack of itself as a name, the name of the unnamed "X" standing for the void of naming. As an empty instance of tautological self-reflexivity that lacks grounding in the missing name, a source-name stands in the relation of reflexive opposition to itself. Recall, once more, the case of H.M. His deficit only pertained to the olfactory mode, meaning that he was able to name the objects by sight or touch, but not by smell. H.M.'s remark about the "lemon" not smelling like a "lemon" points precisely to the aforementioned inner gap of reflexivity: the self-identity of an entity is thwarted by a difference separating the entity from itself.

This chapter began with the maximum opposition, an antinomical relation between names and smells. But the discussion of source-names that are commonly used as lexical stand-ins for the missing proper names has perhaps—and perhaps surprisingly—led us to affirm the equivalence of names and smells. Is not every proper name ultimately an empty name, a "rigid designator"[78] of an object irreducible to the cluster of its positive descriptive properties, in turn designating the unnamed property "X"? Or is there a difference between the two, one that ultimately makes them irreducible? A proper name, say "Peter," stands for a number of descriptive properties of its referent; but contrary to the central claim of the Frege-Russell description theory of names, these properties are never exhaustive and are only exhausted in the name that covers all of these properties, including the empty excess of singularity that they themselves do not and cannot exhaust. However, considering our discussion of smells and naming, another crucial element must be added to the philosophical notion of the proper name. The mysterious property "X," designated by the name "Peter" and unnamable in terms of the descriptive properties that determine "Peter's" biographical identity, can be "rigidly designated" by the name "Peter" only because this name is itself a stand-in for a lacking name. There are many Peters: Peter differs from Peter and Peter from Peter, but not in name and not only in respect to his positive descriptive properties. "Peter" is singular and distinctive (from any other "Peter") not because of the properties he *has*, nor because of the properties he *lacks*, but because of the property he *has lacking* ("X"). A proper name like "Peter" is a taking possession, a rigid nominal containment of the property lacking the name.

The parental ritual of picking the newborn's name testifies to this logic. When picking the child's name, I am not merely assessing the qualities of available names while considering their personal (familial) or social meaning as it relates, for instance, to factors of custom, religion, political ideology, class, ethnicity, or education. In addition to relating them to identifiable *meanings*, I am also relating these sonorous and literal qualities to my (unborn) child's supposed singularity, to his or her unnamed "X," and determining which name best fits that which is ultimately *meaningless*. In short: I am effectively searching for a name that would be the best stand-in for the missing proper name, that is, for a name that could, would it not be lost, directly name, and thus fit, the quality "X."

The parent's occasional obsession with what we (as mere observers) inevitably perceive as "made up names," is symptomatic of this process: such neonyms are attempts to bypass the bypass, that is, to bypass the choice inherent in the process of naming, to find a way around the available stand-ins and to directly conjure up the lacking name that would fit the quality "X" without a remainder. (Without a remainder—or should we say without the spectral, surplus flesh from the biblical story that emerges in the place of the lack, never quite filling and befitting it?) Such use of neonyms could be deemed part and parcel of "new age obscurantism," as understood by Žižek.[79] They are desperate attempts at reclaiming the primordial Unity of Being, undermined by language and its subjectivizing effects. But as such, the obscurantism of naming mirrors the formalism of science: what is formalization if not a conjuring up of the lacking name that fits the quality "X" without a remainder? However, the already discussed impasse traversing scientific formalization also applies to the obscurantism of the name: neonyms succeed in capturing the Real *as long as they are not repeated back*. What the parents in their quest for a unique linguistic expression of the singular object tend to overlook is the fact that the available collection of names already consists of nothing but such attempts at directly naming the unnamed. That is to say, they overlook the fact that the history of names is itself already a historical archive of structurally failed attempts of naming the singular. The parental attempts of directly naming the "X" usually backfire in effecting the opposite of what was intended. They often amount not to a fortuitous complete overlapping of Being and Sense, but rather to a metamorphosis of the supposed sublime singularity of the precious object into an obscene linguistic parody of a ridiculous abject. Again, the neonymic figuration fails to prefigure the subject and is consubstantial with the disfigured stain of subjectivity.

The investigation of the olfactory is the investigation of everything else.
—Hans J. Rindisbacher, *The Smell of Books*

METAPHYSICS OF DUNCES

Freud had a good nose for bullshit. He had a good nose for detecting speech that appears convincing while disregarding any reference to truth. Phenomena generally grouped under the label of "occultism" were blossoming in turn-of-the-century Europe and the world. And Freud had good reasons for concern. The pseudoscientific spiritualists were further eroding the already shabby reputation of psychoanalysis, sharing with it several privileged objects, most notably that of dreams. The beliefs in clairvoyance, telepathy, the Kabbalah, levitation, astrology, and theosophy shared with psychoanalysis the terrain of "psychic research," effectively spurring doubts as to whether psychoanalysis can aspire to the status of science. The "partnership" between psychoanalysis and occultism intensified in the 1920s. Their convergence was supported by the trend to align psychoanalytic findings with the principles of positivist rationalism. That which was supposed to bring psychoanalysis closer to science effectively brought it closer to the occult.[1] Psychoanalysis and occultism both focus on forces that clandestinely guide human behavior but—importantly—remain inaccessible to sensory experience. Occultism thus concerns the internal organization of being, which emphatically escapes sensual forms, in turn revealing a peculiar causality that can do without any reference to sensibility.[2]

Considering this proximity between occultism and psychoanalysis, we are not surprised that Freud addressed the issues of the occult in a series of his books and articles. A closer look reveals that the themes related to the occult are a constant in most of Freud's texts, starting with *The Interpretation of Dreams*

(1900), intended to deliver this ancient object from the stronghold of pre-scientific explanations,[3] and *The Psychopathology of Everyday Life* (1901), with its concluding chapter on superstition. Occult phenomena in the strict sense are addressed in the texts "Animism, Magic and the Omnipotence of Thought" (1912), *Das Unheimliche* (1919),[4] "Psychoanalysis and Telepathy" (1921) and "Dreams and Telepathy" (1922), *The Future of an Illusion* (1927), and, finally, in the section on "Dreams and the Occult" from the *New Introductory Lectures on Psychoanalysis* (1933). The following Feuerbachian comment gives us a good idea of Freud's general attitude toward spiritualism:

> The proceedings of the spiritualists meet us at this point; they are convinced of the survival of the individual soul and they seek to demonstrate to us beyond doubt the truth of this one religious doctrine. Unfortunately they cannot succeed in refuting the fact that the appearance and utterances of their spirits are merely the products of their own mental activity. They have called up the spirits of the greatest men and of the most eminent thinkers, but all the pronouncements and information which they have received from them have been so foolish and so wretchedly meaningless that one can find nothing credible in them but the capacity of the spirits to adapt themselves to the circle of people who have conjured them up.[5]

The occultic "metaphysics of dunces" was certainly in the air.[6] But instead of closing itself off in its own detached sphere outside of science, it focused its efforts on finding the scientific basis for understanding occult phenomena. This union of scientific knowledge and superstition, or of *vernaculus* and *occultus*, is characteristic of modernity in general and of modern science in particular, such that the scientific "disenchantment" of the world coincides with its simultaneous "re-enchantment."[7] The "disenchantment of the world" is the myth of the Enlightenment, with Reason giving birth to its own stupidity. Importantly, the latter is the result of its progress, rather than a simple regression to the premodern world of superstition.[8]

The history of science has abundantly documented this entanglement of modern scientific discourse with the occult interests of scientists. Think of Newton, who devoted himself not only to mathematical sciences but also and above all to the study of alchemy and biblical chronologies. In this regard, John Maynard Keynes challenged the conventional image of a great physicist, reducing physics to Newton's side hustle:

> In the eighteenth century and since, Newton came to be thought of as the first and greatest of the modern age of scientists, a rationalist, one who taught us to think on the lines of cold and untinctured reason. / I do not see him in this light. . . . Newton was not the first of the age of reason. He was the last of the magicians.[9]

And think of Saussure, whose scientific breakthroughs in the field of lin-guistics were accompanied by the study of anagrams, that is, of random graphic displacements that produce unsuspected meanings that linguistics supposedly cannot account for and explain.[10] Or think of Descartes and his infamous vol-untarism. The veracity of scientific knowledge requires an extrascientific guar-antee: $5 = 2 + 3$, says Descartes, *because God wills it.* Finally, think of Emanuel Swedenborg, the Swedish mystic, who charged the Enlightenment principles of modern science—its rationalism, mechanicism, and materialism—with the secular repression of the occult.[11] Such views received a special boost during the Romantic era. Here, we must mention Franz Mesmer and his influential vitalist theory of "animal magnetism," a kind of precursor to hyp-notism, which attributes to all living things an invisible life force that exerts its influence in the physical world. And we must make a passing mention of the current within avant-garde art, which explicitly connected the tradition of Mesmerian magnetism with the Freudian concept of the unconscious. Surre-alism strived to abolish the Western aesthetic tradition to be replaced by occult practices of "automatic writing," capable of transmitting the hidden "uncon-scious." After 1919, Freud exchanged a series of letters with André Breton, and in 1921 they also met in person. Freud's letter to Breton dated December 26, 1932, nicely summarizes Freud's attitude toward the coupling of surrealism and psychoanalysis: "And now a confession, which you will have to accept with tolerance! Although I have received many testimonies of the interest that you and your friends show for my research, I am not able to clarify for myself what Surrealism is and what it wants. Perhaps I am not destined to understand it, I who am so distant from art."[12] So: *"Was will der Surrealist?"*[13]

With a reference to hypnosis, Freud draws a connection between animal magnetism and the taboo,[14] while reducing the modern interest for the occult to the old religious interest: "That being so, it will be hard for us to avoid a suspicion that the interest in occultism is in fact a religious one and that one of the secret motives of the occultist movement is to come to the help of reli-gion, threatened as it is by the advance of scientific thought."[15] With the assis-tance of the occultist movement, the old religious interest undermined by science is gaining new relevance, thus undermining the enlightened, though utopian, "dictatorship of reason."[16] However, we should immediately add that the occultic revival of religious interest is not acknowledged by the occultists who, in their quest for truth, disguise themselves as scientists. A good example of this is the Theosophical Society, established 1875 in New York, and its slogan "There is no religion higher than the truth."

To quote Adorno:

Monotheism is decomposing into a second mythology. "I believe in astrology because I do not believe in God," one participant in an American socio-psychological investigation answered. Judicious reason, that had elevated itself to the notion of one God, seems ensnared in his fall. Spirit is dissociated into spirits and thereby forfeits the power to recognize that they do not exist.[17]

A further twist must be given to the formula of the study participant quoted by Adorno. Not just: "I believe in astrology because I do not believe in God," but rather: "No, I don't really believe in astrology, but all the same I *don't not believe* in it." Along the same lines, Ernest Jones brilliantly summarizes the gist of occult beliefs in spirits: "No, I don't really believe it, but all the same it is very odd."[18] Jones's formula is found in the third volume of his Freud biography first published in 1957. In it, we recognize the (disavowed?) source for the famous formula of fetishistic disavowal proposed by Octave Mannoni in 1969: "Je sais bien, mais quand même" (I know, but all the same I believe).[19]

FROM THE NOSE TO THE STARS . . . AND BACK

Returning to the relationship between occultism and science, Jones compiles a long list of modern scientists with a pronounced penchant for the occult:

> The vogue of . . . mediums has shown a certain periodicity. Thus it reached special heights in 1860 (the Daniel Home period), in 1880 (leading to the formation of the Society for Psychical Research), in 1900 (the period of the great physicists), and again at the present day. At the end of the last century an impressive list of men of science may be quoted as having, after careful investigation, subscribed to the truth of many of the mediums' claims: T. H. Flournoy, Lombroso, Richet, and Schrenk-Notzing on the Continent; William James and others in America; Sir William Barrett, Sir William Crookes, Sir Arthur Conan Doyle, Sir Oliver Lodge, F. W. H. Myers and Sir George Stokes in England. Some of these were highly distinguished exponents of the physical sciences and so thoroughly conversant with scientific modes of thought. Nevertheless in every single case the mediums who had produced the evidence that convinced these gentlemen of the truth of their claims have been exposed as tricksters who played on the vein of credulity present in the distinguished investigators.[20]

Here, we leave aside both Freud's multifaceted interest in tackling the problem of the occult, as well as the psychoanalytic interpretation of worldviews generally and "the world outlook of simpletons" specifically.[21] Our intention is not to provide a general theory of occultism, even though, due to the requirements imposed on us by this text, we will, finally and incidentally, arrive at a definition of the occult object. Occult phenomena and occult practices are notoriously branched out, making it difficult to precisely define their scope. However, this indeterminacy has its paradoxical flip side: no one knows or can discursively state what exactly occultism is, yet everyone spontaneously knows what is meant by it—which itself is an example of telepathic "transference of thought."

Rather than sketching a general theory of occultism, we will focus on the germs of the occult in Freud's own theory. We will focus on a blind spot of Freud's critique of the occult, that is, on those viewpoints he considers scientific and therefore does not scrutinize. This blind spot has a privileged source in the person of Wilhelm Fliess. In today's views of the history of psychoanalysis, Fliess plays the role of Freud's sparring partner whose presence provided the relationship of transference that propelled Freud's self-analyses, thus paving the way for his first psychoanalytic breakthroughs. The two men, who met in Vienna in 1887, had—apart from their names, which seem barely distinguishable on the printed page—much in common:

> Of the undeniable personal attraction something will be said presently, but it is important to remember that there were many more objective bonds of serious interest linking the two men. To begin with, their situation in life had much in common. Young medical specialists, emerging from the Jewish middle class, they were both concerned with establishing a practice and maintaining a family. . . . They were both educated in the humanities and so could make allusions to both classical and modern literature. . . . The scientific background of the two men was very similar, almost identical. The teachings of the Helmholtz school of physics and physiology, which extended to Vienna from Berlin, were those in which Fliess also was brought up. . . . The bearing this common education had on the scientific outlook and aims of the men is of the greatest importance. The scientific interests in common between Freud and Fliess were so interwoven with Freud's personal aims and needs that to give a coldly detached account of them alone would leave a misleading impression.[22]

Freud greatly appreciated Fliess's scientific work, even though their friendship eventually ended explosively and polemically. Fliess had a tremendous influence on Freud's understanding of bisexuality as a constitutional feature of human sexuality, while the dispute between them was ignited by *Sex and Character*, Otto Weininger's notorious 1903 book. According to Jones, Fliess was convinced that a young psychologist and friend of Weininger's named Swoboda was a student of Freud's, and that Freud had shared with Swoboda the details of Fliess's research that then found its way into Weininger's book. Freud denied the connection and the accusation (another case of a telepathic transfer of thoughts?), and his friendship with Fliess did not survive the confrontation.[23]

If we follow a little further along the trail of Fliess's conceptions, which, among other things, formed the background of his theory of bisexuality, it

must be said right away that Fliess's scientific interests—similar to the interest of Newton, Saussure, et alii—far exceeded his central expertise in medicine and biology. Fliess took his cue from two facts "on which he then built
an enormous superstructure of hypotheses."[24] He posited that menstruation
occurs monthly and that there is a connection between the mucus membrane
of the nose and genital events. The mucus membrane was said to often swell
during menstruation as a result of genital irritation. Fliess called this syndrome "nasal reflex neurosis."[25] For Fliess, the causes of this syndrome, which
included a plethora of unrelated symptoms, were either organic or functional,
and he treated it with the nasal administration of cocaine. The syndrome, so
it seemed to Freud, was clearly connected with neurasthenia, or with what he
himself called "actual neuroses."

Science did not confirm these hypotheses, but Fliess clung to them. In particular, the claim regarding menstruation, attributed to both sexes, gave rise to
Fliess's theory of periodicity (!) at work in all vital activities. And this brings
us to the central point: Fliess was looking for the key to this periodicity, and
he found it in the interplay of two numbers, 28 and 23. The first (feminine)
number marks the number of days between the beginning of the previous and
the beginning of the next menstrual cycle. The second (male) number measures the number of days between the end of the previous and the beginning
of the new menstrual cycle. These two numbers supposedly determine the
entire life processes in both sexes. According to Jones,

> These sexual "periods" determined the stages in our growth, the dates of
> our illnesses, and the date of our death. The mother's periods determined
> the sex of the infant and the date of its birth. They operated not only in
> human beings but also throughout the animal kingdom and probably in
> all organic beings. Indeed the remarkable extent to which these numbers
> explained biological phenomena pointed to a deeper connection between
> astronomical movements and the creation of living organisms. From the
> nose to the stars, as with Cyrano de Bergerac![26]

Fliess, unlike Freud, had a talent for mathematics, possessing an ability
of fending off criticisms with intricate calculations. But crucial here is the
fact that these theories not criticized by Freud effectively and obviously rest
on occultic assumptions of numerology, with the nose situated at their very
center. Except in private conversations and correspondence, Freud did not
publicly accept these theories; however, in his private life, he continued to
entertain Fliess's ideas of periodicity long after the two had lost contact. Jones
notes that Fliess's hypothesis effectively provided support for Freud's earlier
superstitions:

Then we have the extraordinary story of how extensively Freud accepted his friend Fliess's "biological" doctrine of the fateful influence of the portentous numbers 28 and 23; . . . Freud's interest in mystic numbers long antedated Fliess's influence. Insofar as calculations based on them were thought to predict the future the doctrine may fairly be said to appertain to the occult. Even when Freud had emancipated himself after years of severe struggle from the influence of his old friend, indeed after a painful quarrel had parted them forever, he retained something of the former beliefs. In his correspondence there are many current allusions to the mysterious numbers. If he tells Ferenczi that an attack of migraine came on 23 plus 2 days after his birthday, or reproaches Jung that he has had no letter from him even 28−3 days from the last, we are bound to conclude that such pointless remarks, half-jocular as they doubtless were, indicated some lingering belief in the significance of such numbers.[27]

Though not warming up publicly to the doctrine of periodicity, Freud certainly publicly accepted the occultic implications of the coupling of sexuality and the sense of smell. In his analysis of "Rat Man," he states:

It turned out that our patient, besides all his other characteristics, was a renifleur [sniffer]. By his own account, when he was a child he had recognized every one by their smell, like a dog; and even when he was grown up he was more susceptible to sensations of smell than most people. I have met with the same characteristic in other neurotics, both in hysterical and in obsessional patients, and I have come to recognize that a tendency to taking pleasure in smell, which has become extinct since childhood, may play a part in the genesis of neurosis. And here I should like to raise the general question whether the atrophy of the sense of smell (which was an inevitable result of man's assumption of an erect posture) and the consequent organic repression of his pleasure in smell may not have had a considerable share in the origin of his susceptibility to nervous disease. This would afford us some explanation of why, with the advance of civilization, it is precisely the sexual life that must fall a victim to repression. For we have long known the intimate connection in the animal organization between the sexual instinct and the function of the olfactory organ.[28]

Here, suffice it to highlight the astonishing connection between the nose and knowledge. The nose knows—the nose knows without being subject to the discursive criteria of knowledge. In "The Freudian Thing," Lacan follows Freud's line of thought, drawing a connection between the truth and the nose. Addressing the reader in the first person, the Truth emphatically asserts: "Let a sense of smell surer than all your categories guide you in the race to which I challenge you."[29] I will return to this, as well as to Freud's thesis regarding the atrophying effect of human bipedalism on the sense of smell.

THE CROOK OF THE ELBOW

Writing a philosophical history of smell is tantamount to tracing an history of the ahistorical. In his novel *Perfume: The Story of a Murderer* (1985), Patrick Süskind says of his nosewise character Jean-Baptiste Grenouille that "if his name . . . has been forgotten today, it is . . . because his gifts and his sole ambition were restricted to a domain that leaves no traces in history: to the fleeting realm of scent."[30] In the German original, the subtitle of *Perfume* reads *die Geschichte*,[31] meaning "story" or "history," which makes Süskind's story a history of the ahistorical. Grenouille embodies a variety of smell-characteristics discussed so far. Crucially, there is the antinomy between names and smells, alluded to in the passage above and reiterated throughout the novel. His genius residing in his nostrils, Grenouille "had never in all his life handled speech well."[32] His aphasia mirrors universal olfactory anomia; his personal shortcoming emulates that of language itself: "our language is of no use when it comes to describing the smellable world."[33] Süskind's novel reproduces the Proustian dichotomy, but with a twist. In the figure of Grenouille, words and smells, the mouth and the nose, swap places. This inverted world consists of scents forming a differential system more complex and sophisticated than language itself. In contrast to our inability of memorizing them, Grenouille had no problem holding on to scents "and had gathered tens of thousands, hundreds of thousands of specific smells." Apart from easily recalling them, he "could also actually smell them simply upon recollection."[34] Moreover, he was able to form "smelled sentences" by "sheer imagination" (*in seiner bloßen Phantasie*) creating "odors that did not exist in the real world":

> It was as if he were an autodidact possessed of a huge vocabulary of odours that enabled him to form at will great numbers of smelled sentences [*Geruchssätze*]—and at an age when other children stammer words, so painfully drummed into them, to formulate their first very inadequate sentences describing the world.[35]

While olfactory cues typically present obstacles to naming, Grenouille's linguistic capacity was prompted solely by his nose. When, at the age of four, he finally started speaking, "he used only nouns, and essentially only nouns for concrete objects, plants, animals, human beings—and only then if the objects, plants, animals or human beings overcame him with their odour."[36] He only spoke when—unawares, *ex abrupto*—odors overpowered and subdued him, *ihm unversehens geruchlich überwältigten*. Instead of suppressing verbal signs, olfactory indices incite them: "He had seen wood a hundred times before, had heard the word a hundred times before. . . . But [until its smell overcame him] the object called wood had never been of sufficient interest for him to trouble himself to speak its name."[37] Unlike the rest of us, Grenouille only spelled when he smelled, consequently having had great difficulty with "words designating non-smelling objects, with abstract ideas," which he "confused . . . with one another, and even as an adult used them unwillingly and often incorrectly: . . . what these were meant to express remained a mystery to him."[38] But "everyday language would soon prove inadequate for designating all the olfactory notions [Begriffe] that he had accumulated within himself. . . . Soon he . . . could clearly differentiate them as objects in a way that other people could not have done by sight." The "poverty of language" could not measure up to "the richness of the world perceivable by smell." Names fail to capture the self-othering essence of smells: why should things possess only one name, "when from minute to minute, second to second, the amalgam of hundreds of odours mixed iridescently into ever new and changing unities . . . each filled at every step and every breath with yet another odour and thus animated with another identity"?[39]

Grenouille's nose exhibited great power of discrimination, figuring as a means of a "dividing of being." With the sole aid of it, he could make out in minute detail the entire edifice of his world, accounting for all objects within it. But at the limit of this methodically organized order of self-identical entities lied division itself. Though nosewise, possessing an unmatched sense of smell that he hid from the world, Grenouille had no odor and hence was nose-blind when it came to himself, giving a twist to the biblical dictum "Noses they have, but they do not smell" (Ps 115:6). His ability to sense the subtlest of odors across great distances was underpinned and necessitated by the nose's incapacity of reflectively relating to itself. If in his world odors are words, sentences, language itself, then his "huge vocabulary of odours" was lacking a name (𐌢) with which to capture his own identity.[40]

What do humans smell like, according to Grenouille? "Normally human odour was nothing special, or it was ghastly. Children smelled insipid, men urinous, all sour sweat and cheese, women smelled of rancid fat and rotting fish. Totally uninteresting, repulsive—that was how humans smelled."[41] Hence, "there was a basic perfumatory theme to the odour of humanity, a rather simple one, incidentally: a sweaty-oily, sour-cheesy, quite richly repulsive basic theme that clung to all humans equally." But at the same time, "the odour of human being did not exist, any more than the human countenance," such that above the basic perfumatory theme of humanity, "each individual's aura hovered only as a small cloud of more refined particularity. / That aura, however, the highly complex, unmistakable code of a *personal* odour, was not perceptible for most people in any case."[42] It is this imperceptible aura that animates, *beseelt*, a person's identity. But does it have a source? Where does the aura emanate from?

He laid the index and middle fingers of his left hand under his nose and breathed along the backs of his fingers. He smelled the moist spring air spiced with anemones. He did not smell anything of his fingers. He turned his hand over and sniffed at the palm. He sensed the warmth of his hand, but smelled nothing. Then he rolled up the ragged sleeve of his shirt, buried his nose in the crook of his elbow. He knew that this was the spot where all humans smell like themselves. But he could smell nothing. He could not smell anything in his armpits, nor on his feet, nor around his genitals when he bent down to them as far as he possibly could. It was grotesque. He, Grenouille, who could smell other people miles away, was incapable of smelling his own genitals not a handspan away![43]

He searched every nook, crook, and cranny of his body, but found no smell. Fingers, hands, armpits, feet, genitals emit the odor of humanity as such, its basic perfumatory theme, while the source of human variation, of the aura of individuality and personal identity, is tucked away in the crook of one's elbow.[44] The conditions there certainly appear ripe for the task. A rich microbiome, the crook of the elbow hosts six tribes of bacteria, busy cooking up scents.[45] But why should the aura emanate from the crook of the elbow, exactly? The crook is the spot where the exteriority of the body folds back on itself, relating to itself, and thus forming an interior, self-relational pocket. This hollowed-out inner pocket is merely a fold of the Outer, the spot where the Outer relates to, or affects, itself. Thus, according to Deleuze,

> folds and folding . . . together make up an inside: they are not something other than the outside, but precisely the inside of the outside. . . . This derivation or differentiation must be understood in the sense in which the *relation to oneself* assumes an independent status. It is as if the relations of the outside folded back to create a doubling, allow a relation to oneself to emerge, and constitute an inside which is hollowed out.[46]

While the odor of humanity as such is the mere *effluvium* of the body, the aura results from the body's folding back on itself, reflexively relating to itself. But since it is a single self-identical surface of the body's exteriority that, through folding back on itself, creates an "intimate exteriority," interiority is exterior's self-difference, an outside excluded into itself, that is, *the extimate*.[47]

The aura that Grenouille now sets out to manufacture is the aura of the reflexively opposed ($a \neq a$), not the aura of the self-identical ($a = a$). Grenouille has no smell, but to pass as human, he must emulate not the smell of humanity but the imperceptible odor of a human, thus veiling his own odorlessness with an odorless odor. To emulate such an odor, one must imitate the human being's folding back on itself: "It was a strange perfume that Grenouille created that day. There had never before been a stranger one on earth. It did not smell like a scent, but like a *human being who gives off scent.*" The self-reflexive doubling is crucial here: "If one had smelled this perfume in a dark room, one would have thought a second person was standing there. And if a human being, who smelled like a human being, had applied it, that person would have seemed to have the smell of two people, or, worse still, to be a monstrous double creature [*Doppelwesen*]."[48] Creating this veil-scent, Grenouille deceives us into thinking there is a human being behind the scent. Such is the triumph of the scent he created over the nose.[49] The doubling is important: to pass for a human, he must mimic not a human in its self-identity, but a human identity self-dissipating, that is, not the human but the human stain. In terms of the biblical story, Grenouille's perfume emulates the self-splitting of man(kind), man as *Doppelwesen*.

One final note before moving on. A godless creature, Grenouille aspires to a godlike status. Born *inter urinas et faeces*, his aspiration is that of a modern self-made man, singlehandedly accomplishing the impossible transition from *Kot* to *Gott*. As a genius perfumer, he is certainly in the business of creating that which prior to his creation did not exist in the world. His supernatural nose figures as an appendix, an artificial extension of his body, an instrument of the unnatural by which he exercises his mastery over the natural world. In this sense, he is what Freud called "a prosthetic God," *ein Prothesengott*:

> These things that, by his science and technology, man has brought about on this earth, on which he first appeared as a feeble animal organism and on which each individual of his species must once more make its entry ("oh inch of nature!") as a helpless suckling—these things do not only sound like a fairy tale, they are an actual fulfilment of every—or of almost every—fairy-tale wish. All these assets he may lay claim to as his cultural acquisition. Long ago he formed an ideal conception of omnipotence and omniscience which he embodied in his gods. To these gods he attributed everything that seemed unattainable to his wishes, or that was forbidden to him. One may say, therefore, that these gods were cultural ideals. Today he has come very close to the attainment of this ideal, he has almost become a god himself. Only, it is true, in the fashion in which ideals are usually attained according to the general judgement of humanity. Not completely; in some respects not at all, in others only half way. Man has, as it were, become a kind of prosthetic God. When he puts on all his auxiliary organs he is truly magnificent; but those organs have not grown onto him and they still give him much trouble at times.[50]

The episode just analyzed sheds a new light on Freud's famous passage. Grenouille is a prosthetic God, but the prosthesis he creates is paradoxically intended to *humanize him.* His auxiliary organ, the nose, fits him all too well, and to become human, a gap must be introduced, ever so slightly detaching the organ from the body. Grenouille's perfume unveils a dialectic inherent in Freud's text. It is not only the case that, through acquiring his auxiliary organs, the human becomes God-like. It is equally true that only by acquiring them, does the human become human-like. Prosthetic divinization effects humanization. The gap separating the human from God is the gap humanizing the human.

A CRUMB OF PHILOSOPHY

Grenouille's story, however, truly began with an encounter by means of which the divided subject becomes unconscious of himself. His great ability of historicizing smells, that is, of allotting them their proper places within the olfactory system, stumbles upon the ahistorical. This fatal event was brought about by Grenouille's encounter with a scent that had no place in this world. Moreover, this scent was not just inexistent and hence previously unencountered by him in the real world; rather, it was *both inexistent and unimaginable*, eluding the creative capacities of his splendid olfactory imagination, *Phantasie*. As such, the scent was, strictly speaking, undifferentiable: it had a freshness, but Grenouille could not relate it to any of the source-names: it was not the freshness of "limes," "pomegranates," "myrrh," "cinnamon bark," "curly mint," "birch," "camphor," "pine needles," "May rain," "frosty wind," or "well water." It had a warmth, but its warmth was not that of "bergamot," "cypress," "musk," "jasmine," "narcissi," "rosewood," or "iris." It was like "silk," yet also like "pastry soaked in honey-sweet milk," *wie honigsüße Milch, in der sich Biskuit löst.*[51] Incomparable, beyond description, and lacking a name, this scent renders Grenouille's world incomplete while figuring as the disfigured stain of his own (dispossessed) subjectivity. The singularity of this scent is not defined by what it has or lacks, but by what it *has lacking*.

Before this fatal encounter, Grenouille, like Proust, was living a dreary, *langweilige*, existence; and like Proust's search, Grenouille's quest was triggered by *a crumb*:

> He was just about to leave his dreary exhibition and head homewards along the gallery of the Louvre when the wind brought him something, a tiny, hardly noticeable something, a crumb, an atom of scent; no, even less than that: it was more the premonition of a scent than the scent itself—and at the same time it was definitely a premonition of something he had never smelled before.[52]

Though already at "the age of six he had completely grasped his surroundings olfactorily," such that there was "no spot [*Fleck*] be it ever so small, that he did not know by smell, could not recognize again by holding its uniqueness firmly in his memory,"[53] this scent-crumb was something else entirely. It had no spatial consistency, no extension, or else he would have spotted the spot, the *Fleck*, sooner. Not only does the crumb not have a place in the organizational structure of his olfactory world, but it is also out of this world, its externality reduced to the passing of time. Lacking spatial consistency, the crumb is also temporally unlocalizable. Its self-othering reduces it to the irreducibility of the Now, that is, to the ungraspable interval between "not yet" and "no longer." Doesn't the lack of spatial consistency testify to the *occult* character of the crumb? Of the crumb as the "real core" of the unknown?

Encountering this atom—*less* than an atom—of scent, Grenouille is smelling as if for the very first time.[54] This less-than-an-atom first announces itself as the clinamen of Lucretius's atomism. Imperceptible, the clinamen is the minimal swerve that disrupts the laminar flow of olfactory atoms through the void.[55] Though introducing turbulence into the orderly "primordial chaos" of Grenouille's olfactory world, the new odor simultaneously provides the initiative for and premonition of an establishing of a new order. Met with this obstacle, the virtuoso becomes an everyman. The crumb is not only a stranger in our world, but also in Grenouille's inverted world: it is *out of this and that world*. The smell is barely noticeable, the narrator tells us: less than an atom, a crumb, a particle, a fragment, a leftover of something undefinable, "the premonition of scent [rather] than the scent itself," *eher die Ahnung eines Dufts als ein tatsächlicher Duft*. The crumb is a presentiment of a scent—in a word, a prescentiment. Recall that Grenouille's speech was prompted by smells overpowering him *ex abrupto, unversehens*, without prior warning, catching him unawares. The smell-crumb, however, was all premonition of scent rather than the scent itself. Though his speech is typically prompted by scents, this smell-crumb renders Grenouille speechless.

The smell-trace lacks the ontological consistency of anything. Though nothing at all, the crumb is not nothing. Less than something and more than nothing, neither being nor non-being, the smell-trace signals the domain of the unborn or unrealized.[56] Not yet a scent, but rather a premonition prefiguring the first appearance of a scent, the smell-crumb is a prescentiment: "The scent was inconceivable, indescribable, could not be categorized in any way—it really ought not exist at all. And yet there it was as plain and splendid as day."[57] The scent is, we could say, *ein Duft der nicht sein dürfte*, a smell that ought not be, and yet here it is in its *Selbstverständlichkeit*, its matter-of-factness, as something self-evident, though also something never smelled before, the Neversmelled, *das Niegerochene*.

The odor forces itself on the subject with the logical solidity and veracity of a material implication: *If a smell like that existed (which it does not), it would be such that it ought not exist*. In *Seminar XX* (1972–1973), Lacan makes use of the logical structure of material implication to account for "the other, female satisfaction" irreducible to the male, phallic one, while stressing that material implication "was perhaps what was most solid in logic."[58] Is Grenouille's smell-crumb not an instance of an Other enjoyment unbefitting his mapped out olfactory universe? Lacan's formulae of sexuation map out two distinctive—male and female—forms of totalization. In *Portnoy's Complaint* (1969), Philip Roth nicely captures their duality. As a child, Portnoy would discover in every woman the unmistakable identity of his own mother, the ultimate shapeshifter, whose transformations and reincarnations he tried time and time again to catch a glimpse of but perpetually failed. His father, on the other hand, is described as perpetually suffering from poor bowel movements, finding no relief:

> Her ubiquity and his constipation, my mother flying in through the bedroom window [to transform herself back into her familiar shape], my father reading the evening paper with a suppository up his ass . . . these, Doctor, are the earliest impressions I have of my parents, of their attributes and secrets.[59]

The dichotomy corresponds precisely to the "attributes and secrets" articulated in Lacan's formulae of sexuation: the male totality is essentially *constipated*, the female *ubiquitous*. The male form is predicated upon a constipating exception (the totality of Grenouille's olfactory universe relies on him remaining odorless), while the ubiquitous totality of the female form is premised on the impossibility of a constipated totalization, accentuated by the smell-crumb rendering Grenouille's universe untotalizable.

The smell-crumb is the everything *else* that must be accounted for and contained, or else *everything* falls apart. It is only a premonition, yet it is a "certain premonition," a hunch that doesn't deceive. Interestingly, Rousseau already mentions the nature of smells as presentiments: "Smells by themselves are weak sensations. They move the imagination more than the sense and affect us not so much by fulfilment as by expectation."[60] The expectation has the sinister character of a premonition of something still eluding him. As a crumb of the unsymbolizable Real, the prescentiment triggers an almost "sickening excitement" and "exited helplessness"[61] akin to anxiety. He "suspected [*er ahnte*] that it was not he who followed the scent, but the scent that had captured him [*ihn gefangengenommen hatte*] and was drawing him irresistibly to it [*zu sich zog*]." The scent is the point of *Anziehung*, the primordially repressed crumb effecting an irresistible attraction that arrests Grenouille, making him a prisoner of his own fate. And the closer the scent had pulled him, the stronger was its power of attraction, its *Anziehungskraft*: "Grenouille walked with no will of his own."[62]

Incidentally, Lacan explicitly relates anxiety to *prè-sentiment*: "Anxiety is this cut that opens up, affording a view of what now you can hear better, the unexpected, the visit, the piece of news, that which is so well expressed in the term *pressentiment*, which isn't simply to be heard as the premonition of something, but also as the pre-feeling, the *prè-sentiment*, that which stands prior to the first appearance of a feeling."[63] Süskind describes this anxiety-producing *prè-sentiment* as follows:

> He had the prescience of something extraordinary—this scent was the key for ordering all odours, one could understand nothing about odours if one did not understand this one scent, and his whole life would be bungled, if he, Grenouille, did not succeed in possessing it. He had to have it, not simply in order to possess it, but for his heart to be at peace. / He was almost sick with excitement.[64]

Possessed by the scent, he has to possess it. The crumb is unsettling, disturbing Grenouille's *geruchliche Ruhe*, the "olfactory quiet" (translated as "olfactory peace") that characterizes his *lautlosen Geschäft*, his otherwise "noiseless business" (translated as "soundless procedure") now disturbed by a loud smell.[65] If we refer once again to ancient atomism, then the starting point is the orderly chaos of the olfactory universe, disrupted by the *clinamen*, a minimal deviation that triggers an anxious premonition of something incomprehensible. And just as the less-than-an-atom of odor is not an odor but only a premonition of an odor, *clinamen* is nothing but a excarnate deviation.

The noiseless business of smelling is best captured by a passage from Rilke's novel *The Notebooks of Malte Laurids Brigge* (1910). The scene takes place in a mansion that was recently partially destroyed by fire. The gathered company suddenly and anxiously catches a whiff—not of smoke but—of the premonition of smoke:

> She made a distinctly strained impression, like someone who does not want to be disturbed. She made slight, dismissive gestures with her soft, beringed hands; somebody said "Psstt!" and suddenly there was complete silence. / Behind the people in the room, the huge objects from the old house were thrusting upon the scene, far too close. The weighty family silver gleamed, looming as if seen through the magnifying glass. My father looked round, somewhat taken aback. / "Mama can smell something," said Viera Schulin behind him. "We always have to be quiet. She smells with her ears." She herself stood attentively with her eyebrows raised, all nose.[66]

Unable to hear with their nose, they smell with their ears, desperate to spell it out.[67] Entering the quiet of the olfactory world is akin to entering the realm of the death drive: the "clamour of life," the lively laughing and chit-chatting, is suddenly interrupted by the appearance of a smell that renders the lively company mute, keeping their tongues on their toes.[68] The smell is acousmatic, its originating cause unknown. In the face of it, the company goes quiet like Pythagoras's pupils, the *akousmatikoi*. The prescentiment is indicative of something about to happen, a change looming large, appearing in threatening, magnified form. As words recede, things stand out, "thrusting [themselves] upon the scene, far too close" to us. Suddenly, inert matter comes to life, objects seem to have taken a deep breath, expanding, blowing up, appearing "as if seen through the magnifying glass." But which of these newly animated objects is breathing and, hence, emanating the smell? The company sets out to locate its source, but its neither here nor there; the smell cannot be pinned to anything:

> Zoë, a practical and thorough person, busied herself at the stove. The Count went about, pausing in every corner and waiting. "It isn't here," he would announce. The Countess had got up without any idea where to look. My father turned slowly on his heel as if the odour was behind him. The marchesa, who had instantly assumed that it was an offensive smell, held her handkerchief over her mouth and looked at everyone in turn to ascertain if it was gone. "Here, here," Viera called from time to time, as if she had found it. And around each word was a curious silence. As for myself, I had been busily sniffing away along with the others.[69]

The scene is halfway between a police investigation and a séance, a methodical search for clues that might reveal the ghost's identity:

> But all at once . . . I was overcome, for the first time in my life, by something akin to a fear of ghosts. It dawned on me that all these assertive, grown-up people who had just been talking and laughing were going about bent over, occupied with something invisible; that they conceded something was there that they could not see. And the terrible thing was that it was stronger than all of them. / My fear grew apace. I imagined that what they were looking for might suddenly break forth from withing me, like a rash; and then they would see it and would point at me.[70]

The child notices the curious power that the ghost holds over the adults who purportedly don't believe in them. The presentiment of a scent takes a hold of them, much like the occultic beliefs in spirits grab a hold of the scientific spirits of modernity. Emphatically invisible, the smell is a prescentiment, that is, something structurally prior to its own appearance. The company is not only puzzled about where it is coming from; they are unsure whether it even exists. But the smell isn't nothing; rather, it *is* "not nothing" as irreducible to "being."[71] The initial hermeneutics of faith soon turns into a hermeneutics of suspicion, where everything and everyone is suspect. Moreover, the suspicion is dialectical, folding back on itself: one even suspects oneself. Will the suspicious and suspecting finger finally point at *me*? Will they single *me* out, am I the ghost? Will the self-othering dissolution of my reflexive identity suddenly break out of its bodily prison like a rash? Does it show already?

Occultism fundamentally presuppose the existence of "beings" in space that cannot be attached to a spatially extended body: "From the dawn of history until quite recent times," writes Jones, "man has believed firmly in the existence and activity of discarnate beings."[72] Süskind's smell-crumb and Rilke's spectral scent are "spiritual" bodies without a bodily body. However, to claim that the crumb is a discarnate being is not entirely accurate. Though disembodied, the crumb is not discarnate. The already quoted Adornian shift from Spirit to spirits can be read as a move from Spirit incarnate to *spirits excarnate*. Moreover, the crumb is not an excarnated *being*, but rather an *excarnated not-nothing*. From here, we can return to our discussion of psychoanalysis and the occult. We immediately see that psychoanalysis ultimately centers on this excarnated object. The excarnated scent is not and cannot be an object of science—it can only be its oozing remainder, breaking forth from within it like a rash. And ultimately, psychoanalysis will focus its efforts on conceptualizing this excarnated ooze of scientific modernity to wrest it from the spiritists, thus countering the modern occultist revival of premodern religious interest. All of this will come at a high price. In relation to the occult, psychoanalysis will be faced with a double and continuous challenge: that which the occultists are after will break out of its findings like a rash. And psychoanalysis will be forced into anxious self-inquisition (*Am I, psychoanalysis, this occult spirit?*), as well as into efforts to bone out the false pretender, reducing him to his Real core.

The occult concerns an object without spatial consistency, an object that escapes the domain of sensibility. And what is the psychoanalytic name for this occult discharge of sensuality, if not sexuality—sexuality as an excremental increment of sensibility? Fliess's numerological doctrine of bisexuality had an influence on Freud and on Freudian theory, but ultimately was an occult offspring of Freud's own theory of sexuality. The occultic core of Freud's theory of sexuality thus found a displaced echo in Fliess's occultism of periodicity and bisexuality. To catch a whiff of the difference, one must listen with one's nose.

MURDER MOST FRAGRANT

The Neversmelled leads Grenouille to a young girl, a barely pubescent virgin. To merge with the (less than an) atom of scent, he must strip it of its bodily shell. Grenouille's encounter with the girl is reminiscent of Adam's encounter with the void of naming, though the repetition once again comes with a twist. Like Adam, who has familiarized himself with "every beast of the field and every bird of the heavens," Grenouille is thoroughly familiar with the city's constipated smellscape, unsurprised by it, until catching a whiff of the unnamed. The smell-trace eventually leads him to a girl in the rue des Marais. For the first time in his life, Grenouille couldn't believe his nose and had to briefly resort to eyesight to assure himself that she was in fact the source of the smell.[73] "Funny, it doesn't smell like a human!" we imagine him saying. Better still: "Funny, it doesn't smell like a smell!" Just like no "helper" could measure up to Eve, "every perfume that Grenouille had smelled until now, every edifice of odours that he had so playfully created within himself, seemed at once to be utterly meaningless. A hundred thousand odours seemed worthless in the presence of this scent. This one scent was the higher principle, the pattern by which the others must be ordered."[74]

His olfactory memory, impeccable as it was, could never have done it justice. He had to stay with the girl long enough to decipher the scent's higher principle. This, at long last, was "the flesh of his flesh," but was he the flesh of hers?[75] Adam, like Grenouille, "had never felt so wonderful," but had Eve, like the girl in the rue des Marais, "felt the air turn cold"? The girl, too, had a premonition, "was uneasy, sensed a strange chill," and "felt as if a cold draught had risen up behind her, as if someone had opened a door leading into a vast, cold cellar."[76] Frightened, Grenouille's virgin offered no resistance when he "put his hands on her throat" so as "not to lose the least trace of her scent."[77] Met with this scent, the virtuoso became an everyman, and the everyman became a murderer. If it weren't for the book's subtitle, the murder scene would have caught us by surprise. By killing its support vehicle, isn't the intoxicating substance bound to dissipate? Wouldn't it have been more prudent to take in her smell from afar, rather than grabbing her by the throat?

Grenouille could have been driven to murder in a desperate attempt at restabilizing his world suddenly disturbed, devalued, its structural integrity threatened by this piece of the Real. But no; such a restoration would have been impossible, he could never "let it be," meekly returning to his old world. But as a child of the Enlightenment, Grenouille could have the cake and eat it too. Though uneducated, he displays the thought patterns of a scientist. Instead of the thing considered scent's mere accidental support-vehicle, he is after the odorant, the principle, the formula, "a model, . . . a scent diagram."[78] And what is the word, the principle, the formula, if not the murder of the thing, that is, the phallic signifier prophylactically re-constipating his fractured olfactory universe? The narrator says it plainly: "Her form did not interest him. She no longer existed for him as a body, but only as *a disembodied scent*."[79] The German original does not speak of an *entkörpert* (disembodied) scent, but rather of a *körperlos* (bodyless), incorporeal scent. The English translation brings out a crucial aspect merely implied in the original term: as an organ without the body, the scent is not merely incorporeal but rather excarnated by way of a subtraction of Being. Moreover, as a perfumer, Grenouille was in the business of "extracting the scent from inert objects": more precisely, *die Gewinnung der Düfte lebloser Dinge* (distilling the excarnated essence of lifeless things).[80] The ability "to snatch [*entreißen*] the scented soul from matter" fascinated him and "kindled his enthusiasm [*Begeisterung*]." *Entreißen*, that is, extracting the soul from matter, literally endows Grenouille with Spirit, *begeistert ihm*, for the "scented soul, that ethereal oil, was in fact the best thing about matter, the only reason for his interest in it. The rest of the stupid stuff . . . were of no concern to him. They were mere husk and ballast, to be disposed of."[81] However, the murderer disembodying scents is disembodied himself: "The murderer seemed impalpable, incorporeal [*körperlos*], like a ghost."[82] Moreover, immediately prior to Grenouille's taking possession of her disembodied scent, the girl in the rue des Marais was busy pitting yellow plums. She was removing the kernels from the fruit and Grenouille will do the same. But unlike the girl who is discarding the kernels, Grenouille will discard the fruit so as to excarnate the precious kernel of scent. Indeed, "on wild trees the flowers are fragrant, on cultivated trees, the fruits."[83]

We only smell that which inhabits the excarnated edge of Being. In his discussion of the physical senses, Hegel singles out this crucial aspect of smell in very precise terms: "Denn zu riechen ist nur dasjenige, was schon in Sichverzehren begriffen ist" (For we can smell only what is in the process of wasting away).[84] From the point of view of the murder scene, two opposing meanings can be attributed to Hegel's *Sichverzehren*. If we abstract from their reflected senses and consider their immediate linguistic meaning, "wasting away" implies a lack, particularly a lack of nourishment required to sustain me, thereby signifying a process of weakening and of a gradual loss of strength. On the other hand, *Sichverzehren* also signifies the process of being devoured, ravenously eaten up, avidly enjoyed to the point of destruction. But the two meanings of lack and excess should be read together. Think of Kafka's "hunger artist."[85] Hunger artists were very popular in turn-of-the-century Europe, attracting large crowds of pleasure-seekers willing to pay to witness their fasting. The aesthetic practice of Kafka's protagonist, however, exceeds mere fasting. A hunger artist is not simply a hungering artist wasting away. Instead of not eating, of abstaining from food, the hunger artist emphatically eats nothing—hunger *is* his nourishment. Perhaps a keen sense of smell is required to fully grasp this point, for another of Kafka's protagonists, a dog, would say it best: to truly comprehend the notion of nourishment, one needs to sink one's teeth into hunger. I will return to this.

Furthermore, *Sichverzehren* is also a *self*-devouring, enacted not by an external agent but by the very substance undergoing its own dissolution. Montaigne writes of smells: "He who complains of nature that she has left man without an instrument to convey smells to his nose is wrong, for they convey themselves."[86] We can smell only what is in the process of self-devouring (*Sichverzehren*). The cannibalism of things is the condition for smelling. It indicates, for lack of a better word, an epithanatotic process of self-dissolution as the dissolution of the Self, of one's own reflexive identity. To briefly return to Proust, we see him highlighting the same absorptive capacity of smells. No sooner, he writes, I had raised "a spoonful of the tea in which I had soaked a morsel of the cake" than

> a shiver ran through me and I stopped, intent upon the extraordinary thing that was happening to me. An exquisite pleasure had invaded my senses, something isolated, detached, with no suggestion of its origin. And at once the vicissitudes of life had become indifferent to me, its disasters innocuous, its brevity illusory—this new sensation having had the effect, which love has, of filling me with a precious essence; or rather this essence was not in me, it *was* me.[87]

Adorno and Horkheimer emphasize this aspect of self-devouring as a devouring of the self in their famous line from the *Dialectic of Enlightenment*: "Im Sehen bleibt man, wer man ist, im Riechen geht man auf" (When we see we remain who we are, when we smell we are absorbed entirely).[88] The touch of the eye is theatrical, that of smell absorptive.[89] Smell encroaches on the eye and the "I." The moment I smell, my self-identical Self comes undone, dissipating, ceasing to be itself. When I smell that which is in the process of wasting away, my Self wastes away. Such a reading is confirmed by Grenouille's crumb. Instead of the more common word *Krümel*, cognate with English "crumb," Süskind makes the uncommon choice of *Bröselchen*, whose etymology proves revealing. A diminutive of *Brösel*, the word is related to Old English *brosnian*, "to corrupt," "to decay," "to perish," "to rot." A few pages earlier, the adjective *bröselig* is used: "aromatic flakes of resin odour crumbled from the pinewood planking of the shed,"[90] *von der Fichtenwand des Schuppens fiel in der Wärme bröseliger Harzduft ab*. The decaying, perishing, rotting resin-smell *fiel ab*, "crumbled from" the pinewood planking. The verb is important, for it underscores the *decaying* smell *wasting* away (*Abfall* = waste, refuse). We only ever smell *Bröselchen* (crumbs of decay).

After the encounter, Grenouille did not remain who he was; the experience was transformative, for it was through becoming unconscious of himself that he realized what he was destined to be. Returning home in possession of the phallic scent diagram, he felt

> as if he had been born a second time; no, not a second time, the first time, for until now he had merely existed like an animal with a most nebulous self-awareness. But after today, he felt as if he finally knew who he really was: nothing less than a genius. And that the meaning and goal and purpose of his life had a higher destiny: nothing less than to revolutionize the

odoriferous world. . . . He had found the compass for his future life. . . . He must become . . . the greatest perfumer of all time.[91]

His nose, prophylactically employed in the girl's murder to re-constipate his universe, thus finds its true calling: the prophylactic artistry of perfumery. The virtuoso became an everyman, the everyman became a murderer, and, finally, the murderer became a genius. But his story does not end here. The very final scene of the novel repeats the initial murder scene, but by adding an extra element. Grenouille ends up back at the cemetery where he was born (the first time around, at least). Pouring an entire bottle of the excarnated scent onto his body, he draws a crowd of criminals who find his scent irresistible, eventually disembodying him to eat his excarnated flesh.

THE OTHER SENSE OF SMELL

Here, the other sense of smell is revealed. Thus far, we've been focusing on smells that arise from sources external to the body and enter the body upon inhalation. The process is called *orthonasal smelling* and proceeds through sniffing. However, there is "a second way of smelling." "To which of our senses," asks Henry Fincks in 1886, "are we most indebted for the pleasures of the table?" He answers:

> To name the sense of taste in answer to this question would be quite as incorrect as to assert that we go to the opera to please our eyes. More incorrect, in fact, because many do attend the opera chiefly on account of the spectacle; whereas, in regard to gastronomic delights it is safe to say that at least two-thirds of out enjoyment is due to the sense of smell. . . . There is a second way of smelling, of which most people are quite unconscious—viz., by *exhaling through the nose* while eating and drinking. In the directions often given to children to clasp their nose when taking a nauseous medicine, this process is instinctively recognized; but it has never been made clear, so far as the writer is aware, that on it is based the whole art and science of cookery.[92]

Anosmics often complain that since losing their sense of smell, food has lost its taste. This loss of flavor has nothing to do with being unable to smell the food on our plate, but rather concerns odorants that are released from inside our mouth during consumption. These odorants stimulate the olfactory epithelium upon exhalation through the back of the throat and out the front of the nose. This other way of smelling is called *retronasal olfaction*.[93] If it wasn't for retro-smell, food would have taste but no flavor, meaning that we could distinguish, for instance, "salty" from "sweet," but not "apple" from "pear." The mouth deterritorializes into a dissipation machine long before uttering the first word. The division further supports the extimate nature of smells, split between internally and externally sourced olfactory inputs, between extra- and intra-nasal smelling.

Thus, One divides into Two. Does the duality of ortho- and retro-smell not provide the key to distinguishing the murder of the girl from the novel's cannibalistic finale? Immediately after the totemic meal, the cannibals search their hearts for the higher motive, the principle behind their murder. And before long, they find it: Love. The way to a man's heart is through retronasal smelling:

> Though the meal lay rather heavy on their stomachs, their hearts were definitely light. All of a sudden there were delightful, bright flutterings in their dark souls. And on their faces was a delicate, virginal glow of happiness. Perhaps that was why they were shy about looking up and gazing into one another's eyes. / When they finally did dare it, at first with stolen glances and then candid ones, they had to smile. They were uncommonly proud. For the first time they had done something out of Love.[94]

The scene should remind us of Freud's famous scientific myth of the murder and subsequent devouring of the primal father by the pack of his sons. In *Totem and Taboo* (1912–1913), as well as in other texts, Freud draws a link between cannibalism and identification: by devouring the primal father, the sons took possession of his qualities. Hence, their cannibalism served a "higher motive": "The higher motives for cannibalism among primitive races have a similar origin. By incorporating parts of a person's body through the act of eating, one at the same time acquires the qualities possessed by him."[95] The cannibals become what they ate, fusing with the other in an act of organic identification:

> Cannibal savages as they were, it goes without saying that they devoured their victim as well as killing him. The violent primal father had doubtless been the feared and envied model of each one of the company of brothers: and in the act of devouring him they accomplished their identification with him, and each one of them acquired a portion of his strength. The totem meal, which is perhaps mankind's earliest festival, would thus be a repetition and a commemoration of this memorable and criminal deed, which was the beginning of so many things—of social organization, of moral restrictions and of religion.[96]

Was love the driving force behind Grenouille's initial murder? If love is the driving force behind both of these murders, a distinction introduced by Kierkegaard may be of some help. In *Repetition* (1843), Kierkegaard retells a story of a young acquaintance "deeply, passionately, beautifully, and self-effacingly in love."[97] He confessed his love and found it reciprocated; yet instead of consuming it, the love was his "melancholy preoccupation," such that "he was already, in the earliest days, in a position to recollect his love. He was basically finished with the whole relationship. Simply by having begun, he advanced such a terrific distance that he had leapt right over life."[98] Such was the young man's *recollection's love* that is bound to make a person unhappy. By recollecting his love, he is repeating it backward as something already past. But the unhappiness is also a haven, for "the great advantage of recollection is that it begins with a loss. This is its security—it has nothing to lose."[99] Grenouille's love for the virgin is a recollection's love premised on loss. As such, it has the metonymic structure of desire as conceived by Lacan. Grenouille treats the love object as already dead, with its intoxicating essence safely committed to memory and recollected at will. "It would make no great difference if the girl died tomorrow," Kierkegaard comments on his young friend's love, "He would still throw himself into his love. . . . Her existence or non-existence, in a certain sense, actually meant nothing to him."[100] Following Kierkegaard, we can say that Grenouille's virgin was not his beloved; permeating every aspect of his being with her excarnated scent, she awakened the perfumer in him and thus signed her own death sentence.[101] In removing the spectral flesh from her body, he finds his calling. For what is perfumery if not the art of excarnation, of extracting carnal essences from bodies?

After the initial encounter, and after committing the ortho-scent to memory, Grenouille was back to his old unhappy self. His enjoyment was indeed just as solitary as the young man's love. Recollection's love relies on *Erinnerung*, a historical interiorization and hence universalization of the ahistorical crumb. It remains subject to the experience of fundamental fantasy as fantasy of a relation, which, as Kierkegaard notes, can only be a rapport with a corpse.

The melancholy recollection's love relies on orthonasal incorporation by identification. The final scene of the novel, however, mobilizes another aspect of *Erinnerung*: retronasal interiorization by way of cannibalistic ingestion. Here, the love object appears to be consumed, and a move is accomplished by which, to quote Lacan, "the experience of the fundamental phantasy becomes the drive."[102] For Lacan, the drive is consubstantial with repetition, so could the final scene of the novel be depicting *repetition's love*? Steeped in disembodied scent, Grenouille becomes the partial object of the partial drives. It is not his body that is being consumed here, but rather the disembodied scent, the smell-crumb of surplus-enjoyment. They "formed a circle around him,"[103] mimicking the circular path of the drives: "Everything Freud spells out about the partial drives shows us . . . that circular movement of the thrust that emerges through erogenous rim only to return to it as its target, after having encircled something I call the *objet a*."[104] Does the circularity of the drive not entail a duality inherent to smell, with ortho-smell standing for the initial thrust emerging from the erogenous rim of the nose prompted by an external object, and with retro-smell emerging once the movement is folded back onto itself, encircling and consuming the smell-crumb in its twofold circular movement? The cannibalistic dismembering and devouring of Grenouille's body is indicative of the impossibility of relating to the love object in a unifying way. They aren't after his body, but rather aim at the retro-scent released by the mouth-machine. By tearing him apart, the cannibalistic criminals turn Grenouille into a partial object of their partial drives. Theirs is a cannibalism of indifference toward the unified totality of the Other, or its globalizing bodily integrity. If the killing makes no difference to them, it is because the drive is indifferent to the object of satisfaction. Instead of identifying with the bearer of the scent, they aim at the less-than-an-atom of excarnated scent situated beyond identification.[105]

If not Love, what then do the cannibals find in the end, after their totemic meal? They find an impossible solidarity, a kinship, premised upon their irreducibly partial and helplessly solitary drives. Their mistake is twofold: first, they mistake solidarity for love, and second, they reverse the causality, assuming solidarity had led them to devouring Grenouille, not realizing that solidarity had resulted from cannibalistic fusion.[106]

Their idiotic enjoyment, revealed by childishly embarrassed glances (not to be confused with feelings of shame) and dumb smiles of blissful satisfaction, finds its primordial expression in the scene of "a baby sinking back satiated from the breast and falling asleep with flushed cheeks and a blissful smile." For Freud, "this picture persists as a prototype of the expression of sexual satisfaction in later life."[107] Moreover, there are "good reasons why a child sucking at his mother's breast has become the prototype of every relation of love."[108] The cannibals' finding of the object is essentially a refinding of it; their cannibalistic fusion finds its prototype in breastfeeding. Crucially, for Freud, breastfeeding is not about feeding—the enjoyment of sucking trumps any need for taking nourishment.[109] Sucking is incremental to feeding, yet the drive is only after sucking as the excremental increment of feeding. Furthermore, breastfeeding turns out to be an occult practice: like ticks, neonates are drawn to the breast by the smell (and not by hunger)[110] and find satisfaction in sucking (and not in taking nourishment). In light of the duality of the sense of smell, a corollary is warranted: attracted to the breast by orthonasal smelling, infants find satisfaction in retronasal smelling. The latter is inseparable from sucking and parasitically attached, though irreducible, to the taking of nourishment.

As a partial object of the partial drive, the breast is detached not merely from its biological function but also from the mother's body. In a cryptic passage, Lacan speaks of the vampiric nature of the breast as an excarnated organ sucking the mother's organism.[111] That is meant to say that the infant's sucking and the breast are structurally inseparable. The partial drive is irreducibly fused with the partial object and hence structurally attached to the organism's detachable organ. If the cannibalistic baby is indifferent to the body of the mother, it is because he is after the satisfaction rather than the object. Circumvented by the drive, the breast is constituted by it: the breast is sucking as an object of the drive.[112] Incidentally, the vampiric nature of the baby appears to extend well into its life as a fetus. Counterintuitively, the fetus bathing in odorous amniotic fluid has open airways. In addition, amniotic fluid is odorized by smells of foods and drinks consumed by the pregnant mother,[113] which places the fetus in the structural position of smell parasitically attached to the maternal dissipation-machine.[114]

The fusional nature of the relationship between the drive and its object sheds light on the imperative nature of the scent worn by Grenouille in the final scene of Süskind's novel. The scent applied to his body is not an irresistible object of sniffing, but rather sniffing excarnate, that is, sniffing itself as an object, fully detachable from his body and enjoyed by way of cannibalistic consumption. The cannibalistic consequence serves to stress the effect of mutilation as pertaining to Love insofar as it finds its prototypical expression in the function of the drives: "I love you, but, *because inexplicably I love in you something more than you—the* objet petit a [or the excarnated scent]—I mutilate you. / This is the meaning of that breast-complex, that *mammal-complex*, . . . except that the orality in question has nothing to do with food, and that the whole stress is placed on this effect of mutilation."[115] The passage is very precise. Orality has nothing to do with food; rather, it relates not to mutilation as such but the effect of mutilation. And what is the quintessential effect of such a mutilating consumption if not precisely retro-smell?

THE SNIFF-KISS

Having sniff-kissed Grenouille, the cannibals had already become him. To then proceed to devour him is tantamount to them kissing themselves. Smell entails a cannibalistic consequence: "Carnal enjoyment," writes Kant, "is cannibalistic in principle (even if not always in effect)."[116] The duality is strictly correlative with the duality of smell: ortho-smell is cannibalistic in principle, retro-smell also in effect. Jean-Claude Milner points out that historically carnal enjoyment was conceived in two opposing ways.[117] According to *the doctrine of fusion*, the sexual act is a merging of Two into One. Such a notion, Milner points out, is modeled on the incorporation of food and best exemplified by the dark vision of sexual fusion presented in Lucretius's *De Rerum Natura*:

> Its imaginary goal is fusion, but this goal cannot be reached; sexual
> partners' moans and physical efforts prove that they are lost in the pursuit
> of an illusion. Because the most obvious example of a successful fusion is
> the incorporation of food, the partners seek to bite each other's flesh or

to drink each other's fluids; but they immediately grasp that such tactics never succeed. Lucretius concludes that there is no such thing as sexual pleasure; even between the most beautiful and loving bodies, coitus results in suffering and disappointment. In the fruitless quest for the impossible, it cannot avoid the constant risk of brutality, savagery even.[118]

For Lucretius, sex is unsatisfiable—its cannibalistic effects undermine all desire for unity. With the incorporation of food and drink,

> easily the desire for water and bread is met. But from a pretty face and rosy cheeks nothing comes into the body to enjoy but images, thin images, fond hopes. . . . To sow the fields of love, they cling together mouth pressed to watering mouth and lips to lips drawing deep breaths as body calls to body. In vain. For they can rub nothing off from it, neither can body be absorbed in body. . . . They can find no device to cure their ill, bewildered and confused they waste away, the helpless victims of an unseen wound.[119]

If the doctrine of fusion, with its insistence on unity, necessarily entails the cannibalistic consequence, a way out may be provided by the competing *doctrine of use*. The latter posits an irreducible duality and finds its privileged example in the use of tools. However, according to Milner, the use of another's body as a tool for achieving sexual pleasure entails two detrimental consequences. First, either the subject or the other is reduced to a mere thing, and second, both become users of another human being, thus negating their own humanity. Kant's solution to this problem is the contractual form: the partners retain their humanity by freely consenting to the use of each other's bodies, thus also averting the cannibalistic consequence.[120]

Smell is fusion's paradigmatic example. In the realm of olfaction, no duality can be maintained—but neither can unity. The smell's absorptive capacity underscored by Adorno and Horkheimer effects an excorporation. The two murder scenes from Süskind's novel attest to this. Though brutally abusing the girl to the point of her death, she does not appear to be Grenouille's mishandled tool. As is made clear by the narrator, Grenouille couldn't care less about the girl's body and does not use her body for the purpose of extracting his precious kernel of enjoyment. As essentially useless, her body is effectively an obstacle to his fusion with the excarnated scent. If, by definition, a tool is a detachable extension of the human body used to modify external reality, then it is her scent (rather than her body) that is the tool. Grenouille clearly considers this scent the missing part of the puzzle, undermining the coherence of his olfactory universe while promising to provide it with its higher principle. Unbeknownst to her, she used the tool of scent to modify him and his world. (Did he, in an act of expropriation, snatch the tool away from its user by relieving the scent of its bodily shell?) Grenouille does not track down the girl so that Two would become One. He is already consumed by her; the fusion always already took place, undermining his self-identity and shattering the organizational unity of his olfactory universe.

The girl has no use-value, but she's so money, so to speak. In Marx's terms, use-value relates to the natural form of a thing, that is, to its intrinsic properties as means of satisfying human needs. Marx's account of use-value has led commentators to regard it as an essentially empirical notion of an external appendage to the commodity, an appendage that is a necessary component of the commodity, but only insofar as the commodity is always already an external thing with useful properties that satisfy human needs. This, however, is not Marx's concept of use-value. For upon writing that use-values "constitute the material content of wealth, whatever its social form may be," Marx immediately continues: "In the form of society to be considered here they are also the material bearers [Träger] of . . . exchange-value."[121] Thus, on the second page of the first chapter of *Capital* (1867), Marx moves beyond the generalized notion of use-value as it exists independently of any particular social form, so as to consider the specificity of use-value as it appears solely within capitalism. Is the girl's useless body not useful in this precise sense? Is it not merely the bearer of the spectral materiality, or "phantom-like objectivity," of scent?[122] It is this spectral materiality, rather than use-value as a means of satisfying his needs, that Grenouille is truly after. As we have seen, it is at this precise point in the story that Grenouille discovers his destiny: to become the world's greatest perfumer. And perfumery is a capitalist art par excellence: the materiality of a perfume is a mere support vehicle of the volatile molecules of scent, just like use-values are mere bearers of the immaterial, spectral substance of value. Grenouille's squeezing of the girl's neck is a process of distillation by means of which all her empirical properties are extinguished to "extract that unholy essence."[123]

If smell is the paradigm of cannibalistic fusion, we must pause to consider its position among the physical senses. From Aristotle to Hegel, sight and hearing are considered *theoretical senses*, and it is precisely their theoretical nature that grants them philosophical priority. Essentially theoretical, both operate at a distance from their object and hence are capable of perceptually grasping the object without coming into direct contact with it. Consequently, the perceived object remains intact, untouched by perception and hence unblemished and unmodified. In Hegel, such a philosophical notion of the senses results from the function of conceptual thought:

> The theoretical study of things is not interested in consuming [*verzehren*] them in their particularity and satisfying [*befriedigen*] itself and maintaining itself sensuously by means of them, but in coming to know them in their universality, finding their inner essence and law, and conceiving them in

accordance with their Concept. Therefore theoretical interest lets particular things alone [gewähren] and retreats from them as sensuous particularities, since this sensuous particularity is not what intelligence tries to study.[124]

The paragraph is overflowing with visual metaphors that have always informed philosophical discourse. In *Negative Dialectics* (1966), Adorno criticizes the Western metaphysics' concept of the subject as essentially "locked up in its own self."[125] To emphasize this crucial aspect of the subject's self-enclosing prison, Adorno speaks of a "peephole metaphysics," a term that nicely captures the incessant and overwhelming reliance of Western thought on its visual metaphors. Suffice it to think, for instance, of the notions of "theory" (from ancient Greek theōréō, "I look at," or "view"), "speculation" (from Latin speculātiō, "watching," or "looking at"), "reflection," the Platonic noesis, which stems from noeîn, "to see" in the sense of providing insight into the very essence (eidos) of the thing (the latter once again deriving from eídō, "I see"). In the passage just quoted, Hegel mentions "theory" and "study" (die Betrachtung), which are fused in the pleonastic term die theoretische Betrachtung (theoretical contemplation). Then there is the implicit distance of the theoretical gaze (another pleonasm), the interest of which maintains itself at a distance toward sensuous particularities that remain untouched by it. Intelligence does not strive for contact with the thing so as to reach sensuous satisfaction (verzehren, "to consume," "devour," "eat up," "dissipate"). Rather, intelligence is after the thing's "inner essence and law." Intelligence touches upon and grasps the essential Being in its universality precisely by breaking off contact with the immediate materiality of the sensuous object.

To theoretical contemplation Hegel opposes a practical relation to the object, one demanding contact, proximity, a traversing of all distance, and hence an immediacy of the subject–object relation. *Practical senses* therefore entail the consuming of the object in its immediate sensuous particularity. The subject of practical interest aims not at grasping the inner essence and law of the thing in its universality and its essential being, but rather surrenders the object to destruction. The practical senses include touch and—its special form—taste.[126] Essentially, they demand proximity and contact. On the one end, we have the theoretical senses of sight and hearing, which operate at a distance from the thing and are therefore capable of observing it from the point of view of its universal essence. On the other end, we have touch and taste, which traverse the distance separating the perceiving subject from the thing, thereby risking deforming, modifying, and ultimately destroying it.

Which of the two sides does smell belong to? Smell occupies a paradoxical intermediate position between the two perceptual categories. Süskind's description of the girl's murder exemplifies this point: Grenouille's quest for the elusive scent is theoretical in the sense that it is not guided by consumption but rather oriented by the pursuit of the "higher principle." But letting the object be so as to contemplate its inner essence is impossible, for the object has already reached and consumed us. Hence, on the one hand, smell operates at a distance, and this feature places it on the side of sight and especially of hearing with which it shares its perceptual medium.[127] On the other hand, smell relates most intimately to the immediate sensuous materiality of the object, such that it is impossible to claim that it reflects anything beyond the object's immediately given sensuous determinations. Despite sharing their key feature, the sense of smell is at odds with the two theoretical senses. But nor does it fit the category of practical interest, as conceived of by Hegel. The first feature distinguishing smell from the practical senses of touch and taste is that distance toward the object is the material condition of olfactory perception. But aside from this external distinctive feature, which smell shares with sight and hearing, there is also an internal difference distinguishing smell from the practical senses. If the practical senses are directed at the thing in its particularity, effecting sensuous satisfaction as the result of the object's consumption, in the case of smell it is the subject that is consumed by the object, with the latter remaining at a distance from it.

Due to the relation of contiguity and immediate proximity, touch necessarily modifies its object. Taste as a subspecies of touch takes the relation of proximity even further: instead of modifying its object, taste enacts its destruction. Hence, for Hegel, taste is the prototype of touch (and of the practical sense), deriving its satisfaction from the devouring of its object (*verzehren*). In the case of smell, Hegel points out, this devouring is a devouring at a distance and hence can only be conceived of in terms of a self-devouring. There is a split separating the object from the thing, or the self-dissipating scent from its support vehicle. Moreover, the analysis of smell as it relates to the distinction between theoretical and practical senses points to a common ground of these disparate perceptual categories. The distinction concerns only the senses' relation to their objects but says nothing of the effects of physical perception on the perceiving subject. In seeing and hearing, the object and the subject remain intact; in touching and tasting, the object wastes away, while the subject once again remains intact. In smell, neither remain intact: the subject is consumed and absorbed by the self-consuming object. Moreover, the intermediary position of the sense of smell as neither purely theoretical nor purely practical is confirmed by it being split between ortho- and retro-smell, that is, between distance and proximity.

Hegel's distinction between theoretical and practical senses echoes Kant's typology of the organic senses, split between the two categories of the senses of cognition and the senses of enjoyment. Those of cognition are considered more objective, meaning that "as empirical intuitions they contribute more to the *cognition* of the external object than they stir up the consciousness of the affected organ," while the senses of enjoyment are more subjective, meaning that "the idea obtained from them is more a representation of *enjoyment* than of cognition of the external object."[128] The first category includes sight and hearing, but also touch, while the second includes taste and smell. However, here, too, the paradoxical intermediate position of smell comes to the fore. For Kant, smell is situated at the very interface of distance and proximity. In smell, the most distant proximity coincides with the nearest of distances. As a unique subspecies of taste, smell is *Geschmack in der Ferne*, "taste at a distance."[129] But despite its unique perceptual capacity for consuming objects from afar, smell's perceptual contact with olfactory objects is no less immediate. On the contrary: "taking something in [*Einnehmung*] through smell (in the lungs) is even more intimate [*noch inniglicher*] than taking something in through the absorptive vessels of the mouth or throat."[130] The distance implied in smelling presupposes that the object remains untouched, untouchable even, yet this distancing cut effects the most intimate proximity. Rather than the sublation of the cut, smell's *innigste Einnehmung* is a touching of the cut, that is, a touching of the untouchable.[131] In his discussion of olfaction, Kant only considers ortho-smell as "taste at a distance." To orthonasal smelling as *distant tasting* we must add retronasal olfaction as *proximate smelling*.

Kant's insight is confirmed by the structure of olfaction's neurobiological interface, subverting the ontological divide between interiority and exteriority. Here, the intimacy mentioned by Kant is radicalized. Out of the twelve pairs of cranial nerves (not counting the recently canonized *nervus terminalis*), only the olfactory (CN I) and the optic nerve (CN II) emerge directly from the brain, with the others emerging from the brain stem. But what makes CN I truly unique is this: housed in the roof of the nasal cavity, the olfactory nerve is the only nerve of the human body that is directly exposed to the environment.[132] One important philosophical consequence of this is: *The great outdoors is housed in the roof of our nasal cavity.*[133] Smell is the site where our brain directly touches upon the world, quite literally providing the brain–world interface. The metonymical nature of smell seemed to have implied that smell is the epitome of a correlationist sense: a smell is always a "smell of (something)," lacking substantial footing outside of the correlation with the object-source. However, this correlationality of smells as embodied in their step- and source-names, is the flip side of the impossibility of olfactory abstraction and denomination, which in turn incites us to think of smell as the anti-correlationist sense par excellence.

If cannibalistic fusion proceeds by way of incorporation, then—following Kant's insight—incorporation of the object through smell is more intimate and profound than simple ingestion. Moreover, the radical nature of olfactory incorporation exceeds Kant's physiological point: to smell is not to consume the object but to be colonized by it; the incorporation of the object effects an excorporation of the dissipating subject. Georges Bataille purportedly suggested that a kiss is the beginning of cannibalism. If a kiss is the beginning of cannibalism, a sniff is the beginning of a kiss. Pierre de Ronsard, the sixteenth-century French poet, understood this: "When from thy half-closed lips / Rose-scented breath I smell . . ." Quoting these lines, Robert Mandrou comments that though "today smell and taste are relatively unimportant by comparison with the other three senses, the men of the sixteenth century were extremely susceptible to scents and perfumes. . . . For Ronsard, a kiss was not a contact; it was not connected with touch, but with scent."[134] Mandrou neglects the Kantian point: if smell is a subspecies of taste and if taste is a form of touch, then to sniff is to make contact from a distance.

A sniff is a kiss at a distance. The insight into the olfactory origins of the kiss may no longer be evident to us but is confirmed by the Thai *haawm kaem*, or the *sniff-kiss*. Instead of making direct mouth contact with the other, the practice of sniff kissing consists of placing the nose near the cheek, hair, or neck of the other and inhaling their scent.[135] In his 1907 paper on the sniff-kiss, E. Washburn Hopkins demonstrated that this seemingly unusual manner of kissing is surprisingly common. Examples include: the Eskimo kiss, which "is really only an inhalation of breath or a sniff"; "among the African Negroes it is customary to show affection by means of a vigorous sniff"; the Malayan "nasal salutation" was described already by Darwin and Spencer; on "the North-east frontier of India . . . people do not kiss but sniff at or smell each other. . . . they do not say 'give me a kiss' but 'smell me.'"[136] Thus, "the cult of kissing" finds its protype in the sniff-kiss. Washburn Hopkins is surprised by the fact that after "a real kiss-word appears" in Indian texts, the word for "sniff" remains in circulation. It strikes him as "quite strange" that the meaning of the words for a sniff-kiss and a lip-kiss appears to be "touch." He fails to make the connection: a sniff-kiss is a lip-kiss at a distance.

PHILOSOPHY, DOGGY-STYLE

"When we see we remain who we are, when we smell we are absorbed entirely."[137] Returning to this proposition, we could object to it by saying that seeing may very well modify us. However, what is at stake in Adorno and Horkheimer's claim is not a mere modification of the self. Rather, the question is: Can we be consumed by what we see to the point of self-dissipation? Can seeing effect a subjective destitution? It would seem that in the optic field we are only consumed in such a way not by something we see but by something we *cannot unsee*, that is, by a traumatic event. Smell provides the model for this: it is "trauma," the "unseen wound,"[138] of our sensibility.

But what about music? Prefiguring Henry Fincks's thesis that we don't go to the opera to please our eyes, Kierkegaard points out the spatial distance required for properly experiencing it. Read along the lines proposed by

Adorno and Horkheimer, visual perception thwarts the musical experience: the eye prevents the dissolution of the I, thwarting the aim of disappearing completely in music:

> It is a common experience that to strain two senses at the same time is not pleasant, and thus it is often disruptive to have to use the eyes a great deal at the same time as the ears are being used. Therefore, one is inclined to shut the eyes when listening to music. This is more or less true of all music, and in *sensu eminentiori* [in an eminent sense] of [Mozart's opera] *Don Giovanni*. As soon as the eyes are involved, the impression is disrupted, for the dramatic unity that presents itself to the eye is altogether subordinate and deficient in comparison with the musical unity that is heard simultaneously. My own experience has convinced me of this. I have sat close to the front; I have moved back more and more; I have sought a remote corner in the theater in order to be able to hide myself completely in this music. The better I understood it or thought I understood it, the further I moved away from it—not out of coldness but out of love, for it wants to be understood at a distance. There has been something strangely enigmatic about this in my life. There have been times when I would have given everything for a ticket; now I do not even need to pay one rix-dollar for a ticket. I stand outside in the corridor; I lean against the partition that shuts me off from the spectators' seats. Then it affects me most powerfully; it is a world by itself, separated from me; I can see nothing but am close enough to hear and yet so infinitely far away.[139]

What is required for music to truly colonize its listener, however, is not mere spatial but also a temporal distance separating us from it. It is only in silence following a musical performance that the listener fully fuses with the musical. Is our immersion in and by smells not analogous to being absorbed and cannibalized by the musical world? In volume 4 of his *Mythologiques* (1971), Lévi-Strauss relates the absorptive power of musical enjoyment to that of smell:

> The phenomenon is even more curious; as Proust shows so well, the pleasure of music does not stop with the performance and may even achieve its fullest state afterwards; in the subsequent silence, the listener finds himself saturated with music, overwhelmed with meaning, the victim of a kind of possession which deprives him of his individuality and his being: he has become the place or space of the music, as Condillac's statue was a scent of roses. Music brings about the miracle that hearing, the most intellectual of the senses, and normally at the service of articulate language, enters into the sort of state that, according to the philosopher, was peculiar to smell, of all the senses the one most deeply rooted in the mysteries of organic life.[140]

In his 1754 *Treatise on the Sensations*, Condillac famously imagines an inanimate, statuesque figure of the human being gradually "moved" by sense perceptions, starting with the smell of the rose.[141] A tabula rasa dispossessed of any of the other senses and of any notion of the object, when smelling the rose the statue directly experiences itself as being that smell: *Olfacio, ergo sum*—I smell, therefore I am (that smell). Music, Lévi-Strauss suggests, has the same effect: the moment I hear it, the moment I take it in or am taken by it, I am deprived of my individuality and being. However, and more precisely, for Lévi-Strauss this deindividuating and annihilating effect is only achieved "in the subsequent silence," that is, when the music has stopped. Music achieves its teleological end at the point of suspension of the musical.[142] The discussion takes its cue from the well-known philosophical conception of smell as the least intellectual of the five physical senses. Its intention, however, is to propose a striking equivalence between the least and the most valued of the senses.[143] Just like music, which only arrives at the pinnacle of its sublimity once it has ceased, the most intellectual of the senses is brought to completion in its extreme opposite. The loud business of listening to music finds its apogee in the deafening silence immediately following it, that is, in the silence as the object-voice at its purest.[144] With listening finding its model in the noiseless business of smelling, music is only truly heard once we begin listening with our nose. For the voice-object cannot be spoken, it occupies the position of the unspeakable, that is, the position structurally effected by the primordial antinomy between smelling and spelling.

From Lévi-Strauss to Kafka, from Condillac's statue to Kafka's own inquisitive Quoodle. In Kafka's short story "Investigations of a Dog," written in 1922, the young dog encounters seven musical dogs, finding himself in a Lévi-Straussian predicament:

> the music gradually got the upper hand, literally knocked the breath out of me . . . and quite against my will, while I howled as if some pain were being inflicted upon me, my mind could attend to nothing but this blast of music which seemed to come from all sides, from the heights, from the deeps, from everywhere, surrounding the listener, overwhelming him, crushing him, and over his swooning body still blowing fanfares so near that they seemed far away and almost inaudible.[145]

The dog's encounter with music mirrors Grenouille's encounter with the smell-crumb. The music filled and absorbed him, disrupting his daily canine life. Facing the music that was coming from everywhere, exposing him to a destructive dissipation, the dog lost his canine "individuality and being." The music crushed him beyond mere destruction, his most intimate interiority colonized by an irreducible exteriority. The colonizing auditory object is at once "near" and "far away" from him, at once externally volatile and inti-mately violating. Though coming as if from "the remotest distance," it com-mands him to co-enjoy, "forcing me to my knees."[146] The distance of nearness is the greatest of all distances: it distances the dog from itself, interrupting "those inexplicable blissful states of exaltation which everyone must have experienced as a child."[147]

Facing the music, the "terrible sounds such as I had never heard before,"[148] Kafka's dog is not experiencing the Lévi-Straussian pleasure in listening. His feeling is not one of sublimation, but of frustration. Music exposes him to a fragmentary, partial, excarnated object. It is this auditory (yet, it turns out, inaudible) crumb that triggers the dog's investigations. At one point in the story, the gravity of the pressing enigma of music is captured by a dark can-nibalistic vision. The investigated experience pertains to dog's species-being, and to get at the core of it, the dog would have to feed on the core, the poi-sonous bone marrow, of his own species: "That sounds monstrous, almost as if I wanted to feed on the marrow, not merely of a bone, but of the whole canine race itself. But it is only a metaphor. The marrow that I am discuss-ing here is no food; on the contrary, it is a poison."[149] The stakes of the dog's research are extremely high, and conducting it properly may entail, however metaphorically, filial cannibalism, the eating of the flesh of his flesh: "I under-stand my fellow dogs, am flesh of their flesh, of their miserable, ever-renewed, ever-desirous flesh."[150] This aspect gives the investigations a distinctive flair of transgressing the laws not put in place by dogs themselves. Yet these musical dogs are "holding firmly to laws that are not those of the dog world, but are actually directed against it."[151] The transgression finds its model in the Leviti-cus. If you abhor my laws, God says, the final punishment for your disobe-dience will be that "you will eat the flesh of your sons and the flesh of your daughters" (Lv. 26:29).

The sense of smell plays no central role in Kafka's story. But could the struc-ture of olfaction and the libidinous model it delivers nevertheless provide the key to its interpretation? The cited encounter with the seven musical dogs sets him off on his investigative path. Though music is a persistent compan-ion in any dog's life (and hence is *nothing*), the canine researcher now hears it as if for the very first time (and hence is *not nothing*): "the music . . . liter-ally knocked the breath out of me."[152] But where is the music coming from? "They did not speak, they did not sing, they remained generally silent, almost determinedly silent; but from the empty air they conjured music. Everything was music, the lifting and setting down of their feet, certain turns of the head, their running and their standing still, the positions they took up in relation to one another."[153]

What are the musical dogs up to, exactly? What is the source of their music? Since the latter is the constant companion in any dog's life, they seem to be displaying the most typical, everyday behavior—*sniffing about*. The music of the musical dogs, Kafka tells us, is neither a matter of language, that is, of singing or talking, nor is it a matter of mere sounds uttered by the rest of the "wretched, limited, dumb creatures who have no language but mechanical cries."[154] In fact, it is an entirely noiseless business, emerging at the point at which singing and talking are consumed by an acousmatic silence, to use Mladen Dolar's term.[155] Singing, talking, and sniffing are intimately related to breathing, but while singing and talking (as well as mechanical cries) demand that we exhale, sniffing requires us to inhale. If the dogs are "generally silent, almost determinedly so," if their music is essentially silent,[156] it is because they are inhaling and therefore sniffing. After all, right before encountering the musical dogs, the pup "had run in darkness for a long time, up and down, blind and deaf to everything, led on by nothing but a vague desire, and now I suddenly came to a stop with the feeling that I was in the right place, and looking up saw that it was bright day, only a little hazy, and everywhere a blending and confusion of the most intoxicating smells."[157] If the dogs are actually there, and not merely conjured up by the pup's imagination, they must be taken in by these "most intoxicating smells." Their sniff, sniff, sniffing would provide the rhythmic basis of the musical, and they in fact, we are told, never skip "the stroke of the beat . . . , keeping the rhythm so unshakably."[158] When asked what they're up to, the musical dogs fail to respond. By failing to respond the "dogs were violating the law"[159] or maybe following a new law, the existence of which was still unknown to him. Had they responded, the music would have stopped. Their intense musical performance must not be interrupted, except for the occasional *Luftpause*, a breath-break from sniffing: "their tongues, whenever the tension weakened for a moment, hung wearily from their jowls."[160] The musical sniffing is at odds with the tongue as the metonym for language: the sniffing only appears once the tongue disappears and vice versa.

The role played by smell in Kafka's story also explains its key twist, when the dog's attention is diverted quite unexpectedly from the inquiry into the source of music to the seemingly completely unrelated question: "Whence does the earth procure its food?"[161] There seems to be no relation, no obvious point of passage linking the initial question to the problem of nourishment. The only connection between the two seems to be the dog's strange method of inquiry: the music's essence is only properly revealed in silence; the essence of food is only revealed through hunger and starvation: "for today I still hold fasting to be the final and most potent means of my research."[162] The speculative move from inquiring into the origins of music to an inquest into the nature of nourishment appears obscure to the reader but not to the dog. He proceeds as if the connection between the two questions is something entirely evident. If it is so utterly obvious to him, then music and food must share a common origin.

The following line unties the two domains together: "music had surrounded me as a perfectly natural and indispensable element of existence ever since I was a suckling."[163] As far as the dog is concerned, music and food came into being simultaneously: at sucking time. The dog's encounter with the musical dogs is a refinding of this object, now subtracted from any idea of nourishment. Inquiring into it requires getting one's "teeth into hunger."[164] The fasting has the immediate effect of an awakening, and opens up a world: "the world, which had been asleep during my life hitherto, seemed to have been awakened by my fasting."[165] The fasting awakens him—but to what? It awakens him to an entire smell-world: refusing to eat, "the smell of food began to assail me, delicious dainties that I had long since forgotten, delights of my childhood." The fasting opens a universe of smells, and in a Proustian twist the smells take him back to his long since forgotten childhood. The dog is catapulted to his period as a suckling, discovering music for the very first time: "yes, I could smell the very fragrance of my mother's teats; I forgot my resolution to resist all smells, or rather I did not forget it; I dragged myself to and fro, never for more than a few yards, and sniffed as if that were in accordance with my resolution, as if I were looking for food simply to be on my guard against it."[166] Deciding that fasting was the way of his science, sniffing is deployed prophylactically: not to find food, but to fend it off. Despite his resolution, he is, to quote Adorno and Horkheimer, "allowed to indulge the outlawed drive if acting with the unquestionable aim of expunging it."[167]

It is through eating nothing (abstaining from food) that the olfactory essence of his "mother's teats" is revealed to him. And therewith so is the essence of food, its auratic aroma. Once again, the sniff-kiss is shown to have priority over the lip-kiss, the sniffing over the sucking. Smell is situated at the juncture, in the "border region" between music and nourishment: "So for penetrating into real dog nature, research into food seemed to me the best method, calculated to lead me to my goal by the straightest path. Perhaps I was mistaken. A border region between these two sciences, however, had already attracted my attention. I mean the theory of incantation, by which food is called down."[168]

Die Lehre von dem die Nahrung herabrufenden Gesang—"the theory of incantation, by which food is called down." The sentence joins together the two disparate domains of music and food, yet Kafka's choice of words remains enigmatic. They supposedly meet in a new science that is neither a science of food nor a science of music, though intimately related to both. At their intersection, or "border region," there perhaps emerges *smell as food's song*. Smell is food's charm, its spell or incantation. The dog is under the spell of smell, determined to spell out its secret. Like in the scene from Rilke's *Malte*, the dog's encounter with the musical dogs is spellbinding; it raises spirits. The least intellectual meets the most intellectual of the senses: like smell, incantation operates at a distance, magically turning the distant into the immediately proximate. The dog puts forth two basic ways of acquiring nourishment. Once "the mother weans her young ones from her teats and sends them out into the world," food is provided mostly by the earth. But not without some effort, for the general rule of food production demands: "Water the ground as much as you can."[169]

For the most part, dogs are immediate producers, reliant on the earth from which they have not yet lifted their nose. In Marxian terms, their labor is very much still attached to the means of its realization, namely to the earth and to their organic and undetachable watering tool. However, a second means of acquiring food is mentioned and "should not be forgotten," one that subtracts them from the earth and makes their watering tool useless: the process "can also be hastened by certain spells, songs, and ritual movements."[170] This second method should not be forgotten, while itself entailing active forgetting. The dog should not forget to forget: the musical dogs "chant their incantations with their faces turned upwards, . . . forgetting the ground," the *cloaca*, wishing "to take flight from it forever."[171] Here, the dogs are no longer immediate producers: food is only acquired via a detour through market economy premised on an incantation- or payment-capable need. Unlike the watering of the earth, which was a by-product of a preexisting need, a need too imperative not to be satisfied, incantations are a form of labor, resulting from a demand to work (I unpack this duality in chapter 4 when discussing Marx's concept of primitive accumulation). In the *Dialectics of Nature* (1883), Engels treats labor as a step in the transition from ape to man. The ape's means of subsistence are generally found in its immediate surroundings. The horde of apes would sometimes be forced to "win new feeding grounds," but could not hope to extract from it anything beyond what the ground had to offer by its very nature. With one key exception: "the horde unconsciously fertilized the soil with its own excrements,"[172] watering the ground. All this seems to be common canine knowledge, but until encountering the musical dogs, the pup hasn't paid it any mind: "I swallow down my food, but the slightest preliminary methodical politico-economical observation of it does not seem to me worth while."[173] But there's yet more to the story.

Typically, J. G. Fichte remarks in his *Foundations of Natural Right* (1797), "the eyes of the animal, because of their position, are riveted to the earth, which brings forth its nourishment."[174] Nourishment comes from below, not from above. But Kafka's dog does not rely on the eye, directed downward to the earth, instead listening with his nose to the song calling food down from above. Fichte draws a sharp contrast between the animal, whose eyes "are riveted to the earth," and "the human species [that] has freely lifted itself up from the earth."[175] Is Kafka proposing his canine version of the osmological narrative? Osmological narratives (discussed at length in the next chapter) claim that the onset of culture was conditioned by a suppression of smell, brought about by the landmark evolutionary advent of human bipedalism. Freud adopted such a narrative (moreover claiming its authorship), proposing that anthropogenesis, the becoming man of man, was in fact conditioned by an "organic repression" of smell. Come to think of it, the musical dogs, "much older than me, certainly, and not of my woolly, long-haired kind,"[176] are on their hind legs, unriveted to the earth and its nourishment. The inquiring dog almost failed to notice it: "Because of all the music," he reports, "I had not noticed it before, but they had flung away all shame, the wretched creatures were doing the very thing which is both most ridiculous and indecent in our eyes; they were walking on their hind legs. Fie on them!"[177] Is Kafka imagining the evolutionary advent of canine bipedalism, the dawn of the *canis erectus*?[178] If the dogs "had flung away all shame," they must be standing erect, exposing their genitals. This, too, would seem against the law, this time against the canine law of propriety, the *sensus decori*. Moreover, from the pup's perspective, the posture of the dogs—"carrying out their evolutions"[179]—violates the laws of Nature:

> when, obeying their better instincts for a moment, they happened to let their front paws fall, they were literally appalled as if at an error, as if Nature were an error, hastily raised their legs again, and their eyes seemed to be begging for forgiveness for having been forced to cease momentarily from their abomination. Was the world standing on its head? Where could I be? What could have happened?[180]

With the emergence of culture, conditioned by the landmark evolutionary advent of canine bipedalism, Nature becomes an error and the young dog's world is radically inverted, "standing on its head." Is the dogs' previous, unlawful refusal to answer his questions the result of the evolutionary event by which a new species was born? Did they not speak his language? The dog effectively entertains the inexplicable possibility of them not being dogs at all: "Perhaps they were not dogs at all? But how should they not be dogs? . . . And as for walking on their hind legs, perhaps, unlike other dogs, they actually used only these for walking; if it was a sin, well, it was a sin."[181] The two disparate modes of production mentioned earlier are symmetrical opposites: as immediate producers, dogs must water the ground as much as they can, lifting their hind legs; but to enter the economy of incantation, they must lift their front legs from the ground: "forgetting the ground, they wished to take flight from it forever. I took this contradiction as my starting point."[182]

The dog ends his investigations into "this contradiction," or the border region of music and nourishment, with the science of freedom: "Freedom! Certainly such freedom as is possible today is a wretched business. But nevertheless freedom, nevertheless a possession." [183] Is this freedom, discovered at the very end of the story, a natural emergent of the emerging canine biped? This would certainly be in line with Johann Gottfried Herder's influential 1784 version of the narrative of hominization: "Man the first of the creation left free he stands erect." [184] What is "the theory of incantation, by which food is called down," if not osmology? The musical dogs, standing erect, are the first liberated beings of creation. With the assumption of the erect posture, food is no longer found where they smell it, at nose level, the latter having been raised from the ground. "For the animal," Fichte remarks, "the earth serves as both bed and table; the human being [and the canine biped] raises his bed and table above the earth." [185]

As far as the infant (and the story's dog) is concerned, the breast once served as both bed and table, the original bed-and-breakfast. Is "Investigations of a Dog" a story about *the trauma of weaning, which prefigures castration?* [186] Weaning would certainly explain the starving, for it is only after this defining event that fasting (and libidinal frustration) becomes key to understanding the very idea of nourishment. With the dog weaned off the breast as his enjoyment-providing bed-and-breakfast, enjoyment is re-found by imploring the Other: it is no longer down here (where I am), but up there (where I am not), called down by way of incantation. With the emergence of the Other, the voice-object begins to embody the logical consistency first encountered in the smell-object. The voice is correlative with symbolic castration prefigured in weaning as it relates to smell as food's song. But why would this move entail the idea of freedom? And why is this freedom "a wretched business," but "nevertheless a possession," something worth holding on to? Is the freedom not a possession that the dog—not simply lacks but—*has lacking?* Immaterial and untraceable, yet real, this surplus-scarcity is revealing of the irreducibility of enjoyment to nourishment and signification, and hence is a surplus-scarcity situated at the juncture between the insatiable (the eating of hunger) and the unspeakable (the hearing of the voice).

Kafka's story unfolds in between these two moments. Having weaned off the breast, there is nothing that the dog desires latching on to. The descriptions of the voluntarily starving dog bring forth the imagery of anorexia nervosa, the "eating of nothing": "There was blood under me, at first I took it for food; but I recognized it immediately as blood that I had vomited." [187] The scene ought to remind us of several Kafka's stories, most notably "A Hunger Artist"—another weaning story written in 1922—but also of his own eating disorders and personal preoccupations with fasting. [188] The hunger artist, uttering his last words, explains the reasons behind his fasting: "I couldn't find the food I liked. If I had found it, believe me, I should have made no fuss and stuffed myself like you or anyone else."[189] Upon clearing his cage, the hunger artist was replaced by a panther as his symmetrical opposite. Unlike the hunger artist and the dog, the panther knew what food he liked and experienced no libidinal frustration. Though caged, the panther was untethered to the Other. His satisfaction required no incantational detours and his body, "furnished almost to the bursting point with all that it needed, seemed to carry freedom around with it too; somewhere in his jaws it seemed to lurk."[190]

Civilization is waste, *cloaca maxima*.
—Jacques Lacan, "Conferences in North American Universities"

FLUIDUM LETALE

I already mentioned Franz Mesmer and his vitalist theory of "animal magnetism," attributing to all living things an invisible life force that exerts its
influence in the physical world. In Süskind's *Perfume*, we encounter the Mesmerian figure of the Marquis de la Taillade-Espinasse. Like all great men of
the Enlightenment, the marquis's scientific endeavors cannot do without a
pinch of the occult. Having abandoned his social obligations, the marquis's
old age (old for the times—he was only forty) is devoted strictly to science. A
truly enlightened spirit, his work touches on dispersed scientific fields, from
national economy (he proposes, for instance, a progressive income tax, which
would hit the poor and awaken their entrepreneurial spirit) to experimental
agriculture (to obtain milk, he is attempting to create an animal-plant hybrid,
a kind of "milk-yielding udder flower").[1]

Süskind presents the marquis in an exaggerated way as a satirical embodiment of Enlightenment ideology. Among the most bizarre of his ideas is his
theory of *fluidum letale*: "His thesis was that life could develop only at a certain
distance from the earth, since the earth itself constantly emits a corrupting
gas, a so-called *fluidum letale*, which lames vital energies and sooner or later
utterly extinguishes them."[2] The miasmatic theory, he believes, deserves wider
recognition and should not be limited to the small esoteric circle of its fer-
vent followers. Grenouille provides such an occasion. After living in a cave for
seven years, he travels to the South of France, finally arriving in a small town:

> He looked awful. His hair reached down to the hollows of his knees, his
> scraggly beard to his navel. His nails were like talons, and the skin on his

arms and legs, where the rags no longer covered his body, was peeling off in shreds. / The first people he met . . . ran off screaming at the sight of him. But in the town itself, he caused a sensation. By the hundreds people came running to gape at him. Many of them believed he was an escaped galley slave. Others said he was not really a human being, but some mixture of man and bear, some kind of forest creature.[3]

Grenouille, who had been for seven years "completely encapsulated by the corrupting element of the earth,"[4] might be the (barely) living proof for the reality of *fluidum letale*. The marquis thus brought him to his laboratory to examine him. He had his theory confirmed to the minutest of details. To restore him to health, the marquis set out to perform "the wholesale expulsion of the fluidum, using a vital ventilation machine"[5] he designed and build himself. The five-day treatment of "decontamination and revitalization" worked. Turning to Grenouille, the marquis began his self-praise:

> "Monsieur," he began at last, "I am thrilled with myself. I am overwhelmed at my own genius. I have, to be sure, never doubted the correctness of my fluidal theory; of course not; but to find it so gloriously confirmed by an applied therapy overwhelms me. You were a beast, and I have made a man of you. A veritable divine act. Do forgive me, I am so touched!"[6]

Though undoubtably bizarre to us today, in the eighteenth century similar theories were considered sound science. In *The Foul and the Fragrant* (1982), Alain Corbin analyzes "the fashion for the pneumatic experiments" much like the one performed by the marquis, while meticulously combing through the vast continent of miasmic pathology.[7] Here, however, I want to bring the discussion of *fluidum letale* back to Freud. We can certainly smell the proximity of Freud's osmological assumption with the doctrine of Süskind's marquis: if, in the course of evolution, the human animal adopted an erect posture, it was so as to detach its nose from the *fluidum letale* of sexuality.

November 12, 1897, is a forgotten date in the history of psychoanalysis. On that day, a peculiar idea came to Freud's mind not fully formed, announcing itself as a prescentiment: "Strangely enough, I have a presentiment of such events a good while beforehand":

> I have often had a suspicion that something organic plays a part in repression; I was able once before to tell you that it was a question of the abandonment of former sexual zones, and I was able to add that I had been pleased at coming across a similar idea in Moll. (Privately I concede priority in the idea to no one; in my case the notion was linked to the changed part played by sensations of smell: upright walking, nose raised from the ground, at the same time a number of formerly interesting sensations attached to the

earth becoming repulsive—by a process still unknown to me.) (He turns up his nose = he regards himself as something particularly noble.)[8]

Man's break with his animal prehistory, the initial onset of culture and civilization was effected by the "organic repression" of smell, brought about by man's assumption of an erect posture. The realms of Spirit, history, culture, and civilization are, as it were, founded upon and perpetuated by what is ultimately an extinction of smell, an immemorial or primordial act of deodorization. In his letter to Fliess, dated just two days after gaining his new insight, Freud went out of his way to construct the idea's *Geburtsanzeige*, the "certificate of its birth," thus stressing its fundamental relevance to psychoanalysis: "'It was on November 12, 1897,'" he writes, placing his narrative in quotes, "'the sun was precisely in the eastern quarter; Mercury and Venus were in conjunction—.'"[9] With the insertion of the dash, the tone of the narrative changes and a break, a disjunction, is introduced. Freud omits the scare quotes, tones down on the pathos, and abandons the narrative of a perfectly aligned cosmic order, as if signaling that the *cosmological* narrative is totally unbefitting to his *osmological* claim. After all, what is at stake in it is not the cosmological study of the origin and evolution of the universe, that is, of *everything*, but rather an osmological study of the universe's remainder, that is, of everything *else*: "No," Freud continues,

> birth announcements no longer start like that. It was on November 12, a day dominated by a left-sided migraine, on the afternoon of which Martin sat down to write a new poem, on the evening of which Oli lost his second tooth, that, after the frightful labor pains of the last few weeks, I gave birth to a new piece of knowledge. Not entirely new, to tell the truth, it had repeatedly shown itself and withdrawn again, but this time it stayed and looked upon the light of day.[10]

If smell is essentially characterized by *Sichverzehren*, or "wasting away," synonymous with odorization, then the osmological narrative postulates the wasting away of the wasting away, accounting for the process of deodorization. What is rather striking about the cited passage is the fact that, well into his old age, Freud remained convinced of the centrality of this simple, and arguably bizarre, idea that persisted as if in complete disregard of the breaks and rapid advancements of his own psychoanalytical theory. The idea's disruptive disjunction remained untouched by the course of all the disjunctions that followed upon it. Even more striking is the fact that the idea of the atrophying effect of the adoption of the upright gait on the human sense of smell, supposedly born of Freud's "frightful labor pains" ("I concede priority in the idea to no one"), wasn't Freud's invention at all. In fact, one can trace its origins at least as far back as the age of Enlightenment.[11] Already in 1777, this idea is presented in an article on smell, included in the French Encyclopédie, quoting Albrecht von Haller as its original author (literally commemorating him in the year of his death): "The sense of smell was less important to [man], for he was destined to walk upright; he was to discover from a distance what might be his food; social life and language were designed to enlighten him about the properties of the things that appeared to him to be edible."[12] (Traces of this brief description are found in Kafka's story: the food is placed at a distance and becomes edible by sociolinguistic incantation.) The idea recurs. We find it in Herder's *Outlines of a Philosophy of the History of Man*, originally published in 1784, where Herder, too, treats it as his own brainchild:

> Had man been nearer to the ground, all his senses would have been circumscribed within narrower circle, and the superiour ones depressed by the predominancy of those of the inferiour order, as the instances of wild men show. Smell and taste, as the brute, would have been his leading guides. Raised above the earth and plants, smell no longer bears the sway, but sight. . . . With the erect gait man becomes a creature endued with art. . . . Man, by being formed to walk erect, acquired free and skillful hands, the instruments of the most delicate operations, and of an incessant feeling after new and clear ideas.[13]

For Herder, all uniquely human cultural artifacts (e.g., language, decency, religion) are seen as emerging from this evolutionary, that is, natural, break. Kant picks up the idea in his 1785 *Reviews* of Herder's book, pausing to discuss, in a mere variation on "Herder's" argument, the correlation between man's upright posture and reason as naturally emerging from it:

> It was not because he was destined to be rational that man was endowed with the erect posture which allows him to make rational use of his limbs; on the contrary, he acquired reason as a result of his erect posture, as the natural effect of that same constitution which he required in order to walk upright. . . . Elevated above the earth and the plants, it is no longer the sense of smell which predominates, but the eye.—With his upright gait, man acquired free and inventive hands and became a creator of artifacts. Only in conjunction with his erect gait does true human language appear.[14]

Though making no mention of smell, but stressing the emerging primacy of the eye, Fichte (in a passage already quoted) addresses the idea of bipedalism as a key evolutionary event in his 1797 *Foundations of Natural Right*, once again failing to credit any of his predecessors:

> In my view [!], the human species has freely lifted itself up from the earth and has thereby earned for itself the capacity to cast its gaze in every direction, in order to survey half of the universe in the skies. By contrast,

the eyes of the animal, because of their position, are riveted to the earth, which brings forth its nourishment. By lifting himself up from the earth, the human being has wrested from nature two instruments of freedom: two arms that, relieved of all animal functions, hang from the body only to await the will's command and be made suitable for its ends. Through its daring, upright gait—an everlasting expression of its audacity and skill—the species, in maintaining its balance, also maintains its freedom and reason in constant practice; it remains perpetually in a state of becoming, and gives expression to this. By its upright position, the species transports its life into the kingdom of light, and constantly flees from the earth, which it touches with the smallest possible part of itself. For the animal, the earth serves as both bed and table; the human being raises his bed and table above the earth.[15]

And the list goes on, eventually leading us to (Kafka and) Freud, who couldn't have been unaware of the idea's massive history, yet somehow managed to forget it. The extent of this amnesia in litteris is quite striking, making the osmological narrative modernity's incessantly and spontaneously rediscovered myth of human origins.

Despite its arguable centrality, the status and subsequent destiny of Freud's breakthrough could hardly be farther removed from the notoriety of the event of July 24, 1895, the official birth date of psychoanalysis. The event of that day, or rather of that night, is well known. During his stay at the Bellevue sanatorium, Freud had dreamed the notorious dream of "Irma's injection." The dream was of utmost importance to Freud, presenting him with the opportunity for his very first successful dream-interpretation. In 1900, soon after the publication of The Interpretation of Dreams, which was born out of this first successful attempt and in which the dream of "Irma's injection" was placed center stage, he famously wrote in a letter to Fliess: "Do you suppose that someday one will read on a marble tablet on this house: Here, on July 24, 1895, the secret of the dream revealed itself to Dr. Sigm. Freud."[16] The Bellevue was demolished in the 1960s, but, as if in a variation on the dreamlike theme of "the grin without a cat," in the midst of an empty, deserted field, a monument commemorating the nocturnal advent of the new science was erected, marking the mythical birthplace of psychoanalysis. If not one but two monuments were erected in honor of the latter discovery—namely the marble tablet of the monument and the paper tablet of The Interpretation of Dreams—the event of November 12, 1897, remained reduced to a few brief mentions, mostly in footnotes to Freud's own texts, as if embodying the persistent yet elusive and incommemorable nature of smell situated at the center of the narrative and "repeatedly showing itself" only to be "withdrawn again."

If these two dates are to be considered central to Freud's discovery, one striking thing about them is that smell plays a central role in both. Freud had been treating Irma during the summer of 1895. He proposed a treatment that Irma wasn't willing to accept. After a while, Freud visited with a colleague who knew Irma and inquired about her well-being. That night, upon learning that she was doing better but wasn't altogether well, Freud had the famous dream:

A large hall—numerous guests, whom we were receiving.—Among them was Irma. I at once took her on one side, as though to answer her letter and to reproach her for not having accepted my "solution" yet. I said to her: "If you still get pains, it's really only your fault." She replied: "If you only knew what pains I've got now in my throat and stomach and abdomen—it's choking me"—I was alarmed and looked at her. She looked pale and puffy. I thought to myself that after all I must be missing some organic trouble. I took her to the window and looked down her throat, and she showed signs of recalcitrance, like women with artificial dentures. I thought to myself that there was really no need for her to do that.—She then opened her mouth properly and on the right I found a big white patch; at another place I saw extensive whitish grey scabs upon some remarkable curly structures which were evidently modelled on the turbinal bones of the nose.—I at once called in Dr. M., and he repeated the examination and confirmed it. . . . Dr. M. looked quite different from usual; he was very pale, he walked with a limp and his chin was clean-shaven. . . . My friend Otto was now standing beside her as well, and my friend Leopold was percussing her through her bodice and saying: "She has a dull area low down on the left." He also indicated that a portion of the skin on the left shoulder was infiltrated. (I noticed this, just as he did, in spite of her dress.) . . . M. said: "There's no doubt it's an infection, but no matter; dysentery will supervene and the toxin will be eliminated." . . . We were directly aware, too, of the origin of the infection. Not long before, when she was feeling unwell, my friend Otto had given her an injection of a preparation of propyl, propyls . . . propionic acid . . . trimethylamin (and I saw before me the formula for this printed in heavy type). . . . Injections of that sort ought not to be made so thoughtlessly. . . . And probably the syringe had not been clean.[17]

There are at least three allusions to olfaction in this dream report. First, upon looking into Irma's mouth white stains are revealed. Freud relates these white patches to the use of cocaine. Second, these stains are revealed on "curly structures which were evidently modelled on the turbinal bones of the nose."[18] Third, Max Schur suggests that Irma was in fact a patient named Emma Eckstein.[19] Though proving false, the suggestion made sense: Freud had referred Emma to Fliess two months prior to the occurrence of the dream. Fliess performed nasal surgery on her, leaving a good half-meter of gauze in her nasal cavity by mistake, which caused recurrent nasal bleeding and had left her permanently disabled. The dream, Schur argued, was intended to exculpate Fliess for botching the "nose job."

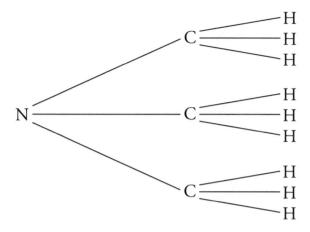

Formula of trimethylamine.

However, there is a fourth olfactory association, doubtless the most important one, namely the mention of trimethylamine. In his interpretation, Freud notes how in the dream "the formula was printed in heavy type, as though there had been a desire to lay emphasis on some part of the context as being of quite special importance."[20] The formula is associated with Fliess who had mentioned to Freud that trimethylamine played an important chemosexual role, arguing that the substance was a product of sexual metabolism. "Thus this substance," Freud adds, "led me to sexuality, the factor to which I attributed the greatest importance in the origin of the nervous disorders which it was my aim to cure."[21] The formula stands for the substance of sexuality, grasping it by and to the letter.

In his reading of the dream of Irma's injection, Lacan insists on the centrality of this meaningless formula for Freud's discovery. The discovery is not exhausted in the "numerological" material presented in the formula as a series of threes (corresponding to the three doctors and the three women appearing in the dream). For Lacan, it is the radical meaninglessness of the formula that holds the key to the meaning of this dream; the formula's "enigmatic, hermetic nature, is in fact the answer to the question of the meaning of the dream."[22] As such, the formula literalizes "this subject outside the subject," that is, the subject excarnate, "who designates the whole structure of the dream."[23] What is designated by this matheme? Trimethylamine, Lacan notes, is "a decomposition product of sperm, and it gives it its ammoniacal smell when it's left to decompose in the air."[24]

Sperm is not the only bodily secretion containing trimethylamine. It has been associated with bacterial vaginosis[25] and found in urine, blood, cerebrospinal fluid, bile, sweat, and breath, giving excreta a distinctive smell of "rotting fish."[26] It is also responsible for the rare metabolic disorder called tri-methylaminuria or "fish odor syndrome." The excretion is socially distress-ing and isolating, turning those affected into perceived social excreta: "What have we here? A man or a fish? Dead or alive? A fish. He smells like a fish, a very ancient and fish-like smell, a kind of not-of-the-newest poor-john. A strange fish!"[27]

The odoriferous nature of this "extracorporeal envoy" is almost unrivaled, and so is its extremely low chemosensory threshold or detection level.[28] The most famous, fateful, and paradigmatic dream in the entire history of psycho-analysis therefore ends with smell as the excremental core of sexuality.

In his reading of the dream, Lacan interprets the formula as "the quest for the word, . . . for signification as such."[29] Structured around an unsymboliz-able navel, the dream's meaning can only be grasped by the formula that liter-alizes the olfactory void of signification. Abscented from speaking beings, the smell is grasped from the outside of language, returning in the guise of an absensed formula: C_3H_9N.

Both events discussed here circle around the olfactory object. Both aim at grasping—by ways of either formalization or mythization—the Irreal, or "the unrealized," defined by Lacan as that which relates to the Real in a manner that eludes us.[30] The theory of the drives is our mythology, Freud claims; the drives are "mythical entities, magnificent in their indefiniteness."[31] The osmologi-cal narrative is the origin story of the drives. This origin story should be read alongside Lacan's own myth about the drive. The organ-libido has the struc-ture of the lamella, described by Lacan as

> something extra-flat, which moves like the amoeba. . . . But it goes
> everywhere. And as it is something—I will tell you shortly why—that is
> related to what the sexed being loses in sexuality, it is, like the amoeba in
> relation to sexed beings, immortal—because it survives any division, any
> scissiparous intervention. And it can run around. / Well! This is not very
> reassuring. But suppose it comes and envelopes your face while you are
> quietly asleep. . . . This lamella, this organ, whose characteristic is not to
> exist, but which nevertheless is an organ—I can give you more details as to
> its zoological place—is the libido.[32]

The lamella is the irrepressible remainder of organic repression, an instance of immortal life deprived of support in the symbolic order. As an organ without a body, the lamella is a being excarnate. Is the excarnated scent as the irrepressible remainder of organic repression not essentially lamellar? Like the lamella, scents survive any division by being the division-into-self of all things self-identical. They run around, doing much more than just envel-oping our faces while we're asleep, instead creeping into our noses, assaulting us at our most intimate.

"I, truth, speak." Lacan's notorious prosopopoeia is the most economical formulation of the critique that the logic of the signifier addresses to classical
ontology (and, by extension, also to structuralism) and its concept of truth.
In its constitution of the object, classical ontology is based on the principle of
reflexive identity. It subsumes the object under its concept, insofar as it can
be "counted as one"—that is, as identical with itself, or as identical with the
concept of the thing. This is the basis of the traditional theory of truth as *adaequatio rei et intellectus*, the correspondence between the concept and the thing.
The philosophical metaphoric of the eye relies on such a conception of truth,
understood in terms of a relational correspondence between the gaze, which
is on the side of the thinking subject, and the being of the object, which is
offered to the mind's eye as "counted as one." The same applies to the metaphoric of the voice. Here, too, truth as correspondence is supported by the
self-identity of the subject *hearing itself speak*.[33] Even the aesthetic use of taste
in the constitution of the beautiful does not escape such a notion of truth,
though referring, in Kantian terms, to a different type of correspondence that
appears as a negative of the concept. Thus, at the core of the classical theory of
truth lies the idea of a conceptual touch.

Commenting on Leibniz's *eadem sunt quorum unum potest substitui alteri salva
veritate*, which follows the classical notion of truth as *adaequatio rei et intellectus* (first formulated by Aquinas and dating back to Aristotle), Jacques-Alain
Miller remarks:

> Those things are identical of which one can be substituted for the other
> *salva veritate*, without loss of truth. Doubtless you can estimate the crucial
> importance of what is effected by this statement: the emergence of the
> function of truth. Yet what it assumes is more important than what it
> expresses. That is, identity-with-itself. That a thing cannot be substituted
> for itself, then where does this leave truth? Absolute is its subversion. . . .
> You will grasp to what extent the preservation of truth is implicated in this
> identity with itself which connotes the passage from the thing to the object.
> Identity-with-itself is essential if truth is to be saved.[34]

The model for such a monstrous entity, standing in a relation of reflexive
opposition to itself, is provided by language—more precisely, by the signifier,
whose principal characteristic is that "it is not as it is."[35] In a passage already
quoted, Jean-Claude Milner remarks that this insight is utterly alien not only
to the philosophical tradition but to thought itself.[36] Now we understand why:
it puts the truth in crisis.

To keep reflexive oppositivity at bay, truth must seek refuge in the concept
and the principle of reflexive identity. A thing not identical with itself must
be reduced to no-thing-at-all and thus banished from ontology. That is why

the truth of classical ontology can never be a speaking truth. Resorting to the utterance "I, truth, speak," entrusting itself to the signifier, it self-dissipates. The quoted prosopopoeia from Lacan's text "The Freudian Thing" is a declaration of war against the classical theory of truth, one waged in the name of a quite different truth, one that the former had to exclude to install itself. But the eliminated and the banished returns in the form of a remainder that the philosophical truth cannot absorb without exuding itself: "Whether you flee me in deceit," says the speaking truth, "or think you can catch me in error, I will catch up with you in the mistake from which you cannot hide."[37] For Lacan, this remainder is revealing of the fact that the classically conceived truth is a "mirage-like truth that can be reduced to the mirage of truth."[38]

Lacan's proposition "I, truth, speak" snatches truth from adequation, correspondence, identity-with-itself, or the principle of reflexivity, all of which become markers of "the mirage of truth." What for psychoanalysis is a mirage of truth, appears, from the other side—that is, from the standpoint of classical ontology—as the truth of a mirage, namely the mirage of a split entity unidentical with itself. But this does not yet exhaust the meaning of the mirage of truth. Lacan does not place the truth discovered by psychoanalysis in a simple external and abstract opposition to the classically conceived truth. Rather, Lacan admits that in its formulation and interpretation, classical ontology has successfully grasped the structure of the mirage-like truth. However, in its gesture of constituting truth as adequation, classical ontology necessarily overlooked something "overdetermining" its own field, namely the secret conveyed by the speaking truth: "Men, listen, I am telling you the secret. I, truth, speak."[39] Expressed in Freudian terms: classical ontology formulated the structure of identification (reflexive identity) but overlooked the structuring field of signification overdetermining its structure, thereby overlooking the inherent share of repression in the establishing of reflexive identity.

The slogan "I, truth, speak" is effectively tantamount to Lacan's famous motto "the unconscious is structured like a language." The truth that speaks is precisely an unconscious truth, the truth of the unconscious, structured like a language, and surfacing in dreams, jokes, slips of tongue, and symptoms, arranged in accordance with Saussurean ontology and its principle of opposition. These formations cannot be counted as one without being discounted. The truth that they epitomize cannot be grasped by way of adequation underlying traditional conceptualization. But here comes Lacan's surprising twist: they can only be grasped by smell, that is, by the sense repressed by the established correspondences between being and thought. A speaking truth is "a speaking nose."[40]

A good illustration of this point may be provided by the image of the Great Sphinx of Giza—and its missing nose. The history of philosophy is permeated by the Sphinx's riddle of smell. Smell is the riddle of the Spirit, of their irreducibility and missed encounter. Half man, half animal, midway between animality and the human Spirit, the Sphinx is a creature apart, epitomizing the endeavors of culture and Spirit to rid themselves of nature and smell. "Out of the dull strength and power of the animal," Hegel writes apropos of the Sphinx as the symbol of unconscious metaphoric, "the human spirit tries to push itself forward [hervordrängen], without coming to a perfect portrayal of its own freedom and animated shape, because it must still remain confused and associated with what is other than itself."[41] For Hegel, the Sphinx is a symbol of tension between the opposing domains of Spirit and nature, or between spirituality and animality. The Sphinx embodies the struggle of the emerging Spirit to leave behind "the dull strength and power of the animal," to push itself ahead and thought it, hervordrängen. But the hervordrängen of Spirit is inherently related to the verdrängen of smell. The Spirit must shake off animality to break through to itself. And is the missing nose of the Great Sphinx of Giza not a doubly adequate depiction of this movement, embodying in the form of an absent object the repressed juncture of spirituality and animality?

On the one hand, the Sphinx can be seen as an embodiment of the classical theory of truth: truth as adequation is forged by eliminating from its field the share of inherent non-identity with itself. The truth as adequation rids itself of this share of non-equivalence by eliminating self-difference:[42] so as not to lose its head, classical ontology must lose its nose. If it is to keep its veritable head, it must rid itself of the speaking nose. However, the missing, repressed nose of truth henceforth haunts the noseless philosophical Sphinx as an excarnated scent. The truth requires a good nose; adequate thought either misses the truth or else ceases being adequate.[43]

Adequate thought circumvents the Real, however the Real persists in this circumvention. Lacan's name for this process is repetition as situated beyond the traditional theory of truth:

> Let us take a look, then, at how Wiederholen (repeating) is introduced [by Freud]. Wiederholen is related to Erinnerung (remembering). The subject in himself, the recalling of his biography, all this goes only to a certain limit, which is known as the real. If I wished to make a Spinozian formula concerning what is at issue, I would say—cogitatio adaequata semper vitat eandem rem. An adequate thought, qua thought, at the level at which we are, always avoids—if only to find itself again later in everything—the same thing. Here, the real is that which always comes back to the same place—to the place where the subject in so far as he thinks, where the res cogitans, does not meet it.[44]

An adequate thought always avoids the same thing. The Real is the limit to this operation of adequation, by which the concept subsumes the thing, counting it as one, that is, as identical with the concept of the thing. Thus, thought is protected against the non-self-identical object—it is only on condition of this expulsion that thought finds itself again "in everything." On the other hand, there is no adequate thought of the Real because there is no adequate thought of a non-self-identical object. Put differently: the only adequate thought is the thought of an object not differing from itself.

An adequate thought always avoids the same thing because the thing in question is never the same, never identical with itself, hence amounting (from the vantage point of adequate thought) to the nonsense of an inadequate thought. "Inadequation" (as non-equivalence) is a term deployed by Lévi-Strauss: "There is always a non-equivalence or 'inadequation' between the two, a non-fit and overspill which divine understanding alone can soak up; this generates a signifier-surfeit relative to the signifieds to which it can be fitted."[45] In Lévi-Strauss, inadequation relates to the non-fit between the orders of signifiers and their signifieds, whereas reflexive opposition (a term I prefer, not least because it is a positive) marks the signifier's relation not to the order of meaning but rather to itself. If there is a non-fit and overspill, it is not due to a signifier-surfeit understood as quantifiable overabundance (of there being more signifiers than there are signifieds). Rather, the overabundance of signifiers is a function of a lack: if signifiers cannot be fitted to the signifieds, it is because a signifier is not what it is and hence doesn't fit itself. Accordingly, an inadequate thought is a thought unbefitting of itself.

For Lacan, the subject of the unconscious is situated in the gap separating adequate thought from itself. As such, it is related to the Cartesian *cogito* insofar as the latter is not the subject of consciousness but rather a subject, devoid of any consciousness-defining content. But upon introducing the thinking subject in its radical emptiness, Descartes mobilized the traditional theory of truth and proceeded by adequating it. The moment it subsumed its object, the empty point of the subject of doubt became an adequate thought: *Cogito, ergo sum*. Thought founds the subject as *res cogitans* (a thinking thing). Thus, a critical move is accomplished: a move from *thinking to thinging*. The constitution of cogito as res cogitans relies on repression as correlative with the establishing of self-identity: the act of repression eliminates the monstrous share of the subject's non-identity with itself.

A SPEAKING NOSE

The elementary error that Lacan attributed to Descartes therefore matches the oversight inherent in the traditional theory of truth in relation to its speaking Other, that is, to the truth capable of saying: "I, truth, speak." For the cogito "certainly cannot be detached from the fact that he [Descartes] can formulate it only by *saying* it to us, implicitly—a fact that he forgets."[46] This forgetting is precisely the forgetting of oppositivity and of the non-self-identity introduced by language. In differing from itself, the Freudian cogito has neither Being nor a Self. Lacan comments on the agreement, or adequation, necessarily entailed by the Cartesian notion of truth, which takes "the famous form Spinoza gave it: '*Idea vera debet cum suo ideato convenire*. A true idea must' (the emphasis falls on the word 'must,' meaning that this is its own necessity) 'agree with its object.'"[47]

The subject of adequate thought (res cogitans) always avoids the same thing that is banished from Being. The Freudian cogito, on the other hand, finds its footing in an inadequate thought that is but a mode of avoiding the same thing insofar as it is unidentical with itself. Sameness as the attribute of the thing always avoided by adequate thought therefore differs from the concept of identity: being the "same" is not the same as being "identical," the "identical" is not identical with the "same." Only a thing differing from itself can ever be the "same." The "same" is not identical with itself and hence not "counted as one"; lacking a signifier, it is impossible in the strict sense of existing at no time (as opposed to the necessity of Descartes's thinking substance that, as substance, exists at all times).[48] It is this Real that repeats itself and can never be encountered by the subject of adequate thought. We should take this in the absolute sense: the subject misses the Real without knowing it had missed it. And vice versa: the subject of adequate thought can only encounter it by ceasing to be the subject of adequate thought—that is, only by ceasing to be (a thinking thing).

The notion of a missed encounter should be given a double meaning. The subject of adequate thought misses the Real because of always only encountering the object in its objectivity. As we have seen, the subject of the unconscious is not simply in an external negative relation to the subject of adequate thought. That is to say, we cannot conclude that the subject of the unconscious encounters the Real *in persona*. Their relationship is more intricate. The subject of adequate thought does not avoid the Real but is entirely indifferent to it, for the Real is nothing to him. It is only at the level of the subject of the unconscious that we can speak of avoiding the Real, for it is only from the vantage point of this subject that the Real is *not* nothing (and hence is *not-nothing*). Interpreters often miss this point by claiming that the Real can only be missed by the subject of consciousness, and by postulating the unconscious subject's immediate encounter with the Real. Lacan subverts such a perspective: "Contrary to all the neurophysiologists, pathologists and others, Freud made it quite clear that, although it was difficult for the subject to reproduce in dream the memory of the heavy bombing-raid, for example, from which his neurosis derives—it does not seem, when he is awake, to bother him either way."[49]

The point goes against the grain of the commonsensical understanding of psychoanalysis. This understanding grasps the unconscious as a face-to-face encounter with the traumatic Real, otherwise pushed aside and neglected in and by our conscious life. Paradoxically, it is not consciousness but rather the unconscious that is avoiding the Real. That is why Lacan can claim that in the waking state the subject indifferently reproduces the trauma of the bombing as if not bothered by it at all. What gives pause to an analysist is the subject persistently avoiding the trauma in his dreams. Not being able to talk about our traumatic experiences is one thing, but being unable to dream of them is an entirely different matter. Herein lies the sharp contrast between remembering (or reproducing), on the one hand, and repeating, on the other. As the subject of dreams, you cannot remember the trauma, but in repetition the trauma remembers you.[50]

Applied to a great number of examples and practices, the concept of interpassivity—coined and developed by Robert Pfaller—has of yet not been applied to traumatism.[51] If that is the case, we have overlooked the conceptual reliance of the notion of interpassivity on the concept of repetition. Taking our cue from the interpassive nature of trauma, we can take issue with the move "from sex to the brain" as proposed by Catherine Malabou in The New Wounded (2007). As the title suggests, Malabou proposes a new theory of trauma, one that is not psychopathological but cerebral. When the psyche is shattered by brain damage, this cerebral traumatism effects the birth of a new subject, unrecognizable to itself and to others, as well as incapable of any regression to its former, now absent self. What is missed in Malabou's critique of Freud is precisely the interpassive nature of repetition. Granted, the new subject of trauma has no history and cannot be accounted for in terms of a regression. While the wound does in fact create "a certain form of being by effacing a previously existing identity,"[52] the new subject is also unable to efface it: the subject might not remember itself, but the Other continues remembering the subject. The truth of the Self, its excarnated identity, is out there in the Other, but no transition from the signifier to being, from cogito to sum, is possible. Commenting on the effects of her grandmother's Alzheimer's disease, Malabou writes:

> If I understood more clearly, I would have tried on occasion to take her back home for a few hours. I would have given her the chance to regain her familiar surroundings, her "things." The point would not have been absurdly to help her to "refresh her memory," but to allow her calmly and without any expectations to perceive "her own absence."[53]

Would the Lacanian point not be that it is precisely such an encounter with "her 'things'" that would have been truly traumatizing for her? The new subject continues to be traumatized by her own posthumous existence outside of herself, in the Other. She may not remember herself, but her things remember her Self in her stead. This is not to deny the validity of Malabou's claim that the autistic, post-traumatic subject as such is radically alien to any notion of biographical identity. As an effect of a strictly external trauma that remains uninterpretable and irreducible to personal history, the post-traumatic sub-ject does in fact present the point of impossibility, or suspension, of herme-neutics.[54] However, in its encounter with the Other, the subject faces not a traumatic *impossibility* of hermeneutics but rather its equally traumatic *inescap-ability*. Quoting Louis Crocq, Malabou rightly observes that such patients "real-ize that a new being is within them, a being whom they do not recognize."[55] The only objection I have to this claim is that, importantly, the unrecogniz-able "new being" is *out there* rather than *within me*. Think of Mike Nichols's 1991 film *Regarding Henry*. Interrupting a robbery, Henry (a wealthy and nar-cissistic lawyer) is shot in the head and suffers severe brain damage. Henry finds himself completely transformed. But though suffering from severe ret-rograde amnesia, unable to recall his former Self, Henry nonetheless inescap-ably encounters his former Self in interactions with others (family members, coworkers, friends). Moreover, from his perspective, this abhorrent former Self, with which he is unable to identify, is the new being emerging out there in the Other.

Let's return to smell and the theory of truth. Unlike Descartes's cogito, the subject of the unconscious lacks not only proper being but also a proper thought that could presentify it. As such, it is represented by a nonsensical signifier to which no meaning can be attributed and under which no object can be subsumed. The subject only surfaces in contingent moments when the impossible appears in dreams, symptoms, and parapraxes as instances of inad-equate thought. The antinomy between thought and enjoyment prompts Lacan to correct the Cartesian formula of *cogito, ergo sum*, the latter only adequately befitting the subject of adequate thought. Not "I think, therefore I am," but rather "I think where I am not, and I am where I think not"—such is the for-mula of the Freudian cogito.[56]

The Cartesian subject (the res cogitans of adequate thought) subtends the classical theory of truth that can never say "I, truth, speak" without self-dissipating. The Freudian subject, on the other hand, only *thinks* where it thinks that it does not think (and therefore is not), and only *is* where it does not think. Unconscious thought is detached from the sphere of being and excluded from the dimension of truth. However, Lacan's speaking truth is pre-cisely the truth of this missing thought that remains adequately inaccessible. Since its object is not identical with itself, conceptual thinking as conceived by classical ontology cannot grab a hold of it.

The excretion of smell in and from the history of philosophy is structur-ally related to its models of conceptual thinking and hence to its theory of truth. Smell is at odds with the principle of reflexive identity as the standard of conceptuality. It stands opposite the concept, *Begriff*, which touches upon the thing in its objectivity, as an *Unbegriff*, a concept lacking, a short circuit of conceptual thought.[57] Smell thus jeopardized the status of truth as grounded in adequate thoughts of the subject. Following the opposition between an adequate and an inadequate thought, between thinking and smelling, between the truth of classical and that of the Saussurean ontology, we arrive at the antinomic relation between the subject of adequation and the olfactory cogito as subject of the unconscious. Smell is the dissolution of the thinking thing, or, in a word, of thinging. As subject, I only exists where I do not smell: *I smell where I am not, and I am, where I do not smell*. Smell is the anamorphosis of objectivity, the speaking truth an anamorphosis of truth as adequation.[58]

Unsurprisingly, then, Lacan's prosopopoeia of the truth eventually leads him to the nose. The smell reference was here all along, right under our noses but too close for us to catch a whiff of it:

> I wander about in what you regard as least true by its very nature: in dreams, in the way the most far-fetched witticisms and the most grotesque nonsense of jokes defy meaning, and in chance—not in its law, but rather in its contingency. And I never more surely proceed to change the face of the world than when I give it the profile of Cleopatra's nose.[59]

There is but a step separating the speaking truth from the speaking nose. Were it slightly different, Cleopatra's nose would change the face of the world. Lacan's reference is Pascal: "Cleopatra's nose: had it been shorter, the whole face of the world would have been changed."[60] Mladen Dolar comments on the passage: "Had Cleopatra's nose been shorter, neither Caesar nor Mark Anthony would have fallen in love with her and the course of history would have been so different that the whole face of the world would have been changed. A minute, contingent cause might have had world-historical consequences."[61]

Had her nose been shorter, would Caesar and Mark Anthony so much as smelled her? Would history by any other length of the nose smell the same? Is the anatomy of the nose the destiny of the world? I am, of course, referring to the line so dear to Freud: "Anatomy is destiny." Freud first proposes it in "On the Universal Tendency to Debasement in the Sphere of Love" (1912).[62] And it is precisely love that is at issue in Pascal's mention of Cleopatra's nose: "Vanity. The cause and effects of love. Cleopatra."[63] The anatomy of the nose provides the key to the psychology of love life and hence to the debasement, *Erniedrigung*, submission, which is not only the submission of Caesar and Mark Anthony, but also the political submission of the world. The keys to amorous debasement and political submission are held by arguably the lowest of the physical senses.

In his slogan "Anatomy is destiny," Freud is paraphrasing Napoleon who, in a discussion with Goethe that took place in 1808 in Weimar, supposedly said, "Politics is destiny."[64] Following the spirit of Pascal's remark, the anatomy of Cleopatra's nose is an emphatically political anatomy. Napoleon's name plays an important role in the enigma of another nose, namely the missing nose of the Great Sphinx of Giza. How did it fall off? What was it that had hit the Sphinx, taking off her nose? What caused this lack? The answer long thought most persuasive was that the nose was taken off by a cannon ball of Napoleon's army. The story nicely joins the two slogans by confronting the supposed world-historic fatefulness of the anatomy of the nose with the fatefulness of political anatomy. The anatomy of the nose nonetheless retains its phantasmatic priority: the submission of Egypt presupposes the submission of anatomy, that is, taking off the Sphinx's nose.[65] This widely circulated story about Napoleon and the Sphinx was finally put to rest by Frederic Louis Norden's drawing of the Great Sphinx of Giza with the missing nose. The drawing was made in 1738, more than thirty years prior to Napoleon's birth on August 15, 1769.

So, is the anatomy of the nose the destiny of the world? Posing the question in these terms, we find ourselves in the regime of adequation, subsuming history as we know it under the concept of Cleopatra's nose, attributing to it the weight of the cause and establishing between the two terms a relation of reflexive identity. The problem of alternate history, implied in the remark, also refuses to shake the regime of adequation, though seemingly relying on contingency: the world is self-identical because it adequately reflects Cleopatra's nose; and had the nose been shorter, history would smell different but remain identical with itself. The seeming priority of contingency is merely the obverse of law and necessity. Cleopatra's nose, as it figures in this reading, is no contingent cause but rather the law of history as a series of effects of a determining cause. Contingency of the contingent cause, on the other hand, is at odds with the law: truth, Lacan writes, resides "in chance—not in its law, but rather in its contingency."[66] The nose in its function of a veritably contingent cause is at odds with the idea that the size of the nose could determine historical processes as a series of its effects. The nose at issue here could only be the nose of the Great Sphinx—not shorter but altogether missing, and hence (as missing) producing historical effects while remaining irreducible to the law of history. Read with Lacan as the embodiment of a contingent cause, Cleopatra's nose is not the law of history but its symptom, a point of contradiction and antagonism determining the historical face of the world.

Anatomy is destiny, but what kind of destiny is it? There are two ancient Greek terms that signify destiny. First, there is Ananke, destiny as necessity, later supplanted by the notion of tyche, that is: destiny as chance.[67] Lacan relates the contingent emergence of the Real to tyche, which in ancient Greek texts denotes the punctual effect of fate on man (the Latin equivalent is fortuna, good or bad luck that befalls us suddenly and without a demonstrable causal connection to our past). Then there is automaton, fate as necessity, pertaining to the unconscious "structured like a language." The two remain irreducible, such that *tyche* as "*the encounter with the real*" lies "beyond the *automaton*"[68] and hence is extrinsic to signification. The notion of anatomy's destiny entails both destiny as (unconscious) necessity and destiny as chance, the latter signifying an incursion into the symbolic order. Etymologically, "anatomy" is related to *the cut*. The two instances of destiny are instituted and untied together by the signifying cut: "If Cleopatra's nose changed the world's course, it was because it entered the world's discourse; for in order to change it for the longer or the shorter, it was sufficient, but it was also necessary, that it be a speaking nose."[69] By way of an example, think of the speaking nose from Freud's fetishism text. There, the fetishistic attachment to a certain *Glanz auf der Nase* is revealed to be a matter of a faulty translation. Though the fetishist had long forgotten the language of his infancy, the nose remembers. Freud can only interpret his fetish by letting the nose speak: *Glanz*, "shine," is revealed to signify "a glance" at the nose as the precondition of the patient's fetishistic enjoyment.[70]

A speaking nose refers us back to our previous discussions. The universal olfactory anomia was related to primal repression, instituted by the first signifying cut, and establishing the antinomy between names and smells, between spelling and smelling. From this perspective, a speaking nose is a monstrous and inadequate entity, and were it to speak, it would be speaking—not in tongues but—in slips of the tongue, wandering about, as Lacan writes, in what we regard as least true and as, by its very nature, undermining the principle of reflexive identity. However, it is precisely as inadequate and reflexively oppositional that the speaking nose comes to figure as the bearer of the primordially repressed truth, announcing itself in contingent encounters, seeping through the cracks of the deodorized history of the world. The nose is structured like a language. Seeping through the cracks in contingent encounters, the speaking nose occupies the position of the divided subject. Split between ortho- and retro-smelling, olfaction foreshadows the linguistic duality of anticipation and retroaction at work in signification. As such, the speaking nose has the temporal structure of a *Sichverzehren*, inhabiting the temporal gap separating the *will* from the *have been*.

THE ORIGIN OF SWEAR WORDS

"A sense of smell surer than all your categories."[71] This is the punchline of Lacan's prosopopoeia of truth. If ever there was someone with a good enough nose and the patience necessary for such a truth (a patience requiring a patient), it was the Rat Man, the foremost nose of psychoanalysis. As already mentioned, the Rat Man's childhood was characterized by a keen sense of smell, such that he was able to identify people by their odors, like a dog.[72] Capable of identifying people solely by their smell with no assistance from the other senses, the Rat Man caught a whiff of the structural share of repression in the constitution of identity, or the share of self-difference dissipating with the establishing of relations of identity. In the already quoted passage, Freud goes on to comment:

> I have met with the same characteristic in other neurotics, both in hysterical and in obsessional patients,[73] and I have come to recognize that a tendency to taking pleasure in smell, which has become extinct since childhood, may play a part in the genesis of neurosis. And here I should like to raise the general question whether the atrophy of the sense of smell (which was an inevitable result of man's assumption of an erect posture) and the consequent organic repression of his pleasure in smell may not have had a considerable share in the origin of his susceptibility to nervous disease. This would afford us some explanation of why, with the advance of civilization, it is precisely the sexual life that must fall a victim to repression.[74]

We stumble upon the same idea three years later, in the passage paraphrasing Napoleon:

> we know that the sexual instinct is originally divided into a great number of components—or rather, it develops out of them—some of which cannot be taken up into the instinct in its later form, but have at an earlier stage to be suppressed or put to other uses. These are above all the coprophilic instinctual components, which have proved incompatible with our aesthetic standards of culture, probably since, as a result of our adopting an erect gait, we raised our organ of smell from the ground. The same is true of a large portion of the sadistic urges which are a part of erotic life. But all such developmental processes affect only the upper layers of the complex structure. The fundamental processes which produce erotic excitation remain unaltered. The excremental is all too intimately and inseparably bound up with the sexual; the position of the genitals—*inter urinas et faeces*—remains the decisive and unchangeable factor. One might say here, varying a well-known saying of the great Napoleon: "Anatomy is destiny."[75]

In Freud's speculative construction, the raising of the nose from the ground is situated at the very point of inception of "our aesthetic standards of culture," at the point of passage from the state of nature to the domain of the Spirit. In this regard, Freud's speculation aligns with the philosophical placement of smell on the side of our animal prehistory whose excremental remainders continue to seep into the cultural domain. The construction presents Freud's speculative response to the Sphinx's riddle of smell addressing the enigmatic beginnings of civilized life. We encounter it once again eighteen years later in *Civilization and Its Discontents* (1930). There, Freud addresses it in two extensive footnotes, while adding additional elements, namely the concept of "organic repression" and the idea of a prioritizing substitution of the olfactory stimuli for visual ones, a prioritizing analogous to the one experienced by Kafka's musical dogs who "chant their incantations with their faces turned upwards, . . . forgetting the ground."[76] But "adding" is not an entirely accurate word here. As we've seen, the construction was first mentioned twelve years prior to its first publication. In his letter to Fliess, dated November 14, 1897, Freud mentions the idea of an "organic repression" of olfactory stimuli as the constitutional factor of culture.

The chapter of *Civilization and Its Discontents* containing the two footnotes is immediately preceded by the following question: "We must ask ourselves to what influences the development of civilization owes its origin, how it arose, and by what its course has been determined."[77] In the already quoted letter to Fliess, we get the idea's "certificate of its birth," which essentially addresses the birth of civilization, its origin, and the determining factors of its course. In a word, we get the birth announcement of the idea of birth. Freud is inquiring into the origin of culture, into its elusive source, and hence into the cause of breaking out of the primordial state of nature. At the mythical point of passage, he discovers the Sphinx's riddle of smell, that is, the riddle of the nose that had to fall off so that civilization might begin: "The diminution of the olfactory stimuli seems itself to be a consequence of man's raising himself from the ground, of his assumption of an upright gait; this made his genitals, which were previously concealed, visible and in need of protection, and so provoked feelings of shame in him. / The fateful process of civilization would thus have set in with man's adoption of an erect posture."[78] In the beginning there was "organic repression" consubstantial with the adoption of an erect posture. Having been lifted from the ground, the nose surrendered its privileged place to the eye and to visual stimuli. However, the osmological narrative is not only about the atrophy of the sense of smell. Rather, it is a story of how the sense of smell was enlisted in the war against excreta, and hence a story of how the newly established primacy of the eye and the I is consubstantial with the birth of smell's prophylactic function.

Freud's osmological narrative is a "theoretical speculation,"[79] but one that fits well with other psychoanalytic discoveries, though ultimately presenting their scientifically unaccountable, if not unaccounted, extrapolation. In addition, we must not disregard the fact that (except for its first mention in the "Rat Man" case) Freud places the term "organic repression" in quotes, hereby indicating that we should use it with caution. Before addressing the question of questionability of these two conceptual choices, let us look at the remainder of Freud's footnote. He mentions the function of smell "in the cultural trend towards cleanliness," immediately adding that any reference to "hygienic considerations" is a form of a *nachträglich* practical rationalization rather than a determining factor in the genesis of cleanliness. The true motive for such a pronounced cultural interest in cleanliness is attributed to the prophylactic function of the sense of smell for which the odor of excreta has become unpleasant. At this point the phylogenetic construction, that is, the idea of "organic repression," is mirrored in ontogenetic development, that is, in teaching and accustoming the child to "cleanliness." Thus, the excremental products that hereto the child has handled without any signs of disgust become the object of the first cultural prohibition. At the same time, Freud adds how this (temporally and spatially localizable) cultural prohibition (resulting from education and other related social factors) would have had zero effect if it weren't supported by the "organic repression" always already preceding and preparing the ground for it. The fate of a child's excreta therefore is merely repeating the fate met by olfactory stimuli in the moment the human nose was lifted from the ground.

Returning to the possible problems with such a speculative construction, it seems that our preceding analysis has already established a rational theoretical core and a suitable starting point for interpreting Freud's speculation and thus for denouncing its supposed involvement in ideological psychologization. The "organicity" of organic repression will not be aligned with notions of "originality" or "primordiality," but reduced to the rational conceptual core of irreducibility, itself conceptually reducible to a separately developed idea of *Urverdrängung*, or primal repression. This irreducibility has to be correlated with the structure of language and hence signifies the irreducibility of the signifying cut. It is correlative with the establishing of the symbolic order, providing the human with linguistic crutches with which it lifted himself from the ground. It is this irreducible foundation of primal repression that prepares the terrain for the—temporally and spatially localizable—prohibitions. The latter play a key role in accustoming the child to cleanliness and should be conceived of as instances of *Nachdrängen*, after-pressure, or "repression proper." Therefore, that which structurally succumbs to repression is not man's own animality, but the share of self-difference introduced by speech. Within this construction, smell represents that share of oppositivity, self-difference or non-identity-with-itself that undergoes repression the moment the first word is introduced. This repressed share, however, returns in the form of an excremental remainder enjoining the thinking and speaking subject to enjoyment, confronting it with its own dissolution.[80]

Herein resides the double—prophylactic *and* libidinous[81]—function of smell befitting the division between, on the one hand, after-pressure as instituted by prohibition (turning the sense of smell into a police agent of disgust and the culturally-aesthetic turning up of one's nose at all things excremental)[82] and, on the other, primal repression and the irreducibly unconscious libidinous impulses expressed in *Riechlust*, the enjoyment in smelling. The relation between the two functions, however, is not one of simple opposition, whereby (the pleonastic) excremental sexuality would yield to the pressures of civilized life while simultaneously displaying an inherent incontinence allowing it to seep through its cracks. Adorno and Horkheimer take note of the double nature of smell, noting how its prohibitive-prophylactic function is out in the service of satisfying the good old pleasure in smelling. Contrary to the denigration hypothesis—highlighting the atrophying effect of organic repression on the sense of smell—civilization is as much in the business of enlisting the sense of smell in its war against excreta as it is in the business of dulling it:

> In civilization, therefore, smell is regarded as a disgrace, a sign of the lower social orders, lesser races, and baser animals. The civilized person is allowed to give way to such desires only if the prohibition is suspended by rationalization in the service of practical purposes, real or apparent. One is allowed to indulge the outlawed drive if acting with the unquestionable aim of expunging it.[83]

Is *mucophagy* not a good example of this? The first population survey of rhinotillexomania, or nose-picking, found it to be an almost universal practice in adults.[84] Though socially deplorable, and its deplorable nature consistently communicated to children, most adults seem to be doing it. Here is Sylvia Plath's detailed account of the sexual pleasures of nose-picking:

> As for minute joys: as I was saying: do you realize the illicit sensuous delight I get from picking my nose? I always have, ever since I was a child—there are so many subtle variations of sensation. A delicate, pointed-nailed fifth finger can catch under dry scabs and flakes of mucous in the nostril and draw them out to be looked at, crumbled between fingers, and flicked to the floor in minute crusts. Or a heavier, determined forefinger can reach up and smear down-and-out the soft, resilient, elastic greenish-yellow smallish blobs of mucous, roll them round and jelly-like between thumb and fore finger, and spread them on the under surface of a desk or chair where they will harden into organic crusts. How many desks and chairs have I thus secretively befouled since childhood? Or sometimes there will be blood mingled with the mucous: in dry brown scabs, or bright sudden wet red on the finger that scraped too rudely the nasal membranes. God, what a sexual satisfaction! It is absorbing to look with new sudden eyes on the old worn habits: to see a sudden luxurious and pestilential "snot-green sea," and shiver with the shock of recognition.[85]

Boogers, or dried nasal mucus, usually extracted with one's finger, are quite often ingested instead of wiped away and thrown in the trash. It would seem that the latter scenario comes to pass only in situations that require us to maintain a heightened public sense of propriety. When no one is (believed to be) looking, and hence no one is forced to co-enjoy, we tend to freely dispose of the little boogers by eating them. The practice is permissible under two conditions. First, that it does not disturb the appearance of decency, that is, the *sensus decori*. Second, and more importantly, that the suspension of *sensus decori* is in the service of the sense of public propriety. In other words: under the condition just defined, one is allowed to indulge in mucophagy because eating a booger is seen as a special form of expunging it. Thus, enjoyment is extracted from the very act of renouncing it.

The inner splitting of smell testifies to the fact that the relation between culture and sexuality is more convoluted than that. In "On the Universal Tendency to Debasement in the Sphere of Love," Freud comments on the following strange possibility: "It is my belief that, however strange it may sound, we much reckon with the possibility that something in the nature of the sexual instinct [*Trieb*, 'drive'] itself is unfavourable to the realization of complete satisfaction."[86]

Freud makes the same strange suggestion in *Civilizations and Its Discontents*: "Sometimes one seems to perceive that it is not only the pressure of civilization but something in the nature of the [sexual] function itself which denies us full satisfaction and urges us along other paths. This may be wrong; it is hard to decide."[87] To account for this, Freud adds a footnote, once again repeating his osmological claim:

> The conjecture which goes deepest, however, is the one which takes its start from what I have said above in my footnote. . . . It is to the effect that, with the assumption of an erect posture by man and with the depreciation of his sense of smell, it was not only his anal erotism which threatened to fall victim to organic repression, but the whole of his sexuality; so that since this, the sexual function has been accompanied by a repugnance which cannot further be accounted for, and which prevents its complete satisfaction and forces it away from the sexual aim into sublimations and libidinal displacements.[88]

Sexuality is complicit in its own repression, meaning that cultural prohibitions against sexuality are always already informing the sexual function itself. The cultural *Nachdrängen* is supported by the *Urverdrängung*, organically (that is, irreducibly) attached to the sexual function as such. Lacan's notion of surplus-enjoyment accounts for the symmetricity of their causal relation, with *plus-de-jouir* signifying both *more* enjoyment and *no more* enjoyment. Surplus-enjoyment is not an amount of enjoyment left over after complete satisfaction has been achieved. The *more* only emerges against the backdrop of *no more*: *Riechlust*, the outlawed drive to smell, is the flipside of cultural prophylactics, its surplus-enjoyment is an addition (of enjoyment) by subtraction (of enjoyment).

Let us return to the eye and the nose. This simple hyperstructuralist dispositif provides the rational anchorage point for the idea of substitution of smell for visual stimuli and the eye as organ of their reception. Two readings impose themselves. First: the eye is an organ of identification and self-identical subjectivity, while smell is on the side of self-difference repressed by processes of identification. Within the libidinal division of labor, smell and sight divide among themselves two aspects of the subject's alienation: the first aspect is that of identification and pertains to the eye; the second aspect is that of repression and pertains to the nose. However, another possible reading imposes itself. According to this reading, the passage from smell to sight is not a matter of progressively substituting the former for the latter, establishing between them a relation of development. Rather, it is the same logical consistency embodied by smell that reappears in the scopic register. This reading is confirmed by the reaction of shame following the passage from smell to sight, effected by the assumption of an erect posture revealing a view of the genitals.[89] Freud emphasized that the shame is caused by the excremental surplus, "intimately and inseparably bound up with the sexual" function born *inter urinas et faeces*, amid urine and feces. Within the scopic register, the excremental surplus emerges as the gaze—that is, it emerges not as the gaze of the subject of adequate thought but as the gaze as the anamorphic stain of objectivity, standing for the share of perception that evades the eye of the I. The reaction of shame thus results from an excarnation of the gaze. Here, smelling retains its value as the paradigm of the drive (including the scopic drive), just as the excremental is the sexual kernel of the genital.[90]

The gaze of the genitals (and not a gaze *at* the genitals) triggers feelings of shame and embarrassment. The explanation for these feelings is provided by the subject's relation to excreta that must remain hidden from the gaze of the other. This explains the curious attitude toward our own excrements, which turn problematic only when appearing in the field of the Other, occupying the position of the object-gaze. The object-gaze is the excrement of the Other, an excarnated embodiment of the void produced by repression as the obverse of identification, of the lifting of the nose from the ground—a rectitude instituted by language. Freud relates this excremental remainder to swear words:

> Thus a person who is not clean [*der Unreinliche*]—who does not hide his excreta—is offending other people [*beleidigt also den Anderen*]; he is showing no consideration for them. And this is confirmed by our strongest and commonest terms of abuse [*Beschimpfungen*]. It would be incomprehensible, too, that man should use the name of his most faithful friend in the animal world—the dog—as a term of abuse [*Schimpfwort*] if that creature had not incurred his contempt through two characteristics: that it is an animal whose dominant sense is that of smell [*Geruchstier*] and one which has no horror of excrement, and that it is not ashamed of its sexual functions.[91]

The excrement is the first swear word. The person not concealing his excreta (*der Unreinliche*, "the unclean one"), insults the Other (*den Anderen*).[92]

But concealment is structurally incomplete. As "taste at a distance," smell presupposes a distance separating the sense from its object; on the other hand, smell has to do with *innigste Einnehmen*, the most intimate incorporation. The penetrating nature of smell, transgressing the distance of objectivity, is but the flipside of smell as taste at a distance. Smell is "taste at a distance" in the precise sense of subverting all distance. As volatile and dissipating, smell is violating and penetrating. As such, Kant remarks, it forces us to co-enjoy: "Smell is taste at a distance, so to speak, and others are forced to share the pleasure of it [*gezwungen, mit zu genießen*], whether they want to or not."[93] There is no private smell; if I smell it, so do you. The analyzed example from Rilke's *Malte* attests to this: one is forced to co-enjoy even when there is nothing to enjoy.

In this sense, the excrement is the paradigmatic olfactory object. Its penetrating and polluting smell offends the other by forcing them to co-enjoy, whether they want to or not. Herein lies another paradox: the concealing of genitals is modeled upon the discarding of the excrement; however, the excrement is the share of the genital that evades concealment, assaulting the nose as it's eluding the other's gaze. Civilization is founded upon the excretion of excreta, yet excreta cannot be excreted, in turn returning as instances of the primordial insult. And the other, drawn into the vortex of pollution, responds by hitting me with a swear word. To talk shit is to refuse to take shit from the other. There is a dialectic to this substitution and displacement: by responding to the excrement (the original swear word) with a swear word (a verbal excrement), the other becomes the founder of civilization.[94]

PHOOEY!

Smell displays a prophylactic function and supposedly tends to civilizational tendencies of suppressing the excremental remainder. The prophylactic function of avoiding the excremental object—a function premised on the prohibition of olfactory contact—is redoubled by the libidinous function of *Riechlust*, or the enjoyment in smelling, which finds satisfaction in this avoidance itself. Culture sets in with a short circuit instituted by the prohibition to touch:

> Right at the beginning, in very early childhood, there was a strong *desire* to touch, the aim of which is of a far more specialized kind that one would have been inclined to expect. This desire is promptly met by an *external* prohibition against carrying out that particular kind of touching.[95]

If in the previously discussed examples Freud highlighted the repression of olfactory stimuli, he now speaks of touch. The conceptual link between the two has already been established. Though "taste at a distance," smell is a form of radical contact, a collapse of all distance, undermining the difference between the Inner and the Outer, subject and object, brain and world. As an abolishing of all distance, smell is the epitome of an inescapable, penetrating, and consuming touch. Accordingly, if the first cultural prohibition is the prohibition to touch, smell is its primordial object, making enjoyment in smelling the paradigm of *Berührungslust*, the enjoyment in touching, or the drive to touch. But is this in fact the case? Freud's footnote added to the passage just quoted seems to dispute such a reading: "Both the desire [*Lust*] and the prohibition relate to the child's touching his own genitals."[96] The note further supports the misleading impression that the prohibition in question relates to tactile contact between the hand (the fingers) and genitalia. However, *tasten* is not the same as *berühren*.[97] *Berührungslust* is not *Tast-* or *Tastempfindungs-lust*: the desire to touch is not a desire to feel or palpate;[98] the enjoyment and drive to touch does not relate primarily to the "feeling fingers" or the "tactile hand" (a term used by Freud in the *Three Essays on the Theory of Sexuality*).[99]

When addressing the tactile erotogenic zone, Freud speaks of *Berührungsempfindungen von der Haut des Sexualobjektes*, "tactile sensations of the skin of the sexual object," while positing that seeing is "an activity that is ultimately derived from touching," *vom Tasten abgeleitet*.[100] Tactility, however, is itself a derivative of the olfactory touch. As an organ of unmediated contiguity, the nose has neither lids nor skin, directly fusing with its sexual object. Accordingly, the primoradial cultural prohibition to touch does not relate to haptic perception or *Tastsinn*. We must altogether abandon the idea that touch is a haptic or tactile phenomenon—touch is intangible. Irreducible to tangibility, smell is the prototype of touch, dealing the subject its "earliest blows" of sexual enjoyment (from *prōto-*, "first," and *-túpos*, "blow"). The sniff-kiss (signifying radical contiguity) is the starting point in the ontogenesis of touch that proceeds as follows: nose (sniffing), mouth (sucking), skin (feeling), eye (seeing), ear (hearing). Hence, the object-smell is touch in the olfactory register; the object-taste is touch in the gustative register; the object-feel is touch in the tactile register; the object-gaze is touch in the scopic register; and—finally—the object-voice is touch in the phonic register.[101]

The proximity between the senses of smell and hearing is brought to light in Mladen Dolar's comparison between auditory and visual perception:

The ears have no lids, as Lacan never tires of repeating; they cannot be closed, one is constantly exposed, no distance from sound can be maintained. There is a stark opposition between the visible and the audible: the visible world presents relative stability, permanence, distinctiveness, and a location at a distance; the audible presents fluidity, passing, a certain inchoate, amorphous character, and a lack of distance. The voice is elusive, always changing, becoming, elapsing, with unclear contours, as opposed to the relative permanence, solidity, durability of the seen. It deprives us of distance and autonomy. If we want to localize it, to establish a safety distance from it, we need to use the visible as the reference. The visible can establish the distance, the nature, and the source of the voice, and thus neutralize it. The acousmatic voice is so powerful because it cannot be neutralized with the framework of the visible, and it makes the visible itself redoubled and enigmatic. [102]

The genesis of the swear word supports our idea of onto-logical development: in the move from dirt to the dirty word, the excremental stench is supplanted by a stinky verbal projectile. In both cases, the subject is defenseless against it, the nose and the ears having no lids. But swear words are not its only embodiments. Freud revisits the genesis of the swear word in his treatment of the dirty joke. Like the one deploying terms of abuse, the teller of a dirty joke is "the unclean one" who assaults the other by displaying that which should have remained hidden. In his jokes book, Freud first defines "smut" (obscene or lascivious talk) as "the intentional bringing into prominence of sexual facts and relations by speech," but immediately adds: "This definition, however, is no more valid that other definitions. In spite of this definition, a lecture on the anatomy of the sexual organs or the physiology of procreation need not have a single point of contact [Berührungspunkt] with smut." [103] If there is no necessary point of contact between a lesson in sexual anatomy and smut, what does smut touch upon? Freud subtracts from further contingencies: though often directed at women, smut can be uttered in their absence, such that both the person telling it and the person hearing and laughing at it are seen as "spectators of an act of sexual aggression." Additionally, and crucially, smut contains "more than what is *peculiar* to each sex; it also includes what is *common* to both sexes and to which the feeling of shame extends." Once again, this commonality refers to the excremental core of sexuality, that is, to "what is excremental in the most comprehensive sense." [104] This most comprehensive sense leads us back to infantile sexuality, seen as "a cloaca within which what is sexual and what is excremental are barely or not at all distinguished." [105] The sexual is "barely or not at all distinguished" from the excremental. If there is a difference, it is a Hegelian difference of the "not undistinguished." At this point in the text, Freud repeats the gradation he proposed in the *Three Essays* (1905), famously written simultaneously with *Jokes*. After concluding that the desire to see the other's sexuality exposed is the original motive of smut, Freud returns to "fundamental facts," once again entertaining the idea that the scopic drive, here substituted for the invocatory drive, is itself the substitute for the drive to touch. [106] Smell is not mentioned in this text, but other passages already quoted—passages compatible with the analysis of smut—confirm its priority. One final word on the homologies between swear words and smut. Unlike smut, swear words don't appear to be intended to trigger sexual excitement in the other. Rather, their aim is to trigger in the other disgust at the (verbal) excrement. However, both disgust and embarrassment are but roundabout admissions of sexual excitement connected with the excremental object.[107]

For Freud, sexuality is situated amid, or in between, *urinas* and *faeces*, flirting with the excremental. This situates enjoyment beyond the pleasure principle, or, empirically speaking, beyond the attraction/aversion divide. (Think, for instance, of foods whose aversive olfactory overtones, and hence their flirting with what we find disgusting, increases our appetite for and appreciation of them.) The second of the two osmological footnotes from *Civilization and Its Discontents* includes an ethnographical comment, bringing together the topics of smell and excreta in reference to folkloristic accounts of sexuality that give off an unmistakable flair of smut: "Nor should we forget that, in spite of the undeniable depreciation of olfactory stimuli, there exist even today in Europe peoples among whom the strong genital odours which are so repellent to us are highly prized as sexual stimulants and who refuse to give them up."[108] The depreciation of genital odors is, in fact, undeniable: "The most perfect smell for a woman is to smell of nothing," writes Montaigne, approvingly quoting the authority of Plautus.[109] Even the woman's use of perfumes is deemed suspicions, for they are thought "to be used to cover up some natural defect in that quarter."[110] Scents are stench in its oppositional determination, much like money, according to Sándor Ferenczi, is only "filth that has been made to shine."[111] I will return to this.

For Freud, "repellent" means that said odors are not "highly prized" in our systems of "civilized" sexual morality intended to limit their enjoyability. But the disgust-inducing effect of such an inhibiting cultural devaluation effectively raises their hedonic value.[112] They are regulated by the scarcity principle raising their surplus-value, or, more precisely, their surplus-scarcity-value.[113] Studies of the effects of female armpit and vulvar odors on men's arousal find that these "repellent" smells lubricate, rather than hinder, sexual attraction.[114] Without (the ultimately unavoidable) disgust elicitors involved in sexual encounters, sex isn't sexy. Henry IV knew this very well, reportedly having said in a message to his mistress Gabrielle d'Estrees: *J'arrive, ne vous lavez pas* ("I'm coming, don't wash").[115] An odiferous "surplus-investment" is required to trigger a paradoxical sexualization of sexuality:

> Human sexuality is not sexual simply because it includes the sexual organs (or organs of reproduction). Rather, there is something in the very constitution of human nature that, so to speak, sexualizes sexual activity itself, endows it with a surplus-investment (one could also say that it sexualizes the activity of reproduction). This point might seem paradoxical, but if we think of what distinguishes human sexuality from, let us say, animal or vegetable sexuality—is it not precisely the fact that human sexuality is sexualized (which could also be put in a punch line like: "Sex is sexy")?[116]

But that is not to say that sexual enjoyment is unaffected by exposure to disgust-inducing odors. Genital sexual arousal has generally been shown to be hampered by exposure to offensive odors.[117] Given the pervasiveness of the strongest disgust elicitors in sexual encounters, one might wonder not only how sex can be pleasurable but how come our species has not yet gone extinct. Though our "cultured" noses like a challenge, the line of demarcation between repulsion and attraction is notoriously and idiosyncratically elusive. For the inhibitory effect (correlative with surplus-enjoyment) to occur, a threshold must be transgressed. But by how much? How much surplus is too much surplus? How much too-muchness is too much?[118] Clearly, surplus-enjoyment is not quantifiable; there is no a priori measure of it. And yet, when we encounter too-muchness, we immediately know it to be too much. There is no rule, yet we all follow it. We can say that the threshold has been exceeded when the sexual no longer merely flirts with (the olfactory disgusting) it but *becomes* it. The moment cannot be determined in advance (and for good), but we know it when we see it. And we know it physically, which makes the knowledge visceral and unnegotiable. George Orwell put it best: "You can have an affection for a murderer or a sodomite, but you cannot have an affection for a man whose breath stinks—habitually stinks, I mean."[119]

Orwell takes note of the "impassable barrier," so central to feelings of disgust: "For no feeling of like or dislike is quite so fundamental as a physical feeling. Race-hatred, religious hatred, differences of education, of temperament, of intellect, even differences of moral code, can be got over; but physical repulsion can-not."[120] Physical repulsion is imperative and unnegotiable. Take, for instance, *surströmming*, canned fermented herring, traditional to Swedish cuisine. Considered one of the world's stinkiest foods, surströmming became the center of YouTube "challenges" undertaken by the uninitiated. The reactions to its pungent smell are visceral and include instant gagging and vomiting. Yet, not experiencing the stench makes its existence hard to believe. In the early 1980s, surströmming was at the center of a German legal dispute. A landlord terminated a resident's tenancy for breaching her contract by willfully spilling surströmming in the building's stairwell on Christmas Eve, and again on the second day of Christmas. The issue was taken to court. That the supposedly foul-smelling food could be reason enough for an eviction seemed dubious. Could anything so pungent exist in the first place? The eviction seemed either frivolous or, worse, a case of magical thinking. It seemed as if the tenant violated a taboo, thereby becoming taboo herself.[121] However, when the landlord's party demonstrated their case by opening a can of surströmming inside the courtroom, the mere "thereness" of the smell was enough to convince the court that the termination was fully justified.[122] The court deemed the co-enjoyment forced upon the co-tenants intolerable, concluding that it "had convinced itself that the bad smell of the fish brine [üble

Geruch der Fischpökelbrühe] far exceeded the degree that fellow-tenants [Mitbe-wohner] in the building could be expected to tolerate."[123]

Like in the case of the Signorelli parapraxis, the European peoples described in Freud's comment as "highly prizing" "repellent" odors once again belong to the Balkan tribe, supposedly uninhibited by the restrictions burdening civilized Europe. Our discussion of the issue, however, sufficiently confirms that the Balkans are but a plain onto which Europe projects its own coprophilic fantasies, once more lending credence to Dolar's old insight that the European unconscious is structured like the Balkans. To substantiate his point, Freud refers the reader to various volumes of Friedrich Krauss's *Anthropophyteia*, a journal on sexual folklore and ethnological study of sexuality. Here is one story from Krauss's journal, titled *The Cunt Sniffer* (*Pizdonjušac*), about a man from the outskirts of Dubrovnik:

> A young nobleman adored a beautiful and, in his mind, honest girl. When he got her to let him spend the night with her, all he did was put his finger in her cunt, smeared it heavily, and then ran it under his nose, sniffing it. He then paid her a fiver and went on his way. This is what he used to do whenever he visited her. / She once said to herself: "If he pays so well, he deserves to have it made up, washed clean and sprinkled with scents!" As thought, so done. In the evening the youth appeared; as usual he put his finger in, but when he placed it under his nose he frowned sullenly, paid without wasting a word and went away never to return again.[124]

Sexuality is prosthetic, hinging on a detachable organ. In mapping out the logical consistency of the *objet petit a*, that is, the excarnated surplus-enjoyment, Lacan highlights its two key aspects of separability and relation to loss. The excrement as the "natural" object of smell is the "natural" incarnation, or rather excarnation, of this schema. The excrement as the object of the first cultural prohibition is precisely "something from which the subject, in order to constitute itself, has separated itself off as organ. . . . It must, therefore, be an object that is, firstly, separable and, secondly, that has some relation to the lack."[125] If the prohibition to touch relates to "touching one's own genitals," as Freud notes, then the sexual quality of genitality relates to the excremental remainder, separable from the subject and inseparably fused with the sexual.[126] And just like genitality is reducible not to the genitals but to the excremental remainder "all too intimately and inseparably bound up with the sexual,"[127] the sexual core of this remainder is reducible not to the excrement as an object of satisfaction but rather to *satisfaction as an excremental object*. If the prohibition to touch is directed at the genitals, it is so because it's impossible to touch the genitals without touching the excrement. Smell is the essence of excreta, as well as its link to the sexual. To further account for this thesis, let us approach it by way of the singular exception that only serves to confirm the rule. All excreta smell, and it is their smell that accounts for their excremental essence so intrinsically bound up with human sexuality. The link is so inherent that odorless excreta would not be considered excreta at all. Excretions of the body, *tears* trigger no disgust or repulsion; as *odorless excreta*, tears are bodily excretions cleansed of all excrementality. Lacking excremental character, one study suggests, tears have a desexualizing effect.[128]

The polluting nature of the excrement has nothing to do with its uncleanliness in the hygienic sense of the term. Excrementality is the excrementality not of shit (as an empirical object) but of enjoyment. That is why we cannot rid ourselves of the excremental nature of enjoyment by simply rejecting, hiding, eliminating the excrement. Freud makes this point in several of his texts, but a quote from Goethe's *Faust* says it best:

Uns bleibt ein Erdenrest
zu tragen peinlich,
und war' er von Asbest,
er ist nicht reinlich.

Freud cites this passage in his "Preface to Bourke's *Scatalogic Rites of All Nations*" (1913). Translated literally, it reads: "We still have a remainder of the Earth, which is embarrassing to bear; and though it were of asbestos it is not cleanly."[129] Our attitude toward asbestos surely has changed since Goethe wrote these lines, yet the point remains valid. The *Erdenrest*, the earth's remainder of our days prior to the lifting of the nose from the ground, the earth's remainder as the object of the prohibition to touch is not uncleanly due to any of its empirical properties—it would not be any cleaner even if it were cleanliness itself. The dirtiness or uncleanliness of the remainder is empirically imperceptible and thus stands for the spectral uncleanliness of enjoyment, "of which," Freud remarks, "the sexual and excretory functions may be considered the nucleus."[130]

In essence, the first cultural prohibition is the prohibition to smell. The disconnect initiated by culture is a loss of touch—that is, of touch as epitomized by smell. This interruption entails the constitution of an object that the subject is subsequently supposed to rid itself of, eliminate it, flush it, emphatically reducing it to an excrement. The excrement thus emerges simultaneously with the emergence of the prohibition in its double structure of identification and repression. It emerges at the point of an interrupted olfactory contact. Ultimately, this break is the break introduced by language. One of Lacan's early slogans is "jouissance [enjoyment] is prohibited to whoever speaks."[131] The prohibition of enjoyment is a prohibition to touch; the drive, however, touches its object precisely against the backdrop of this prohibitional loss of touch. The drive to touch, discussed by Freud in *Totem and Taboo*, is the heir to this first detachment (or detouchment). The satisfaction of the drive to touch occurs against the backdrop of this detouchment and hence essentially as "touch at a distance." Smell is therefore the paradigm of the drive making contact with satisfaction without meeting its object, or: the drive arrives at the satisfaction qua object by bypassing the object of satisfaction. In Lacan's terms, the drive achieves its aim (satisfaction qua object) without reaching its goal (the object of satisfaction).

The prohibition to touch is the constituting cultural prohibition. It is directed at the genitalia only insofar as their nucleus consists of the spectral excremental substance, that is, only insofar as the "genital apparatus remains the neighbour of the cloaca." [132] Ultimately, one of the most fundamental insights made by Freud in *Three Essays* is the necessity to separate the sexual from the genital. The first gesture of this book was to dethrone genitality, which was generally considered the one and only "natural" throne of sexuality, while Freud reduces it to but one of many scenes of its polymorphous actualizations.

In her text "'Anal' und 'Sexual,'" Lou Andreas-Salomé persuasively relates the prohibition against touch to the anal and the excremental. Freud referenced the text in the 1920 edition of the *Three Essays*, calling it the paper that "has given us a very much deeper understanding of the significance of anal erotism." [133] Andreas-Salomé begins her text with resistances against psychoanalysis, especially against its doctrine of the drives, highlighting two of its most neuralgic points. First, there is the discovery of infantile sexuality, smearing the angelic, asexual being of the child with the stigma of sexual life, even worse: of polymorphous perversity. However, she adds, the resistance against the idea of infantile sexuality is still "considerably weaker than [the resistance] against the anally-sexual." [134] The remark may surprise us. First, because today anal sexuality (in the ordinary sense of the term) is nothing problematic. This is true even beyond the comparison with the taboo of infantile sexuality, which presents the only thesis of the *Three Essays* that is still somewhat triggering and offensive to our sensibility. This assertion spontaneously leads to a hypothesis of developmental progress: "Compared to the puritan Viennese public of the time, we have become more enlightened." This hypothesis goes hand in hand with the hypothesis of primitivity: "How dangerously confused the Viennese public must have been, if infantile sexuality appeared to it less triggering than anal eroticism." The hypothesis of homophobia joins hands with that of pedophilia—could anything be more offensive to liberal sensibilities?

However, that is not what Lou Andreas-Salomé's remark is getting at. She highlights a neuralgic point of enduring relevance. The reason why our attitude toward anal eroticism appears less problematic may very well be that due to our liberal attitude toward homosexuality we are more inclined to overlook it. The homosexuality at issue here, of course, is male homosexuality. Female homosexuality can be bracketed due to the role it plays in the male-heterosexual fantasy-space. For this reason, Lacan defined heterosexuals as those who love women, which includes not only heterosexual men but also homosexual women. Moreover, the liberalization of attitudes toward (male) homosexuality may be seen as a mode of a genitalization of anality, that is, a consequence of reducing it to the limited and manageable sphere of sexuality dethroned by Freud's *Three Essays*. Genitalized anal sexuality = sexuality without excrementality. The most reactionary homophobia thus essentially joins hands with its most liberal adversary. Both—the reactionary homophobe in his or her opposition and the liberal in his or her support—are confronted with the premonition that their "genital apparatus remains the neighbour of the cloaca."

With his *Three Essays*, Freud struck two blows to our understanding of sexuality that still retain the power of a taboo: he tainted infancy with sexuality and sexuality with excrementality. If resistance against the second taboo remains much stronger, it must be linked to the fact that the excremental is the object of the very first prohibition:

> While we are in the habit of watching all kinds of childishly gentle touches of the parents' bodies with a moved gaze and letting them have their way unhindered, from the very beginning the second area is emblazoned with the capitalized inscription "Phooey," which we must accept [*das wir in uns aufzunehmen haben*]. This is how the history of the first prohibition, so important and varied, is introduced.[135]

The prohibition to touch is the most economical mark of culture, finding its most economical expression in a minimal word, a mere interjection, which already functions as a full-fledged sentence, a cultural history in miniature: "Phooey!" The prohibition requires no negation and consists of a single word. The word is not so much meaningful as it is imitative, a mere expression of disgust, mimicking the act of spiting, of dejection of an object that has already reached (into) us. Hence, the first cultural prohibition is structured like a swear word, a shame-inducing verbal excrement.

THE PROHIBITION TO TOUCH

The prohibition to touch is intangible in the sense of being irreducible to tactility. Freud sees in it the nucleus of the neurosis: "As in the case of taboo, the principal prohibition, the nucleus of the neurosis, is against touching; and thence it is sometimes known as 'touching phobia' or '*délire du toucher*'. The prohibition does not merely apply to immediate physical contact but has an extent as wide as the metaphorical use of the phrase 'to come in contact with'."[136]

For Freud, the concept of touch extends far beyond the sense of feeling, the "immediate physical contact," to encompass any "coming in contact with." In smell—this paradigm of touch and this object of the first prohibition—there is no difference between the immediate and the remote. It is hence not surprising that taboo persons and objects reflect the penetrating and polluting nature of the excremental: anything that touches such an object or person itself becomes taboo; anything touching the taboo fuses with the excrete object, losing its discrete identity.

Culture begins with a swear word, "Phooey!" is the first cultural prohibition, and the first prohibition is the prohibition against touching the excremental object as the nucleus of sexuality. If smell is the paradigm of a now prohibited coming into contact, the following conclusion must be drawn: *deodorization is the beginning of culture.* The first culture war is the war against smells.

"Dirt is matter in the wrong place," writes Freud in "Character and Anal Erotism" (1908).[137] A "remainder of the Earth" resulting from signifying deodorization, dirt is matter in the wrong place, matter that is not properly localized and kept at bay. Its out-of-place-ness is so intrinsic to it that the moment we localize it, dirt ceases to be dirt and becomes mere localized garbage, cleansed of its polluting excremental function (the word "dirt" comes from Middle English drit, "excrement"). Freud is quoting William James here, probably from memory, unwittingly paraphrasing the original formulation.[138] James writes:

> Here we have the interesting notion fairly and squarely presented to us, of there being elements of the universe which may make no rational whole in conjunction with the other elements, and which, from the point of view of any system which those other elements make up, can only be considered so much irrelevance and accident—so much "dirt," as it were, and matter out of place. I ask you now not to forget this notion; for although most philosophers seem either to forget it or to disdain it too much ever to mention it, I believe that we shall have to admit it ourselves in the end as containing an element of truth.[139]

A "part of no part" of the universe,[140] dirt is not merely matter in the wrong place, but rather is emphatically out of place, that is, placed outside the place as such, or unplaceable. But both definitions—James's and Freud's—should perhaps be read together, such that dirt is matter in-out-of-place. Dirt is matter placed in a place out of place, eluding the distinction between the Inner and the Outer, between within and without. Lacking any substantial footing, or a realm of its own, this in-between forms "an Other scene," *einen anderen Schauplatz*, to use Fechner's term deployed by Freud in *The Interpretation of Dreams*.[141] The excarnated materiality of excreta is neither the external materiality of an object—which can be in the wrong place, but not in-out-of-place—nor the internal materiality of its representation, but rather the materiality of the impossible intersection between the two, between the outside and the inside. Smells are structurally outplaced or extimate: by definition, they refuse to stay put, escaping their sources. But while refusing to be contained by the source-objects emitting them, they also refuse to stay out, persistently penetrating the insides of our bodies.

Smell functioned as the object as well the objectal remainder of the first cultural prohibition: "Phooey!" The prohibition's effected deodorization presents the basis of the inside—outside divide. A paradigm of the abolished contiguity, the olfactory object is radically inadequate, irreducible to essences and hence essentially unaccounted for. James puts this rather emphatically when he writes "of there being elements of the universe which may make no rational whole in conjunction with the other elements, and which, from the point of view of any system which those other elements make up, can only be considered so much irrelevance and accident." However, these feces of totality contain "an element of truth": they undermine the truth of adequation, revealing it as a mere mirage of truth.

Another thing to note is that James's call for the philosophical valuation of undignified and worthless "dirt" finds its model in the infamous exchange between the old Parmenides and the young Socrates, staged in Plato's *Parmenides*. If unexamined life is not worth living, the examination of life must entail "stool analysis" as an analysis of the analytically worthless:

> "And what about these [things], Socrates? Things that might seem absurd, like hair and mud and dirt, or anything else totally undignified and worthless? Are you doubtful whether or not you should say that a form is separate for each of these, too, which in turn is other than anything we touch with our hands?" / "Not at all," Socrates answered. "On the contrary, these things are in fact just what we see. Surely it's too outlandish to think there is a form for them. Not that the thought that the same thing might hold in all cases hasn't troubled me from time to time. Then, when I get bogged down in that, I hurry away, afraid that I may fall into some pit of nonsense and come to harm . . ." / "That's because you are still young, Socrates," said Parmenides, "and philosophy has not yet gripped you as, in my opinion, it will in the future, once you begin to consider none of the cases beneath your notice. Now, though, you still care about what people think, because of your youth." (Prm. 130c-e)

Is there an eidetic essence of dirt? Or is dirt simply "what we see," limited to our erroneous and uncertain sensuous perception? Does dirt resist eidetic reduction simply on account of being devalued by *doxa*, or is it itself premised on something irreducible? What is the eidetic essence of the excrement, if not its smell? And if we were to subject it to the process of eidetic reduction, what would we be left with in the end? Something or nothing? Not nothing?

Freud's thesis regarding the "anal character," characterized by orderliness, parsimoniousness, and obstinacy, was developed out of the transformations of infantile anal eroticism. Freud establishes an astonishing chain of substitutions leading from the excrement to money as its final substitute, such that the eidetic reduction of money unveils its excremental core. The anal zone is the home of the metaphor, of signifying substitutions, and hence the primordial locus of the gift economy, the infant gifting its parents the only object in its possession: the excrement.[142] In 1914, Sándor Ferenczi undertook a bold attempt at just such an eidetic reduction, drawing a detailed ontogenetic account of the interest in money. The question he asks is the following one: what are the stages of this genesis that Freud uncovers "in the ancient civilizations, in myths, fairy tales and superstitions, in unconscious thinking, in dreams and in neuroses" and that introduces "the contrast between the most precious substance known to men and the most worthless, which they reject as waste matter ('refuse')"?[143] Ferenczi first proceeds by summarizing the main elements of this contradistinction, beginning with the child's interest for its own excreta, which it "handles" without a hint of resistance, such that the feces "thus held back are really the first 'savings,'" the excrement effectively being "one of the first toys of the child."[144] He continues within a well-known osmological context. The child—who is still "creeping on all fours," whose eyesight is sharpening, and who is increasingly more skillful in the use of his hands—gives up his toy only when pressured by the first prohibition:

> The child's interest for dejecta experiences its first distortion [Entstellung] through the smell of faeces becoming disagreeable, disgusting. This is probably related to the beginning of the upright gait. The other attributes of this material—moistness, discolouration, stickiness, etc.—do not for the time being offend his sense of cleanliness. He still enjoys, therefore, playing with and manipulating street-mud whenever he has the chance, liking to collect it together into larger heaps. Such a heap of mud is already in a sense a symbol, distinguished from the real thing [vom Eigentlichem] by its absence of smell. For the child, street-mud is, so to speak, deodourised dejecta.[145]

Refering back to Plato's Parmenides, we can say that "real things" (as things containing eidetic essences) are distinguished from the no-thing of an excremental object by the absence of smell. Once more, the birth of philosophy is conditioned by a deodorization of reality. The quote summarizes other key elements encountered so far. It relates individual development to its phylogenetic model, introduced by Freud in his speculative construction; it mentions the very first prohibition directed against touch, which introduces the first break into the child's hereto unproblematic relationship to its own excreta. And this first prohibition targets not tactility (for the child continues to play with and manipulate the *Straßenkot*, "street-mud") but smell. The unabridged version of this first cultural prohibition therefore states: "Phooey, it stinks!" That is why the tactile characteristics of the *dejectum*, such as "moistness, discolouration, stickiness," are not the object of this first prohibition and therefore trigger no disgust. The same is true of visual stimuli, implied in "discolouration," which also do not fall under the prohibition. Feelings of disgust born of the first prohibition thus concern smell and not any of the other senses. These, including the sense of hearing, only gain importance later when a mere mention of the deject is disgust inducing. The cut introduced by the prohibition is hence the cut of deodorizing the deject. The deodorization is at the same time the extraction of smell as the essence of the excremental, which has no other qualities save for the "intangible" olfactory one.

Mud, characterized by the absence of smell, is the "symbol" (better: signifier) managed by the subject (here, a child collecting the deodorized shit into heaps). The signifier "mud" substitutes the missing signifier that underwent repression or deodorization introduced by the first prohibition: "mud" instead of the "deject"—or, more precisely, "mud" instead of the "absent deject," for "mud" is a signifier of absence taking the place of the absent signifier subject to prohibitory repression. Thus, "mud" is split between itself and the absence of itself; a deodorized deject, "mud" is the negative of itself. "Mud" does not merely differ from the deject (external difference); as a negative, deodorized deject, "mud" also differs from itself (self-difference).

The signifier "mud" hence represents the subject for another signifier, namely precisely for the absent signifier that itself is representing in a "distorted," *entstellt* way. The absent, repressed signifier, however, retains a metonymical relation to "mud" as negative deject. This relation is retained throughout the chain of substitutions: "mud" as negative (deodorized) deject; "sand" as negative (dehydrated) mud and thus (metonymically) negative (deodorized) deject; "stone" as negative (solidified) sand and thus both (metonymically) negative (dehydrated) mud and (metonymically) negative (deodorized) deject, and so on, until finally we reach the coin and money as the final links in the chain of negative dejects. The repressed signifier of the olfactory *dejectum* thus travels metonymically through the chain of substitutions as its "missing link," or its subject. In Hegelian terms, "money," "coin," "stone," "sand," and "mud" are the deject in its oppositional determination. "Money" and "shit" differ, even differ absolutely, yet they remain irreducibly undistinguished, whereby their undistinguished sameness is not an identity: the Freudian repression, *Verdrängung*, is not the Hegelian sublation, *Aufhebung*, and if "money" equals "shit," that does not imply that "shit" arrives at itself in its oppositional determination, that is, as "money." Through the mediation of "money" as its displaced substitute, "shit" does not arrive at its "true" identity.

The initial alienation is followed not by sublation but by separation: the ooz-ing remainder is continuously breaking forth from within the chain of sub-stitutions like a rash.

The truth of adequation was based on the operation of the "count as one," that is, on the self-identity of the object as part of objective reality. The exchange of one for another is possible only as an exchange of equiva-lents, presupposing that each of the two is substitutable for itself, that is, self-identical. An object not identical with itself has no equivalent and cannot enter substitutional exchange that is always the exchange of equivalents. To return to Ferenczi's series, we can say that before entering the series of substitutions, the deject had to be objectified, "adequated," purged of its non-identity-with-itself. And the first repression of this share of self-difference was an act of deodorization. The smell of excrement stood for the primordial share of the object's non-identity-with-itself that had to be repressed so as to enable the exchange of equivalents. However, as already noted, this process is not one of sublation but one of perpetual excreting of the unequitable share from within the series of equivalences. As was the case with organic repression, here, too, the "primary" nature of deodorization has to be understood in terms of its irreducibility.

At first, the child's interest in "coins" as the first forms of appearance of money and the first monetary embodiments of the deject is

> less for their economic value than for their own sake as pleasure-giving objects. The eye takes pleasure at the sight of their lustre and colour, the ear at their metallic clink, the sense of touch at play with the round smooth discs, only the sense of smell comes away empty, and the sense of taste also has to be satisfied with the weak, but peculiar taste of the coins.
> With this the development of the money symbol is in its main outlines complete. Pleasure in the intestinal contents becomes enjoyment of money, which, however, after what has been said is seen to be nothing other than odourless, dehydrated filth that has been made to shine. *Pecunia non olet.*[146]

The spectacular development beginning with the deodorization of the deject ends with the coin. The latter brings satisfaction and joy to all the senses, engaged to some extent in the child's handling of the monetary excre-ment. To all but one. Smell is structurally ejected from the final result of the completed chain of substitutions. While the other senses find in the stimulat-ing qualities of the coin an equivalent to the stimulating qualities of the deject, smell remains empty handed and without object. Thus, once again its excre-mental essence is confirmed. The smell-object is not merely the first but the irreducible excarnation of the surplus-object without an equivalent. Just as the truth of classical ontology could only have been the truth of adequate thought, just as it could only keep its head by losing its nose, so the little defecator can engage in his philosophical business by losing his nose: he must lose his nose so as to acquire the nose for philosophy. However, philosophy can only go on against the backdrop of this refuse that called it into being in the first place and which continually emerges from within it.

The eidetically reducing nose can be traced back to the first nose of modern philosophy. In the wax-argument from the *Meditations on First Philosophy* (1641), Descartes subtracts from the intuited characteristics of the piece of wax to arrive at its essential properties:

> Let us take, for example, this piece of wax: it has been taken freshly
> from the hive, and it has not yet lost the sweetness of the honey which it
> contains; it still retains somewhat of the odour of the flowers from which
> it has been culled; its colour, its figure, its size are apparent; it is hard, cold,
> easily handled, and if you strike it with the finger, it will emit a sound.
> Finally all the things which are requisite to cause us distinctly to recognise
> a body, are met with in it. But notice that while I speak and approach the
> fire what remained of the taste is exhaled, the smell evaporates, the colour
> alters, the figure is destroyed, the size increases, it becomes liquid, it heats,
> scarcely can one handle it, and when one strikes it, no sound is emitted.
> Does the same wax remain after this change? We must confess that it
> remains; none would judge otherwise.[147]

Once placed next to a fire, the object's sensuous characteristics are modified. However, according to the text, two of its initial properties are not merely altered but rather disappear: its smell and taste. But, as in Ferenczi's genesis of money, one could argue that here, too, something of the wax-taste survives the reduction, while the smell evaporates entirely. Or, better still, the duality of smell and taste is reducible to the inner duality of smell, split between its ortho- and retro-function. *No cogito without deodorization.*

THE FECES OF LANGUAGE

The impossibility of substitution, or equivalent exchange, epitomized by the olfactory object is the obverse of its prohibition. Let us approach it from yet another direction. Instead of following the genesis of the infant's sense of cleanliness, instead of following the development and transmutations of the excrement, let us focus now on the genesis of the neonate's sense of that particular cleanliness we call language. Potty training and linguistic training as the two principal forms of *orthopedia* (from *ortho-*, "[up]right," "proper," and *paideía*, "upbringing," "training") typically follow immediately upon the child's first steps. Only after assuming an erect posture does the child learn to turn the nose up at its own bodily and linguistic excreta, with ortho-smell assuming its prophylactic function. The structure of the classical philosophical concept of truth is connected to this structural feature of the narrative of hominization. We established a conceptual link between the idea of truth as relying on deodorization (i.e., on the exclusion of the non-self-identical object from classical ontology) and the deodorization supposedly effected by the onset of human bipedalism (i.e., by man's adoption of the upright gait). As already noted, smell was kept at bay and banished from philosophy so that its truth (as *adequatio*, or correspondence, of intellect and thing, that is, truth as relying on the principle of reflexive identity) would be preserved. The truth of *adequatio* is that of predicative rightness. It is truth as *orthós*, or *rectus*, that is, the truth of rectitude and the "upright gait." The idea of the human as *Homo erectus* is structurally tied with the notion of truth as *adequatio*, further reliant on the notion of *orthotes onomaton*, that is, on the deployment of "correct" or "(up)right" names.[148]

My reading reveals the connecting links between smell and truth, rather than leading to a notion of inclination (in Adriana Cavarero's sense of the term) as opposed to the paradigm of verticality: "Next to the paradigm of the vertical axis, appropriated by man because of his inborn rationality, appears the paradigm of an oblique line, reserved to woman because of a constitutive predisposition to maternity, which causes inclination."[149] An insertion of relationality into "egocentric verticality,"[150] Cavarero's concept of inclination differs substantially from my notion of declination as essentially non-relational.[151] As we have seen, for Lacan, the infant relates libidinously not to the (m)other but to the breast (more precisely, the nipple) as the partial object of the partial drive, subtracted from the (m)other's inclining body. Furthermore, in Cavarero vulnerability is the main attribute of the child:

> The infant, meanwhile, is a creature who is completely in the care of the other: infancy is an almost singular form of existence destined to turn itself into an unaware but peremptory solicitation. As such, the infant highlights the originary paradigm of human vulnerability: being defenseless, the infant is archetypal in a double sense, both because everybody's life begins with infancy, and because the principle of infancy returns whenever, in the course of life, one happens to find oneself defenseless.[152]

Contrary to such a notion of vulnerability as central to Cavarero's notion of the infant in its relation to the inclined (m)other, Lacan stresses that the vulnerability effectively pertains to the (m)other, exposed to the superimposed vampiric breast as inseparable from the infant's sucking and as colonizing the (m)other's organism.[153] The concept of declination entailed in this schema is not simply externally opposed to verticality and rectitude, but rather accounts for the inner-heterogeneous declination of rectitude from itself. Hence, verticality is not simply a signifier of masculinity, but rather one of castration. Moreover, as reliant on *orthos logos*, truth as *adequatio* is constituted by excluding, or "organically repressing," the primordial detour, or diversion, which, however, returns in the guise of symptomatic declinations as singular sites of the osmological "return of the repressed." What is lost in the primordial cut is encountered again in the irreducible declinations of the drives.

From here, let us return to the fecal matter of language. Conceptual touch as rooted in adequation, in *orthos logos* or proper speech, rests on the dejection of linguistic differentiality. Adequate thought precludes self-difference as the excrement of reflexive identity. The Saussurian-Jakobsonian ontology accounts for this excrement of conceptual thought, if only to completely ground it in the logic of the signifier, thus dejecting the subject. The structure it introduces is a structure without the subject. Thus, phonology formulates the laws of the unconscious, relying on the principle of differentiality, the laws of substitution and combination, metaphor and metonymy, but can make no use of the speaking nose, that is, of unconscious formations, like dreams, jokes, slips of the tongue. By precluding the subject, structuralist ontology reduces it to mere lack: a slip of the tongue is nothing but a linguistic mistake, regardless of how well it may fit the laws of its ontology. Lacanian psychoanalysis differs from structuralist structuralism in that it assumes the vantage point of its excreta. The structuralist structure dejects the subject, and it is this dejection that grounds its concept of structure as an integral, orthopedic totality. Psychoanalysis, however, relates the dejected subject to the structural incompleteness of structure. This passage entails a transposition that can be formalized as follows:

$$\text{\$}(A) \rightarrow S(\text{\A})$$

The structuralist structure is a totality (A) whose integrality depends on dejecting the subject (\$), reducing it to mere lack. The Lacanian structure, on the other hand, transposes this lack onto the Other, thus placing the subject in a relation to the real: S(Ȧ). To separate the operational field and object of hyperstructuralism from the field and object of structuralist linguistics, Lacan proposes the neologism "linguistricks" (*linguisterie*).[154]

This brings us back to the topic of the linguistic prohibition to touch. The object of linguistricks is "llanguage" as distinguished from language made possible by dejecting the excrement of llanguage. Hence, language is llanguage minus the excrement; language is llanguage purged of the excremental remainder of differentiallity. Language depends on the stock of llanguage and is established by a prohibition to touch. The latter introduces two basic forms of lawful contact, reducible to the two linguistic axes of substitution or association, on the one hand, and combination, on the other. The two axes of linguistic contiguity depend on the prohibition to touch, that is, on *the prohibition of phonic contact*. This prohibition clearly follows from the Saussurian notion of the signifier defined as a bundle of distinctive traits, and established in total abstraction from its phonic materiality. Granted, Saussure's linguistic sign is split between the "sound-image" and the "concept," the signifier and the signified. However, defined as the psychic representative of phonic materiality, the signifier's phonological materiality or "sound-image" is clearly discerned from the physical phonic substance as studied in phonetics. Llanguage, on the other hand, consists of what language has dejected. And if the linguistic structure of language is a whole containing *everything*, llanguage contains everything *else*. Llanguage consists of sound-feces disciplined by the differential structure of language. This linguistic disciplining of llanguage takes two forms. The first entails the dejection of linguistically inadequate terms. These are disciplined by being dejected, but there is a second form of dejection that relates to terms that are dejected by being disciplined. And it is the latter terms that are the driving force behind llanguage. They are called *homophones*:

> Llanguage is made up of a little bit of everything, from what is floating around in the streets and from what we hear in salons. On every page we encounter a misunderstanding, because with a little good will it is possible to find meaning in it, at least an imaginary one. Did he say *"dire"* or *"Dieu"*? Is this *"croate"* or *"cravate"*? *"Was ist das?"* Homophony is the driving force of llanguage. And that is precisely why, I think, Lacan could not have found a better way to characterize llanguage than to draw attention to its phonematic system. [155]

Homophones play tricks on language. Sounding the same, their meanings differ. Did he say "milk" or "silk,"[156] "la langue" or "lalangue," "scent" or "cent," "nose" or "knows," "duh" or "duh"?[157] How do we distinguish between them so that distinctive meaning can be conveyed? How do we uncouple word-couples coupled by a sound-kiss?[158] Contingent matching of sound-images confuses us or at least puts us on the track of a mistaken meaning. We find ourselves at a crossroads of meaning, forced to make a rest stop and ask for directions. We are essentially left with two ways to proceed, and each relates to one of the two axes of language. To distinguish between the phonically indistinguishable, we are forced to rely on the two slopes of linguistic contiguity. Grasping the meaning of homophones requires homonymization, that is, a differentiation of the undifferentiated. In the example of "scent" and "cent," the differentiation is accomplished by the two familiar ways of naming smells, that is, by either substituting the confusing expression for another expression conveying a similar meaning ("smell" instead of "scent"), or by combining it with other expressions ("The scent of burnt pudding . . .").[159] Confronted with homophones, language is briefly derailed, and the speakers lose their linguistic footing. The listeners experience a momentary state of panicked indeterminacy, requiring them to make sense of the deject, bring llanguage back in line with language, reinstate the prohibition of the sound-kiss.

Responding to the question of what came first, llanguage or language, Jean-Claude Milner proposed an ontogenesis of language that closely mirrors the ontogenesis of the infant's sense of cleanliness:

> Given the homophony between *la langue* and *lalangue*, which of the two comes first? Apparently the name *la langue* comes first and its counterpart *lalangue* comes second. In the same way, it would seem that the speaking subject begins by learning *la langue* and reaches homophony subsequently, through his knowledge of *la langue*. The real process is quite different however. Even from the point of view of ontogeny, the child experiments with homophony and word plays before having a complete sense of *la langue*. His babbling has more to do with *lalangue* than with *la langue*. Indeed, what makes a speaking being of the infant is neither *la langue* nor *le langage*, but *lalangue*. Babies seem to play with sounds in the same way they play with water or sand. The main forms of their play imply repeated vowels or consonants, as is shown in baby language: *baby, dada, mama,* etc. But the repetition of sounds is simply a subspecies of homophony. / It is tempting to suppose that the *Fort-Da* represents a first discovery of *la langue* as separated from babbling. It could be considered as a repression of homophonous repetition of phonemes.[160]

The two ontogenetic constructions overlap—coincide, even—in the same object. The child's initiation into the *cloaca maxima* of culture is condition by its ability to manage its own excreta. Shit-management is split between disciplining "bodily" excretions and disciplining "spiritual" excretions. The two ontogenetic constructions are reducible to the phylogenetic model of the osmological narrative: in order to manage its bodily and linguistic excreta, the child must lose the nose. With the emergence of language, the linguistrick dimension undergoes a dejections. However, the moment the prohibition to touch is transgressed by a sound-kiss, the feces of language resurface and effect a phonic contamination of language's differential cleanliness.[161] The contaminating contact is based in similitude and phonic proximity, as opposed to differentiality, non-similarity, or phonologic distance. As a relational and oppositional entity, the signifier has no positivity except for the "positivity" of its distance, or distinctive difference, in relation to other signifiers. To be distinctive, and thus to be signifiers, they must avoid sound-kissing. Hence, the process of dejection and deject-constitution is the same in both ontogenetic constructions: deodorization of the deject is homologous to the dehomophonization of llanguage. If, according to the osmological narrative, the first process results from *hominization*, the second results from *homonymization*. (Did he say "hominization" or "homonymization"?) The two processes are untied together by more than mere homophonic proximity—they are instituted by the prohibition to touch. The child's play is split between playing with phonic and fecal dejects, but the excrement emerges only with the first prohibition intended to accustom the child to bodily and linguistic cleanliness. The prohibition to touch is the birth of touch as the remainder of deodorization/dehomophonization. (We've already stressed this point by saying that touch is intangible and directed at the untouchable.) The prohibition to touch is a suspension, introducing into human experience the sign of an ontological deficit, to use Alenka Zupančič's term.[162] The emergence of speech is correlative with the emergence of surplus-enjoyment:

> Humans are beings roused from indifference and forced to speak (as well as to enjoy, since enjoyment appears at the place of this deficit) by one signifier gone missing. This temporal way of putting it ("gone missing") is an expression of what would be better formulated as the signifying structure emerging not simply without one signifier, but rather with-without one signifier—since this "hole" has consequences, and determines what gets structured around it.[163]

It is here that a new dimension of enjoyment is opened, one split between *Riechlust*, the drive to smell, and the drive to babble. This enjoyment is the surplus-object of the processes of deodorization and homonymization. If their intended effect is scarcity, or lack, their result is surplus-scarcity.

Psychoanalysis, and psychoanalytically infused philosophy, are not settling for a reduction of the homophonic excrement to its meaning, instead turning their nose to the surplus of their irreducibility. The infinite judgment of this book is to reduce the homonymic domains of Spirit and smell to their irreducible homophonic juncture as the inner—heterogeneous—gap of their tautology. In the gap of their tautology, the two touch and contaminate each other, and one cannot differentiate between them without losing their elusive, intangible, and untouchable point of contact. If homonyms imply an identity in expression and a difference in meaning, then the process of homonymization of the homophonic excrement introduces into indistinguishability a difference (in meaning). As entities of llanguage, homophones carry a difference irreducible to signifying difference. What is the nature of the peculiar difference they inhabit? Homophones do not differ—nor do they not *not* differ. As neither same nor different, they are not undistinguished, yet one is unable to distinguish them.

The prohibition against llanguage is a prohibition against touch. If we follow the most fundamental social prohibition, namely that of incest, the prohibition against homophony as constitutive of language yields the following thesis: the phonically closest object is the incestuous and hence prohibited object. The prohibition of incest introduces a break at the points of closest proximity ("dada," "mama"), thus escorting the subject onto the path of differentiality, that is, in search of substitutes. This search aims at expulsing homophony—a homophonic entity knows no substitute; it cannot be replaced with another entity without deodorizing its homophonic nucleus. In homophony, a signifier relates to another signifier based on their phonic similitude, in which language is absorbed entirely. Therefore, what is repressed in the passage from llanguage to language, is the constitutive linguistrick touch epitomized by smell and its object.

In conclusion, we must mention that Lacan introduces llanguage simultaneously with the matheme as the flipside of homophony. For this very reason, Milner asserts: "All Lacanian word plays are mathemes."[164] The point runs counter to the famous Badiou–Cassin polemic, subtitled "Two Lessons in Lacan."[165] According to Milner, there is only one lesson to be learned. And the one lesson to be learned is the lesson concerning the two lessons: there is no incommensurability or radical opposition between llanguage and the matheme. Hence, the one lesson: both linguistrick interpretation and scientific literalization are excarnated articulations of dejected meaninglessness.

The capitalist knows that all commodities, however tattered they may look, or however badly they may smell, are in faith and in truth money, are by nature circumcised Jews, and, what is more, a wonderful means for making still more money out of money.

—Karl Marx, *Capital*

POTTY TRAINING FOR CAPITALISTS

The osmological break was approached from two distinct angles, aligning with the body/spirit distinction. Ontogenetically, the break occurred as the double process of shit-management, split between the domains of bodily cleanliness and the cleanliness of language. The first was propelled by deodorization, the second by dehomophonization, but the two touched in the prohibition to touch. Following the genesis of "economic" cleanliness, that is, the genesis of the value-form, we can now add its third modality.

But first we must return to the primal scene of culture. "Children who are making use of the susceptibility to erotogenic stimulation of the anal zone," writes Freud in the *Three Essays*,

betray themselves by holding back their stool till its accumulation brings about violent muscular contractions and, as it passes through the anus, is able to produce powerful stimulation of the mucous membrane. In so doing it must no doubt cause not only painful but also highly pleasurable sensations. One of the clearest signs of subsequent eccentricity or nervousness is to be seen when a baby obstinately refuses to empty his bowels when he is put on the pot—that is, when his nurse wants him to—and holds back that function till he himself chooses to exercise it. He is naturally not concerned with dirtying the bed, he is only anxious not to miss the subsidiary pleasure attached to defaecating. Educators are once more right when they describe children who keep the process back as "naughty."[1]

He needs to go but can't quite let go. The little one sits on the potty and calculates whether to give up "the subsidiary pleasure," the *Lustnebengewinn*, the side-profit "attached to defaecating." His business is not to do business but to side hustle. Not a pleasure in defecating, his is a surplus-pleasure of holding back the excrement, a surplus-enjoyment attaching itself to defecation as its by-product. This by-product is an excrement of the excrement: as "part of no part" of defecation, it serves the accumulation of enjoyment as irreducible to the satisfaction of need. Etymologically, "to excrete" (from *excernō*) means both "to keep apart" or "to keep away," and "to accumulate" or "hold it back." The infant calculates whether to listen to the waste-managers, entrust the surplus to the adult guardians of defecation, whether to give in to their demand and relieve himself of the burden of the surplus-product. In short: he ponders whether to submit to and enter equivalent exchange. But while the infant calculates, exchange is already taking place. For there is no surplus prior to exchange: the side-profit emerges alongside the disciplining demand of the Other, compelling the subject to enter an exchange-contract and exchange its excrement for acclamation as a sign of love. If the subject adheres to the demand and delivers the excrement, he is lauded as "a good boy." If not, laudation is substituted for denunciation and the child *becomes* the excrement: "Shit, you little shit!" We can imagine the infant contemplating his options: "Shall I give you the excrement in exchange for your love, as you demand of me? Granted, you care much more for this commodity than I do, but by giving it to you, by saving it from circulation, will I not be deprived of the increment of its value?"

Is the little defecator the first capitalist, taking possession of the surplus-product that, strictly speaking, he did not produce and hence does not belong to him? Moreover, is the little defecator's dilemma not premised on the fetishism of capital? Is he not convinced of a virgin conception of his valuable commodity? Does he not believe that the extracted surplus is of his own making, the result of his and no one else's inherent productive force? His disavowal is the one permeating the actuality of capitalism, namely the disavowal of the fact that the surplus is produced only in the relation between the little capitalist and his guardian. And does the guardian not labor away by disciplining the child into producing the surplus? And does the little defecator not snatch it away in the process? Is the little defecator the first capitalist, calculating the profitability of his investment and appropriating the first surplus-value?

Adjusting the perspective, the little one can also be considered a proletarian. Along these lines, the disciplining scene is the scene of the very first expropriation, depicting the loss of control over the means of production, as well as over its product and, finally, also over the excrement of the excrement, that is, the surplus-product or the increment of defecation. In a further turn of the screw, we can say that the defying little shit is the first communist, refusing to give up ownership of the means of defecation and hence the surplus-product, conscious of the traps of the wage-form, its mystification. Did he realize that the other's payment in the currency of love and laudation only repays him for the value of the labor-power of defecation, while robbing him of the surplus-labor, the *Lustnebengewinn* as the germ of the first surplus-value? Is the little one a communist who, through his defiance, succeeds in expropriating the expropriator and thus in starting his first little potty-training revolution?

In a variety of ways, the little potty-training scene is the origin story of capitalism. The first option is to read this scene of *primitive, or originary, defecation* as the primordial scene of capitalism, its *primitive, or originary, accumulation,* in which the little one plays the role of the expropriated proletarian. He takes on the role of the doubly free worker, as understood by Marx. One the one hand, capitalist modernization frees the worker of feudal domination, which relied on relations of personal dependence. Through his disciplining, that is, potty training, the guardian is effectively "emancipating" the child of his most intimate dependence on adults. But there is another side to this emancipation: it liberates him from his own means of production.[2] By becoming disciplined, he loses control over the production process, which hereafter adheres to the demands of the Other, that is, to cultural laws of shit-management.

The myth of primitive accumulation is the primal scene of capitalism, whose goal is to account for the beginning of the count, that is: to account for the accumulation of the first capital prior to capitalist accumulation. This origin story "is told as an anecdote about the past."[3] The anecdote tells us that a long, long time ago there were two sorts of people: the diligent and frugal ones and the hedonistic slackers. The ones leading an ascetic life of hard work and constant renunciation of pleasures gradually came to own the means of realization of labor, while the lazy ones were left with only one possession: their own labor-power. It is immediately clear that the narrative aims at explaining class divisions. In this sense, it plays the role of a metanarrative intended to explain the causality of the primordial cut as the foundation of the elementary class difference, thereby filling in the structural void pertaining to capitalism's origins. Telling its "truth about truth," the capitalist metanarrative is a story of the original sin of capitalism.[4] It explains its inception in terms similar to those used by parents in explaining the defiance of their naughty child: the proletariat is the child of enjoyment and laziness, while the capitalist class was born of discipline, diligent obedience, and hard work. Marx subjects this "idyllic" origin story of capitalism and the capital-relation, this fundamental fantasy of capital, in which the slacker performs the role of his lifetime, to harsh criticism. He shows that the scene of this idyllic metanarrative is also the scene of a primal repression of capitalism's origins in violent expropriations that separate immediate producers from the means of production and subsistence.[5] A comparison between Marx's phylogenesis of capital and Freud's phylogenetic construction of the origins of civilization yields a series of similarities justifying an understanding of primitive accumulation as the primordially repressed nucleus of capitalism.

The historically specific processes of primitive accumulation trigger the passage from feudalism to capitalism and are situated in their intersection. As the primordial cut, primitive accumulation cut off immediate producers from their means of production, thus establishing the original division between capital and labor as the foundation of the capital-relation. The expression "primitive accumulation" already signals a certain ambiguity. Primitive accumulation is capitalism's prehistory. As such, it describes a reality prior to capitalism standing up on its own two feet, lifting its nose from the ground (though not quite). In this respect, primitive accumulation is external to capitalism and to capitalist accumulation. As "primitive," primitive accumulation is an essentially precapitalist accumulation enabling the emergence of capitalism. However, it can enable it only if as "primitive" and "precapitalist" it is also the primitive accumulation of *capital*, hence already capitalist, and therefore already marked with that which follows from it. For this reason, the difference between primitive accumulation and capitalist accumulation is not a mere external difference separating precapitalist accumulation from capitalist accumulation, but rather stands for the inner-heterogeneous split of accumulation itself. That is why the primitiveness of "primitive" accumulation must be placed in quotes as the "So-Called Primitive Accumulation."[6]

Marx establishes a clear link between the two modes of accumulation, that is, between the initial process that produced the two categories of commodity-owners (the owners of labor-power and the owners of conditions of realization of labor), and capitalist production that reproduces this primordial division "on a constantly extending scale."[7] The capitalist production establishes contact between the two categories of commodity-owners separated by the primordial cut. It does not, however, merely preserve it as its presupposition, but rather reproduces it as its own result. Placed at the center of this dialectical movement is the category of "dispossessed labor," which apart from being the condition of *becoming* of capitalist production is also the *result* of its own exploitation, of appropriating its surplus-product. Conditioned by this initial cut, capitalist production retroactively posits its own presuppositions: "These presuppositions, which originally appeared as conditions of its becoming—and hence could not spring from its *action as capital*—now appear as results of its own realization, reality, as *posited by it*—*not as conditions of its arising, but as results of its presence.*"[8]

The Hegelian logic of "resulting presuppositions" implies the temporal logic of retroaction and asserts two modes of heterogeneity. By preceding and enabling the capitalist order, the heterogeneity of primitive accumulation is a strictly external ortho-heterogeneity. Once the system stands on its own two feet, the conditioning ortho-heterogeneity of the primordial cut repeats itself as the retro-heterogeneous result of capitalist accumulation. In relation to each other, the two are therefore not external but continuous, though their continuity is a continuity of discontinuity, that is, the continuity of the cut that makes out the capital non-relation.

The assertion of a conceptual link between Freud and Marx's notions of primary repression and primitive accumulation appears valid. Is the relation between primitive and capitalist accumulation not homologous with Freud's conceptual couplet of *Urverdrängung*, primal repression, and *Verdrängung*, repression as after-pressure, *Nachdrängen*? To account for processes of repression, Freud had to construct the speculative notion of primal repression as the metapsychological presupposition for repression proper. To paraphrase Marx's *Grundrisse*: primal repression appears, first, as the metapsychological condition of becoming of "psychic reality" (and hence could not spring from it) and, second, as the result of its own realization. As a "resulting presupposition," primal repression only has ontological reality in the series of its repetitions. Classical political economy stumbled upon an analogous conceptual problem of determining and explaining the accumulation of the first capital that enabled the emergence of capitalism. "The whole movement, therefore," Marx writes, "seems to turn around in a never-ending circle, which we can only get out of by assuming a primitive accumulation (the 'previous accumulation' of Adam Smith) which precedes capitalist accumulation; an accumulation which is not the result of the capitalist mode of production but its point of departure."[9]

Primitive accumulation thus signifies the pre- or meta-capitalist cut which conditions its subsequent development, while the subsequent and recurrent capitalist accumulation stands for an "after-accumulation" (*Nachakkumulation*). The latter repeats the primal cut, thus reaffirming the capital-relation. However, since the capital-relation is nothing but this cut itself, capitalist accumulation reaffirms and perpetuates the capital non-relation. By initiating the cut, primitive accumulation and primal repression open up the space of (libidinal and capitalist) economy. The initial cut repeats itself as the safeguard of (the symbolic and capitalist) order, as well as the singular point of its inner impossibility, of the fundamental antagonism, or of the (sexual and class) non-relation.

PECUNIA NON OLET

Against the backdrop of this conceptual link between primitive accumulation and primal repression, we can now proceed with a series of correlations between Marx's phylogenesis of capital and Freud's phylogenetic construction. Both posit a break: the break of "organic" repression marking the passage from nature to culture, and the break of "primitive" accumulation situated at the point of passage from feudalism to capitalism. In both instances, the break is irreducible, and it is irreducibility that is the nucleus of their respective "primitiveness" and "organicity." Culture and capitalism begin with the breaking off of contact, that is, with deodorization and expropriation. In both cases, the interruption of organic contiguity is effected by a separation from the earth:

> In the history of primitive accumulation, all revolutions are epoch-making that act as levers for the capitalist class in the course of its formation; but this is true above all for those moments when great masses of men are suddenly and forcibly torn from their means of subsistence, and hurled onto the labour-market as free, unprotected and rightless proletarians. The expropriation of the agricultural producer, of the peasant, from the soil [Grund und Boden] is the basis of the whole process.[10]

"Organic" repression is correlative with man's assumption of the erect posture and hence with the lifting of his nose from the ground, while the "whole process" of "primitive" accumulation has its "basis" in the "expropriation of the agricultural producer, of the peasant" from Grund und Boden (from the ground). Primitive accumulation has literally forced the immediate producer onto his feet, separating him from the ground as his means of subsistence. (Incidentally, the same process was depicted in Kafka's imagining of the advent of canis erectus, emerging with the move away from the watering of the earth as a means of acquiring sustenance and toward incantations resulting from a demand to work.) In both instances, the separation is conceived as a break with immediacy or with the immediate relation of contiguity. Primitive accumulation is Marx's solution to the Sphinx's riddle of the first capital, its origins in the separation of the immediate producer from the means of his livelihood. And in both instances, this break, maintained "on a constantly extending scale,"[11] is not a mere presupposition of culture and of capitalism, but is compulsively repeated once culture and capitalism have been established. It is repeated as their "resulting presupposition," grounded in the ungrounding instituted by the prohibition to touch. The elementary cultural prohibition "Phooey!" therefore figures as the original slogan of enclosures of the commons, of private ownership (of the means of production) now subtracted from the proletariat.

Thus, after bodily toilet training and linguistic toilet training comes "economic" toilet training, instituted by primitive accumulation as the primordial process of cleansing. The proletarian figures in it as the quite literal remainder of expropriation. Once the land is cleansed of peasants, there emerges the proletarian excrement as resulting from the "enclosure of the commons." It is this "epoch-making act" that provided the model for the osmological narrative: labor detached from the means of its own realization. As indicated by Marx, the term and concept of primitive accumulation were established with Adam Smith's "previous accumulation," discussed in his 1776 *The Wealth of Nations*, while the very first known description of the osmological narrative appeared a year later, in the 1777 *Encyclopédie* article on smell. Smith's is an idyllic view of the process. The osmological narrative may be a displaced and distorted origin story of capitalism. However, unlike Smith's idyllic view of the process, osmology, despite its distortions, accurately mirrors its actual beginnings.

The breaking off of phonic contact—correlative with dehomophonization and subject to the linguistic prohibition against touch—was superseded by a new contiguity, that is, by the signifying contact that replaced the interrupted phonic contact. In case of "primitive" accumulation, too, the separation of labor from the means of realization of labor is superseded by the forging of a new contiguity. The old homophonic immediacy of the feudal order had been banished, and in order to subsist, the newly expropriated immediate producer had to learn the language of commodity exchange, of bourgeois freedom and equality, in short: the language of the labor-contract. The contract replaces contact as the new form of contiguity. The two subjects brought into being by the initial cut, that is, the owner of the means of production and the expropriated owner of labor-power, now meet in the production process to set in motion the transformation of money and commodities into capital. Thus, capital is the paradigm of the new contiguity. Born of the initial cut, capital perpetuates, reaffirms, and deepens the capital non-relation.[12]

In the myth of primitive accumulation, the accumulation of money in the hands of the capitalist was explained with recourse to the idyllic primal scene of ascetic renunciation and diligence, while the pauperization of the emerging proletariat was elucidated in terms of punishment for the sins of laziness and wastefulness. The myth's fundamental fantasy served to heal the wound of the actual break, dulling its sharp blade down to the smoothness of a continuous passage. Just as Freud and Ferenczi's money emerged from a long process of substitution, so, too, capital appears in the myth in its deodorized cleanness mystifying its smelly origins. *Pecunia non olet*, "money doesn't stink." From the vantage point of classical political economy, money accumulating in the hands of the few is inodorate. For Marx, in this process the opposite is at stake. *Pecunia olet*, money surely stinks if we have the nose for sniffing out its genesis. Marx intervenes into the origin myth of capitalism to follow the path of its genesis in reverse, reducing its monetary cleanness to the history of expropriation, "written in the annals of mankind in letters of blood and fire."[13] In order to dispel the deodorized politico-economic mirage of truth, Marx's critique of political economy assumes the vantage point of the speaking nose, letting itself be guided by a sense of smell surer than all the categories of classical political economy.

The deodorized Spirit of capitalism, that is, the Spirit of freedom, equality, property, and of universal emancipation, is haunted by the smelly spirits of its origins. This smell is doubly sourced. It refers both to the cut of the initial emergence of the capital-relation, and to its recurrence within the already established capitalist order. Capital reeks of dispossession and exploitation, oozing with dirt: "If money, according to Augier, 'comes into the world with a congenital blood-stain on one cheek,' capital comes dripping from head to toe, from every pore, with blood and dirt."[14] By following his nose, Marx thus hits capital with the first swear word: he shows to capital its own excreta, exposing its excremental origins, its birth *inter urinas et faeces*, amid the feces of the original dispossession and the cesspool of capitalist exploitation.

According to the roman historian Suetonius, the motto *pecunia non olet*, "money does not smell," was coined by the roman emperor Vespasian, who ruled in the years 69–79 AD. The slogan was conjured up in response to the abhorrence expressed by Suetonius's son Titus over the fact that the emperor was making money by taxing public toilets, specifically urine: "When Titus found fault with him for contriving a tax upon public conveniences, he held a piece of money from the first payment to his son's nose, asking whether its odour was offensive to him. When Titus said 'No,' he replied, 'Yet it comes from urine.'"[15]

The example retraces the Freudian genesis of money-interest, leading from waste to value. The urine flowing into the "greatest sewer," the Roman *Cloaca Maxima*, one of the very first sewage systems, was being collected and sold. As a source of ammonium, it was used, among other things, for cleaning and bleaching woolen togas:

> The urine itself was an expensive raw commodity. It was used in the tanning industry, where it was mixed with the hide to soften it, loosen the hairs and dissolve the fat from its surface. It was also used as bleach where tunics were immersed in urine and whitened. The smell of urine was then washed out with water. Wealthy Romans, especially women were willing to pay large sums of money for toothpaste in which urine was the key ingredient.[16]

Vespasian imposed a tax on the disposal of urine, the so-called *vectigal urinae*.[17] Curtesy of this unusual tax, starting in 1830, Vespasian lend his name to the first Parisian public toilets, the street urinals, or *vespasiennes*.[18]

Marx uses the phrase in *Capital*, in the section on money and the circulation of commodities, which takes the form C—M—C, commodity—money—commodity. Simple commodity exchange consists of the exchange of a commodity for money and money for another commodity:

Money is the absolutely alienable commodity, because it is all other commodities divested of their shape, the product of their universal alienation. It reads all prices backwards, and thus as it were mirrors itself in the bodies of all other commodities, which provide the material through which it can come into being as a commodity. At the same time the prices, those wooing glances cast at money by commodities, define the limit of its convertibility, namely its own quantity. Since every commodity disappears when it becomes money it is impossible to tell from the money itself how it got into the hands of its possessor, or what article has been changed into it. *Non olet*, from whatever source it may come. If it represents, on the one hand, a commodity which has been sold, it also represents, on the other hand, a commodity which can be bought.[19]

Commodity exchange first appears as a process of social metabolism. The formula of simple commodity exchange (C—M—C) clearly relies on the order of quantitative equivalences. On each of its two extremes we find commodities that don't resemble one another in the least, since both present two different use-values and thus two different means of satisfying one's needs. Moreover, this qualitative difference is the very condition for exchange. I only exchange a use-value or a useful thing for a qualitatively different useful thing that can satisfy a need that the first one cannot. But under the conditions of commodity production, the exchange of one useful thing for another entails the abstraction from the qualitative difference between them and a reduction of this difference to the order of quantitative equivalences. Qualitatively different use-values must be reducible to a homogenous exchange-value. Thus, the qualitative difference of the first commodity vanishes in the qualitatively indifferent money-form to acquire, via its mediation, the form of a commodity with a different use-value. In Lacanian terms, this movement starts with a need that aims at some use-value as a particular qualitatively specific object of satisfaction. But for the need to realize its object and arrive at its satisfaction, it must be articulated as a payment-capable need (*zahlungsfähiges Bedürfnis*), that is, as need kneaded by the signifier. Need must be articulated as a signifying demand, as money, the pure image of value beyond usability. Referring back to Kafka's dog, we can say that, in capitalism, the satisfaction of needs is mediated by monetary incantations. As "the absolutely alienable commodity," money functions as a "vanishing mediator," a perpetually disappearing means of circulation, mediating the satisfaction of needs. In itself, money has no use-value. However, as the vehicle of universal alienation, money can, depending on its quantity, metamorphize into any commodity, thus satisfying a plethora of needs. By being "all other commodities divested of their shape," money has no smell: in it, the commodity-traces of its first metamorphosis are structurally erased. *Money is a deodorized commodity; a commodity is odorized money.* Yet the monetary deodorization is itself structured like smell. In money, commodities are "divested of their shape" and merely provide the "material through which it [money] can come into being as a commodity." All other commodities are but source-objects dissipating in monetary becoming.

This split is inherent to the commodity as such, divided between its use-value and its exchange-value, that is, between its natural and its social forms. As exchange-value, the commodity is a deodorized and denaturalized entity. Its value only "exists" in a differential relation of opposition to other commodities, with which it forms the universe of mutual exchangeability. The substance of value, which exists in no particular commodity but only in relation between them, does not depend on the usefulness of the commodity as a use-value capable of satisfying a particular need. Rather, it depends on the quantity of labor socially necessary for its production. This is the core insight of the "labor theory of value," formulated by Adam Smith and essentially modified by Marx.

The value of the commodity hence amounts to a "congealed mass of human labour"[20] that forms the substance of its value, while the magnitude of this substance amounts to the labor-time socially necessary to produce the commodity. From this foundation alone, there already follows the paradox that the commodity "linen" (to take Marx's beloved example), sold on the market (and unless it is sold, it is not a commodity), is radically cleansed of particularity that it might owe to the fact that it is produced by Peter and not by Paul (who are both linen producers). As a market-commodity whose value amounts to a congealed mass of homogeneous labor, linen is essentially One linen, it "counts as one," though being produced by isolated private commodity-producers. Marx says it clearly: "All the linen on the market *counts as one* single article of commerce, and each price of linen is only an aliquot part of it."[21] Thus, the commodity is once again a split entity: its twofold character results from the dual character of labor, split between concrete labor (that is: labor in its natural form producing concrete use-values that satisfy concrete needs of concrete consumers) *and* abstract labor as labor in its irreducibly social form: "I was the first," adds Marx, "to point out and examine critically this twofold nature [*die zwieschlächtige Natur*] of the labour contained in commodities." It is this split that sets Marx's *value theory of labor* apart from any previous *labor theory of value*.[22] This split, however, is extinguished in the commodity. As a result of market denaturation and extinction of the commodity as use-value produced by concrete labor, a commodity is essentially One commodity. A congelation of the value-forming substance, the commodity is a doubly deodorized product: it is cleansed of its immediate usefulness, as well as of its origin in concrete labor. It only counts as a commodity as the product of abstract labor and thus as the objectification of the substance of value premised on the "count as one."

My linen and your linen, the linen produced by me and the linen produced by you, are One linen not because they are both "linen," that is, use-values that satisfy the same need. Rather, they are One linen because they are "values" and hence excarnations of the value-forming substance of abstract labor. Linen is One not because of being identical with the concept "linen," but because it is subsumed under the concept "value." Value, however, appears only in exchange that places each commodity in relation to all other commodities. Outside exchange we only encounter concrete labors and useful products satisfying human needs, but never commodities as values. The commodity is value only because of the relation of distinctive opposition to all other circulating commodities. As One, it divides into Two: the minimum of commodities are two commodities, such that the value of each is determined in relation to the other. Outside of the relation, neither has any value whatsoever. The entire identity of a commodity as value therefore amounts to its difference in relation to other commodities. But since this is the case for every circulating commodity, the extreme consequence of commodity's "identity" is that it is also distinctively opposed to itself. "Existing" only in relation between commodities, value has no autonomous form outside of this relation. *The commodity, therefore, is One because it is value, and it is value because it is not One.*

For a thing to become a commodity, it must pass through the double process of deodorization—namely, the extinction of use-value in value and the extinction of concrete labor (producing useful things) in abstract labor (mediating social exchange). The split between the useful and the concrete, on the one hand, and the exchangeable and abstract, on the other, emerges again in the nucleus of the commodity's Oneness, cleansed of concreteness and usefulness, yet once again split and opposed to itself. Since a commodity has value only in a differential relation to other commodities, difference is its only identity. Take, for example, Freud's chain of substitutions "excrement—penis—baby—money" and Ferenczi's genesis of money-interest "excrement—mud—sand—stone—coin." Observed from the vantage point of the simple form of value, as conceived by Marx, two things can be said about these chains of substitutions. First, in its relation to "excrement," "penis" functions as its equivalent, as the equivalent form of "excrement," while "excrement" appears in its relative form of relating to "penis." Accordingly, "penis" is the expression of value of "excrement" and the excarnation of its value. Additionally, and more importantly: this excarnation exists only in their relation. Therefore, Freud does not claim that "penis" is in itself "excrement." Rather, he posits between them a value-relation, which makes the second an expression of value of the first.

We hereby arrive at money. The commodity-universe is a structured totality of relations, and it is only in relation to this structured totality of relations that a commodity has any value. The inner logic of the structure dictates an exception. In the simple value-form, one commodity is related to another commodity expressing its value. And though their relation is reversible, such that the other commodity relates to the first one as the expression of its value, it follows that in each instance merely one commodity expresses its value in another commodity, without the other commodity simultaneously expressing its value in the first commodity. An exceptional commodity (or, rather, an exceptionification of a commodity) is required so that in it any and all commodities could express their value. The totality of the commodity-universe (n) is not whole; it lacks one element (-1), namely precisely the element in which all other elements $(n-1)$ express their value.

Money is precisely such a commodity, the embodiment of the ontological deficit of the commodity-universe. As commodity, value is split, while this split is seemingly healed in money, in which the perpetually circulating value settles down, acquires an independent form (independent of circulation), and enters the relation of reflexive identity with itself. Money is the deodorization of value consolidated in the money-form and hence seemingly purged of self-difference, of the non-identity-with-itself that pertains to it as a commodity. Money as the general equivalent of value is the excarnated, "absolutely alienable commodity" and hence the alienated expression of value of all other commodities. It is the excarnated objectification of the share of their self-difference, and hence of difference as such. As indicated, a useful thing becomes a commodity only by entering exchange and thus an oppositional relation to the integral universe of the remaining commodities. This process is one of (materially, not merely ideationally) subsuming a useful thing under the concept of "value." And due to this relation, commodities are capable of a mutual expression of their values, whereby one commodity takes the relative and the other the equivalent form, the latter expressing the magnitude of value of the former. This, precisely, is the function of the money-commodity as the general equivalent of value. As an excarnated commodity, money functions as a measure of value of any commodity (expressed as its price).

The subsumption of a thing under the concept "value"—a subsumption that only takes place in exchange—is thus followed by assignation of a number, in which the value-forming substance of labor is expressed. Thus, the commodity-value is expressed in the price, and to the concept of "value" something else is added, namely the concept of the "identity" of a thing to the concept of "value."[23] The value-subsumption in money is the extinction of the thing. This mechanism of a redoubled movement of subsumption and assignation is premised on an excretion of non-identity-with-itself as inherent in the commodity-form. Hereafter, it appears as though this particular commodity sold at this particular price already contains within itself the substance of value. What is excreted is the commodity's difference in relation to itself, and hence also its relation to all other commodities. The principle of distinctive opposition is replaced by the principle of reflexive identity, whereby value is substantialized and henceforth seemingly embodied in the particular commodity qua commodity. It therefore *seems* that a commodity has value because it is a congelation of concrete labor, of labor-time, which can be measured wherever the labor takes place. In *reality*, a commodity is the congelation of the value-forming substance of abstract labor that conditions a thing's entry into exchange-relations of distinctive opposition.

Money is a deodorized commodity; commodities are odorized money. The process of simple commodity exchange unfolds as a succession of sale and purchase—a selling in order to buy—and hence as a successive deodorization of a commodity in money (C—M) and an odorization of the money in a commodity (M—C). The odorization of money in a commodity is essentially a reodorization, following the deodorization of a commodity in money; the process ends with the consumption of the commodity bought with the money acquired by the sale of my own commodity. Money is an essential mediating factor in the metamorphosis of commodities. This metamorphosis has the structure of alienation: "If it represents, on the one hand, a commodity which has been sold, it also represents, on the other hand, a commodity which can be bought."[24] Money represents one (sold) commodity for another (buyable) commodity, thus constituting itself as the subject of this movement from one commodity to another: C—M—C. This movement is one of alienation of the monetary subject, disappearing in the identification with the other commodity. This identifying disappearance of the monetary subject, however, takes place against the backdrop of the repression, deodorization, or extinction of the first commodity, from which it has previously emerged as the share of the first commodity's non-identity-with-itself. The process of simple commodity exchange rests on the synchronous processes of metaphorical and metonymic exchange (of a commodity for another commodity): the commodity emerging from the exchange retains a relation to the commodity that was exchanged for it. More precisely: it retains a relation not to the first commodity in its positivity and identity as a use-value, that is, not with its mark, but rather with the absence of its mark. Its mark was extinguished in the money-form, that is, in the monetary signifier of a lack (standing for the other commodity in its oppositional determination).

If I consume the commodity I just bought, if I exclude it from circulation instead of selling it, the share of its oppositivity disappears. Alienation is followed by separation, which, however, is not the Lacanian separation as resulting from alienation. In simple commodity exchange, separation amounts to consumption or satisfaction of need.[25] To arrive at the Lacanian separation as resulting from alienation, we must move from simple commodity exchange to the circulation of capital. Here, separation follows the logic of libidinous satisfaction (as opposed to the satisfaction of need in consumption) and therefore it is here that we witness the emergence of the remainder of deodorization as the object of *Riechlust*, the smell-drive of capital, directed at the excrement of value.

THE CAPITALIST UNCONSCIOUS

In conditions of capitalist modernity, things are dissociated from themselves in two ways. First, they acquire a double existence as objects of utility, on the one hand, and as exchange-values, on the other. And second, with this dissociation set in place, the scale is tipped in favor of one mode of existence at the "expense," so to speak, of the other. In capitalism, things only count as countable, that is, as "charged" with value. They only matter as material bearers of the spectral materiality of economic values. Structured like a language, the capitalist universe consists of a network of differential relations, that is, it forms a structure. The elements of this structure are exchange-values. Ergo: exchange-values = signifiers. But does this equation really follow from a "structuralist" reading of Marx? And is such an equation "structuralist" to begin with?[26]

In part, such an assumption (common in Lacanian readings of Marx)[27] has to do with seeming ambiguities of Marx's account of the two factors of the commodity. Marx first determines the commodity as "an external object, a thing which through its qualities satisfies human needs of whatever kind."[28] The commodity is not just any external object, or material thing. Although any external object has empirically determinable qualities, its being a commodity depends on the character of these qualities as useful for satisfying human needs. And it is only this "usefulness of a thing [that] makes it a use-value," which "has no existence apart from" its "physical properties." "This property of a commodity," Marx continues, "is independent of the amount of labour required to appropriate its useful qualities,"[29] since it is the useful qualities of external objects themselves, that is, their ability to satisfy human needs, that make them use-values. It clearly follows from this, that such a notion of use-value is entirely independent of the social form in which the use-value appears. As already indicated in the course of this book, Marx's account of use-value has led some readers to the conclusion that use-value is an empirical concept referring to an external appendage to the commodity. This appendage may be a necessary component of the commodity, but only insofar as the commodity is a useful thing satisfying human needs. Again, this is not Marx's concept of use-value. Use-values "constitute the material content of wealth, whatever its social form may be," writes Marx, immediately adding: "In the form of society to be considered here they are also the material bearers [*Träger*] of . . . exchange-value."[30] For Marx, use-value is an essentially social, and hence historically specific, category.

At its most elementary, Marx's critique of political economy proceeds by following the established scientific model consisting of three elementary terms: the object, the axiom, and the primary concept. And these three terms are defined in the very first sentence of the first chapter of *Capital*: the *science* is called the critique of political economy; its sole *object*: the capitalist mode of production; its sole *axiom*: the capitalist mode of production is a system of commodity production; and, hence, the *primary concept*: the commodity: "The wealth of societies, in which the capitalist mode of production prevails appears as an 'immense collection of commodities'; the individual commodity appears as it elementary form. Our investigation therefore begins with the analysis of the commodity."[31] Considering the commodity exclusively as the primary concept is to consider it only as defined by the axiom, that is, as the element of the capitalist production. But if the commodity is considered solely as the element of capitalist production as its defining social form, its two factors (use-value and exchange-value) only pertain to it under capitalism. In other words, Marx's concept of use-value only applies to capitalist commodity production, and cannot be extended to usefulness as such, nor can it be reduced to the physical properties of external objects.

But what is it then that makes use-value specific to capitalism? Marx says it clearly: use-values are material bearers of exchange-value. It is this function, and this function alone, which makes use-value a factor of the commodity, and therefore a concept with which to analyze it.

This necessary detour leads us back to the proposed equation: exchange-values = signifiers. The commodity is a *Doppelwesen*, a double entity, consisting of use-value and exchange-value. For Marx, the relation between the two factors of the commodity is a necessary one, just as the relation between the signifier and the signified is defined as necessary by Saussure in his analysis of the linguistic sign. The commodity is like Saussure's wave;[32] it is but a division that results from the encounter between the wind of (ideational) value, and the water of (phonic) use-value.[33] But unlike wind and water, which are things existing in reality before being joined together to form a wave, neither use-value nor value preexist their encounter. Nor is there a commodity if either of the two factors is missing. This necessary relation, however, is at the same time a non-relation, for use-value does not determine the exchange-value, nor does the exchange-value determine the use-value of the commodity. But if neither of the two factors determines its flip side, if there is a non-relation between them, what could possibly make them form a single entity? Underlying this problem is Marx's paradoxical premise: use-value and value are two sides of the same coin, *except that there is no coin*, just like there is no wave outside of the encounter between the wind and the water. It is the resolution of this conceptual problem, however, that makes Marx a structuralist avant la lettre. There is no preexisting coin, no-thing that makes the two sides "stick together." But if the two sides are nonetheless untied together to form a commodity, that is only because of other commodities—just like the two sides of a linguistic sign, its signifier and its signified, are coupled solely by the relation of the sign (that they themselves form) to all the other signs.

What immediately follows from this aligning of Marx's project with Saussure's linguistic theory is the conclusion that Marx's analysis of the commodity (as well as Saussure's theory of the linguistic sign) are not concerned with the issue of representation, nor with the issue of reality.[34] The commodity is not held together by the mutual determination of its two factors, but by its relation of distinctive opposition with all other commodities, whereby this relation of commodity A to commodities B, C, D, and so on, is not one of representation. This is clear already from Marx's examination of the "simple, isolated, or accidental form of value" that takes the form of "an x amount of commodity A equals in value a y amount of commodity B," or x A = y B.[35] The equation states the following: the value of a commodity can only be expressed in another commodity, and can be found nowhere outside of this relation. But this relation is not one of representation. It does not state that the value of the commodity A is represented by the commodity B, or that B represents the value of A. Marx is clear in his use of the terms, speaking of B "expressing" the value of A, rather than "representing" it. But what does it mean to say that the value of A is expressed in B, or that B expresses the value of A? It means, quite simply, that B signifies the value of A, and that the value of A is signified by B. Therefore, B is the signifier of the value of A, which makes A the B's signified. However, B as the signifier of the value of A is no exchange-value, but rather the form of expression of the exchange-value of A. And what is it that expresses the exchange-value of A, thus figuring as its signifier? That which expresses the exchange-value of A is the use-value B. Ergo: *use-values = signifiers, exchange-values = signifieds*.

From here, we can now further specify the point made earlier regarding representation. The commodity as use-value signifies, rather than represents, the exchange-value of another commodity. If the commodity, taken as a unity of use-value and value, can be said to represent anything, it is not "value" but (the idea of) "wealth," just like "smoke" can be said to be the representational sign of (the idea of) "fire." Unlike the relation of signification, which is reciprocally symmetrical (the use-value of A signifies the exchange-value of B, and the use-value of B signifies the exchange-value of A, depending solely on which of the commodities figures in its relative and which in its equivalent form), the relation of the representational sign is not reciprocal ("the commodity" is a sign of "wealth," but "wealth" is not a sign of "the commodity"). The very first sentence of *Capital* can be read as indicative of this theoretical shift away from the classical regime of representation, and therefore away from probing the relation between reality and representation, or between words and things: "The wealth of societies in which the capitalist mode of production prevails appears as an 'immense collection of commodities'; the individual commodity appears as its elementary form."[36] The commodity is the representational sign of wealth; the commodity represents the idea of wealth that "appears" in the capitalist world as an "immense collection of commodities." But Marx is not concerned with the question as to what the commodity as a representational sign might represent, and how. His famous research problem is rather, why do products of labor necessarily take the form of the commodity, and what the structural features of such a value-form might be. His research program is "structuralist" rather than semiotic. Thus, use-value, far from designating a thing that is useful due to its physical properties, and far from figuring as a mere element in the system of needs and their satisfaction, is first and foremost the form of expression of value, that is, the signifier of value.

Hence, the money commodity that presents the final result of the conceptual genesis of the value-form,[37] and that serves as the general equivalent of value, such that it is capable of expressing the value of any commodity, is but a commodity in its pure, and purely "useless" universal equivalent form. If Marx's concept of use-value designates the function of commodities "as material bearers [*Träger*] of . . . exchange-value," then money is use-value at its purest. As such, it is irreducible to the physical materiality of a thing—which is contingent in the sense of being coalesced by "social custom"[38]—and serves not as an object of satisfaction of need, but rather as a means of acquiring such objects of satisfaction. Consequently, if observed from the point of view of a system of needs, disregarding the specific social form, the materiality of a use-value amounts to its "physical properties." The materiality of use-values as "material bearers of exchange-value," however, has nothing to do with physical materiality of its properties, but rather solely with the emphatically non-physical (as well as non-psychic) materiality of the signifier. The appearance of the general equivalent of value does in fact alter the universe of mutually exchangeable commodities, for it is only with the money-form that the universe of commodities begins to form an enclosed, "constipated" totality.

To understand this last point, we have to take another look at the differential nature of the commodity insofar as its value is only expressed in another commodity. Such mutual value-determination of commodities presupposes as its condition a point of impossibility. To say that the value of any single commodity can only be expressed via another commodity, means that it is impossible for a commodity to be the expression of its own value. To say: "an x amount of commodity A equals in value an x amount of commodity A"— this equation expresses no value whatsoever. In logical terms, this implies that the relation of equivalence is not reflexive.[39] Situated at the core of the equivalence-relation is a non-relation: a commodity can only enter the relation of equivalence with other commodities because it is standing in a relation of reflexive opposition to itself, that is, because it is structurally barred from expressing its own value. "It's a pity that I can't kiss myself," it seems to be saying.[40] Underlying the constitution of the commodity-universe is the prohibition of the sniff-kiss.

What does reflexive opposition imply for Lacan's (and, as I claim, also for Marx's) "hyperstructuralist" program? It implies, quite simply, a notion of the subject as effected by the structure. What we encounter in the autonomous interplay of structurality is not any substance of Being, but an immanent contradiction that stands for subjectivity as the point of non-identity of commodities with themselves, that is, for the point of their inherent impossibility. And since a thing is a thing only as identical with itself, or else it is no-thing at all, subjectivity stands for the inherent nothingness of the universe of commodities, or for its constitutive, as well as constituting, lack. This negativity of value, however, is not one of negative determination. A negative determination is essentially a negative determination of a positivity, whose external limits are defined by determining what it is not. In short, it is a limitation. However, commodities and linguistic signs are not positive things, which we could determine by relating them to something they are not, neither are they negatives of a positive thing, the limits of which they would mark. Saussure says it emphatically: "in language there are only differences without positive terms."[41] The commodity is nothing if not negative. It only "is" value as differing from other commodities, which in turn "are" values only in differing from it. Moreover, with the move from Saussure to Marx and Lacan this negative entity that only emerges in relation (with other negative entities), while lacking any substantial positivity, is "internally" redoubled, and thus radicalized to the point of logical reflexivity, such that it "is" nothing but the difference from itself.

From here, let me return to the money and the commodity as two modes of existence of value. To claim that money is but use-value at its purest is not to say that with the emergence of money in the conceptual genesis of the value-form nothing has changed, nor does it mean that the money simply equals exchange-value. What has in fact changed is *nothing itself*. With money, we witness the emergence of a commodity that appears very well capable of expressing its own value, meaning that the value of the money-commodity appears to be directly expressed in the use-value of the money-commodity, just like the master-signifier appears capable of directly expressing its own meaning (bypassing what Lacan terms the "phallic function"), whereas the meaning of other, "regular" signifiers is a mere effect of them differentially relating to one another. In addition, the relation of reflexive opposition is mystified by the money-form in such a way that henceforth the value of each commodity appears not as a social relation between different commodities (and thus between different labors), but as an inherent property of each of the particular commodities. Value, instead of *inexisting* as a purely negative spectral objectivity, now appears to exist as a positive thing in the phenomenal world. This is what Marx means when he underlines that with the emergence of the money-commodity value appears to have acquired an autonomous, or independent, existence: "the money form of value is its independent [*selbstständige*] and palpable form of appearance."[42] This mystifying function of the money-commodity, however, which forecloses subjectivity (or lack), thus totalizing (or "constipating") the universe of commodities, is itself structural (the genesis of the money-form is conceptual, not chronological), and not merely the result of our inability to perceive the structure *sub specie aeternitatis*.

At its most basic, Marx's concept of fetishism concerns this structural foreclosure of reflexive opposition, by way of which value appears not as resulting from the social relation, but as existing as an intrinsic property of things outside of any social relation. Fetishism amounts neither to our treatment of things as use-values, while being unaware of their exchange-value, nor does it amount to treating them as endowed with social characteristics (which they really possess). For Marx, fetishism amounts to the supposition that value is an intrinsic property of an individual commodity, which the latter embodies automatically (by natural necessity), transhistorically (regardless of the social form), and outside of any relation. Accordingly, Marx does not claim that in exchanging the products we are not treating them as values, but as mere objects of utility. Rather, he writes that we in fact only relate the products of our labor with each other as abstract values, but that this is not because we know them to be receptacles of abstract labor: "Men do not therefore bring the products of their labour into relation with each other as values because they see these objects merely as the material integuments of homogeneous human labour. The reverse is true: by equating their different products to each other in exchange as values, they equate their different kinds of labour as human labour."[43]

For A. Kiarina Kordela,[44] under capitalist relations, the pure potentiality of labor to actualize itself, that is, its univocal capacity, is thwarted by the capital-relation, that is, by the cutting of the link between labor (now reduced to labor-power, that is, commodified) and the means of its realization (now in possession of the capitalist). Consequently, and resulting from this commodification, labor only appears as value, and hence as an element of structure. For Kordela, capital taps into the pure potentiality of Being in a way that makes its capacity generative of exchange-value, while at the same time foreclosing this potentiality as it is in itself, that is, beyond the law of value. I can agree with this line of argument to the extent that in capitalism the commodification of labor indeed implies that the worker's capacity for labor is used as a means of generating (new) value. What I must disagree with, though, is that the power of self-actualization is reducible to such a capacity, and hence to a mere historical manifestation of the transhistorical substance of Being, now appearing

merely as value (or structurality). I want to claim that the self-actualizing character of labor emerges only with capitalism—as such, it is, first, historically
specific, rather than transhistorical; second, it is not a capacity, but a relation;
and third, since capitalist commodity production forms the structuring matrix
of its emergence, it is essentially the labor of structure, resulting from the law
of value, rather than ontologically preceding it.

In Marx, such a notion of historically specific self-actualizing power of
labor corresponds precisely to the concept of abstract labor. The latter results
from the double character of the products of labor as commodities. In capitalism, the satisfaction of needs is market-mediated, which means that my concrete labor produces use-values for others, while simultaneously producing
the means of acquiring use-values (as, again, produced by others) for myself
as the producer. It is in this sense that labor in capitalism universally mediates
social exchange. As Moishe Postone has observed, Marx's

> analysis of the double character of labor in capitalism, as a productive
> activity and as a social mediation, allows him to conceive of this labor as
> a nonmetaphysical, historically specific "causa sui." Because such labor
> mediates itself, it grounds itself (socially) and therefore has the attributes of
> "substance" in the philosophical sense.[45]

As such, abstract labor as the value-forming substance is not a thwarted
manifestation of Being's always already foregoing power of self-actualization,
but in itself constitutes social relations as grounded solely in themselves, that
is, as self-actualized. Only in this sense, "labor in capitalism becomes its own
social ground,"[46] such that the capitalist social bond results solely from this
function of labor as a historically specific form of social mediation, which
makes this bond inherently secular. Thus, in capitalism, "thought and bodies," figuring "exclusively as value," far from being "prevented from expressing being qua power-of-self-actualization" because of "its subjugation to the
accumulation of economic value,"[47] rather allow for its emergence for the very
first time in human history. This function of abstract labor as self-propelling
power of social self-actualization—divested of any qualities, and fully independent of any overt relations of social domination—is structurally mystified by the effects of fetishism. It is mystified structurally because fetishism is
"inseparable from the production of commodities."[48] As such, *abstract labor is
tantamount to the capitalist unconscious.*

As Milner writes apropos of the signifier, "the signifier has no reason to be
as it is, and firstly because it is not as it is; because it is not identical to itself;
because it has no self; because every self is reflexive, and because the signifier
cannot be reflexive, without being immediately its own other [*second*], and an
other [*un autre*] signifier."[49] What would it mean, then, that a commodity "is"

only by "not being as it is"? What does it mean to claim that a commodity is not identical to itself because it has no Self? It means, as we have seen, that the commodity cannot be substituted for itself. Things only have a Self by being self-identical, that is, by being substitutable for themselves. This operation of substitution for itself lies at the core of the logical principle of identity: A = A. Object A is identical with itself only because it is substitutable for A, that is, for itself. Commodities are universally exchangeable; in the universe of commodities, each commodity is exchangeable for any other commodity. However, this universal exchangeability is only made possible, and is only driven by, the non-exchangeability of the commodity for itself, that is, by the commodity's non-identity-with-itself. So, why is such an account of the commodity radically secular? It is radically secular because only that which has no Self, that is, only that which is not as it is, thus traversing the ontological divide between being and non-being, truly has no (external) reason to be. Structure is never only structure because it is never itself. Structure can only be by not being itself. And there is no Self against which to measure its own not being itself, just as there is no Substance underlying its fallenness. At the core of the universe of commodities, we once more encounter the logical consistency of the sniff-kiss, and its commodity-circulation enabling impossibility, or prohibition.

PARASITES

Like smells, value is not reflexive, it does not equal itself. As a processing value, an *übergreifendes Subjekt*, it is caught in the incessant process of the valo-rizing accumulation-by-dissipation. Thus, the logic of the commodity led us to reflexive opposition and to capital as subject. This logic, however, is related to something visceral and structurally irreducible. Propelled not by the creation and consumption of use-values, capital is only after the incremental excrement, or the excarnated being, of surplus-value. Hence its undead, para-sitical, vampiric essence underscored by Marx: "Capital is dead labor which, vampire-like, lives only by sucking living labour, and lives the more, the more labour it sucks."[50] In 1909, a *Daily People* editorial compared the capitalist vul-garis to the hookworm:

> The capitalist vulgaris sucks blood, the blood of its employes; the capitalist
> vulgaris produces minute hemorrhage; the wound which its tentacles leave
> after the bloodsucking is done continues to trickle; the capitalist vulgaris
> secretes a substance that acts decidedly as a poison; it is the substance
> which spreads foul corruption and ignorance in the atmosphere; the
> capitalist vulgaris lives on workingmen, women and children only. / So
> the "hookworm" is only a Southern localism for the thing known in
> wormology as "capitalist vulgaris," a nuisance and a pest against which the
> Socialist anti-toxine is being directed the world over.[51]

For Marx, the process of self-valorization is conditioned by the capital-relation, hinging on a social non-relation. The capitalist system of commodity production and circulation is essentially "classified": class divisions spell out the truth of the ideologically deodorized, "odor-free market system." Exploitation as the basis of class divisions is deodorized by capital-fetishism and the mystification of the wage-form. Rather than speaking about classes, we are inclined to use deodorized, "declassified" terms, such as "employees" or "business owners." After all, we are supposedly all in the same boat, playing by the same rules, such that our affluence or our poverty merely reflect our calculable and demonstrable merits. Michael Heinrich is right to emphasize that "talk of classes is in no way in and of itself particularly critical. That's not only the case for conceptions of 'social justice' that aspire to an equilibrium between classes, but also for some allegedly 'leftist' conceptions of bourgeois politics as a sort of conspiracy of the 'ruling class' against the rest of society."[52]

Class differences tend to push to the fore in unusual places. Our belonging to a social class is betrayed by our appetites. Take, for instance, a scene from *The Nanny Diaries*, a 2007 comedy starring Scarlett Johansson. The film tells a story of a college graduate who, following a misunderstanding, starts work as a nanny for an affluent Upper East Side family. Settling into their home, the nanny admires and is drawn to the "immense collection of commodities" gathered there signaling wealth, until finally looking into the fridge. The viewer expects her to be equally taken in by food as she is by other commodities. But no: with a clear expression of aversion she says, "Tofu cutlets? Ugh. Yuck." When it comes to food, the ruling class has no class. The Nanny would have happily swapped places with Mrs. X, but having to eat tofu cutlets is taking it a step too far. Our stomachs are class conscious, observant of the class divide.

Nowhere is this inscription of class into our sensibility featured more prominently than in Bong Joon-ho's 2019 feature film *Parasite*. The film's entire premise and plot revolve around the socially divisive role of smells. A tale of two four-person South Korean families—the affluent Parks and the pauperized Kims—the movie reflects on the well-documented deepening of social inequalities in Asia's fourth-largest economy (and in the world at large). With social mobility declining, the social ladder is replaced by a glass floor, separating the "dirt spoons" (*heuksujeo*) from the "gold spoons" (*geumsujeo*). The Kims are declassed members of the working class, its outcasts. They are (barely) surviving on odd jobs, which they can't do very well and hence are economically useless. They live in a semi-basement flat (*banjiha*), signaling their place at the very bottom of the social ladder, and hence their literal debasement and subordination. To paraphrase the title of Freud's famous paper, theirs is a story of "the universal tendency to debasement in the sphere of capitalist economy."

With their toilet situated at street level (and reached by ascending a few stairs), the Kims live a few steps down from the bottom, below toilet-level, in the sewer. If toilet culture is the bare minimum of culture, the Kims are situated beneath the threshold of civilization. During a severe storm, when sewage overflows their apartment, the toilet is the only seat in the house that is risen above the sewer. The Kims' position *inter urinas et faeces* is further exemplified by their kitchen window looking onto the alley (a dead-end street) where drunks often urinate. Smell is mentioned for the first time when Ki-taek, the father of the family, finds a stinkbug in his food. Soon after, when their street is being fumigated, Ki-taek insists they keep the windows open, welcoming the free pest-extermination. Though overtly intended to rid the family of various parasites inhabiting their dwellings and eating their food (*parásitos* literally means "a person who eats at the table of another"), it is obvious to the viewer that the Kims themselves are the stinkbugs fumigated. The dwellings, surroundings, and their own ways of being are an offense to the *sensus decori*, mapping out the sensorial micro-politics of exclusion.

The Kims do not belong to the working class proper. Rather, they are representatives of the *lumpenproletariat*. An "essentially parasitical group,"[53] the declassed lumpenproletariat was conceived by Marx and Engels as an underclass devoid of (working-)class consciousness, and consisting mostly of petty criminals, vagabonds, and prostitutes, but also, and increasingly so, of the unemployed. They are facing structural barriers to entering the workforce. "Employed by capital to be unemployed," they can only scheme their way into employment.[54] The *Communist Manifesto* defines the lumpenproletariat as the passive *Verfaulung der untersten Schichten der alten Gesellschaft*, variously translated as "the passive dung heap" or the "passively rotting (or decaying) mass."[55] In German, *faul* means both "lazy" and "decaying," the term bringing together the capitalist notion of the poor man's *laziness* (refusal to work, or to participate in the capital-relation) and the self-dissipating and polluting essence of *foulness*. The Kims lack all work ethics. Disillusioned by the system and the very idea of a shared involvement in it, they mirror its chaotic reproduction pushing them deeper and deeper into poverty. Permanently unemployable, they secure their employment by means of deceit, posing as someone they are not, shamelessly fabricating their credentials (the son, Ki-woo, poses as a university student; the daughter, Ki-jung, pretends to be an art therapist; Ki-taek is posing as an experienced driver; and his wife, Choong-sook, a housekeeper providing luxury services).

"The passive dung heap" of society, the Kims soon prove to be stigmatized and set apart by their *Lumpengeruch*, or social-scum-smell. Though successfully infiltrating the Parks household, profitably posing as deodorized members of the working class, their true identity soon seeps through the fake facade. The first one to catch a whiff of the deception is Da-song, the Park family's youngest, who remarks that the four new employees of the household all smell exactly the same. Concerned about their true identities being revealed, the Kims wash their clothes, contemplating about each of them using different detergents. But their presence is not made more palatable by the washing. If they can't shake the scent, it is because they are not wearing it. Ki-jung, the daughter, ponders on the social substance of the smell, saying the smell won't leave them unless they leave this place. But will it? Or will it haunt them forever? Smell, Montaigne observes, "betrays the place I come from,"[56] even if I had long since left the place.

The offensive smell cannot be washed off. It clings to their bodies, betraying the true essence of their excarnated class-being, inscribed into their sensibility. George Orwell's account in *The Road to Wigan Pier* (1937) oscillates between a critical rejection of the toxicity of the ideological narrative of "the stinky poor," and the admission of the existence of the reality described by it. Instead of painting an idyllic picture of the working class, patronizing the poor, he resists the temptation of deodorizing them.[57] In smell, the prophesizing of equality hits the barrier of inequality resisting all equalization. Orwell insists that all social differences between the ruling capitalist class and the ruled working class can be overcome (or, rather, disavowed). The eye and the ear can be fooled into thinking we are all in the same boat. Even the sense of (aesthetic) taste can easily be fooled by the establishing of working-class culture with its own set of aesthetic sensibilities coexisting proudly alongside ruling-class culture, their domains neatly separated and freed of any conflict. The sense of touch, too, entails a neat separation between what is rightfully yours and what is rightfully mine. Our senses of sight, hearing, taste, and touch all play a role in the disavowal, but not our sense of smell. Smell figures as the marker of class difference beyond politico-ideological deodorization:

> Here you come to the real secret of class distinctions in the West—the real reason why a European of bourgeois upbringing, even when he calls himself a Communist, cannot without a hard effort think of a working man as his equal. It is summed up in four frightful words which people nowadays are chary of uttering, but which were bandied about quite freely in my childhood. The words are: The lower classes smell.[58]

Observing in disgust a dirty tramp "taking off his boots in a ditch," Orwell adds: "It did not seriously occur to you that the tramp might not enjoy having black feet."[59] However, upon stressing the fact that the abhorrent smell of the tramp's feet is abhorrent to the tramp himself, he considers a smell-difference that cannot be fully accounted for, a difference of the indifferent, explainable only by people belonging to another social class: "And even 'lower-class' people whom you knew to be quite clean—servants, for instance—were faintly unappetizing. The smell of their sweat, the very texture of their skins, were *mysteriously different from yours.*"[60] Though careful not to cross the line, their "mysteriously different" smell unfailingly crosses the line. Referring to Ki-taek, Dong-ik, the Park family father, is unsure how to describe the smell. Talking to Yeon-kyo, his wife, he says: "That smell that wafts through the car, how to describe it?"—"An old man's smell?"—"No no, it's not that. What is it? Like an old radish? No. You know when you boil a rag? It smells like that. Anyway, even though he always seems about to cross the line, he never does cross it. That's good. I'll give him credit. But that smell crosses the line."

Another key aspect of the lumpenproletariat, emphasized in *The Communist Manifesto*, is treated in the film, namely its readiness "to sell itself to reactionary intrigues."[61] *Parasite* introduces a split in the lumpenproletariat by presenting another character, Geun Se, the former housekeeper's husband, who has been living in a nuclear bomb shelter under the Park house. The Parks are unaware either of his or the shelter's existence.[62] The shelter is literally *ein anderes Schauplatz*, an Other scene, a place in-out-of-place. A parasite, Geun Se is undetected by his host. Himself a member of the lumpenproletariat, Geun Se first took refuge in the bunker four years ago to escape loan-sharks. The parasite is an entity split between its prophylactic and its libidinous function, that is, between Geun Se and the Kims. Unlike the Kims, Geun Se is a congenial, grateful parasite, singing praises to Mr. Park without the latter being aware of his existence. He embodies the historical meaning of "parasite," signifying a bard praising the master in song or poetry,[63] solidarizing with the class enemy. Embarrassed by his financial misfortunes, he blames only himself: "It's all my fault. I started a cake shop—Taiwanese Castella—and it completely bankrupted us." He claims to like living underground, adding, "I just feel comfortable here. It feels like I was born here."

The electrical switches in the bunker control the lights above the flight of stairs leading up to the living room. Every day, Geun Se waits for Mr. Park to arrive home. Upon hearing his footsteps, he flicks on a series of lights one by one as Mr. Park is ascending the stairs, performing a welcome home ritual. Hiding in the bunker and holding the candle to Mr. Park, the first explanation he provides of his unusual ritual is economic (and only found in the film's original screenplay): "We have to conserve energy. It all comes out of Mr. Park's pocket." Thus, his prophylactic function is revealed: energy waste-management. At one point, he accompanies the ritual with an improvised song: "Returning after a day's work," he sings, "I love you so much, Mr. Park! Home from the office, Mr. Park is off duty now." His practice is a politico-theologico-economic ritual, a classified liturgical acclamation, glorifying Mr. Park's rule. It is also an "incantation, by which food is called down," for Geun Se's wife, Moon-gwang (a housekeeper who, following a nasty scheme by the Kims, was later fired and replaced by Choong-sook), brings down food to him from upstairs. Like the *laudes* acclamations—discussed by Ernst Kantorowicz and further analyzed by Giorgio Agamben and Santner—subtending the rites of royal investiture, Geun Se's ritual and song serve to invest Mr. Park's rule with sublime legitimacy. The fact that Mr. Park is oblivious of it brings the practice even closer to its medieval predecessor, for the *laudes* acclamation "was an accessory manifestation, impressive by its festal and solemn character, but not indispensable; for legally the liturgical acclaim added no new element of material power which the king had not already received earlier."[64] Borrowing Santner's terms, we can say there is an *officiant cause*, an "oath of office," motivating Geun Se's acclamation by which he *officiates*.[65] Santner exemplifies the officiating subject with a reference to Kafka's aphoristic text that brilliantly captures Geun Se's predicament:

> They were given the choice to become kings or messengers. Just like children they all chose to be messengers. For this reason, there are only messengers; they race through the world and, because there are no kings, they cry out to one another announcements that have become meaningless. They would happily put an end to their miserable life but because of their oath of office they don't dare.[66]

Geun Se would use the light-switches to send morse-code messages to the outside world. However, in the absence of an addressee, he is merely calling out "announcements that have become meaningless." Geun Se's liturgical fervor is juxtaposed to another reactionary practice: not giving a shit. For Ki-taek, hopelessness is the only truth worth proclaiming. Sharing his advice with his son, he reproduces the free-market economy's indictment of planned economy: "Ki-woo, do you know what kind of plan never fails? No plan at all. If you make a plan, life never works out that way." The depressing truth of his insight is, of course, that neither having nor not having a plan is up to us, and that resigning from (liturgical) labor does not absolve us from it, but rather employs us as officiants of "idle worship."[67]

Like Plato's cave-dwellers, Geun Se prefers remaining in the shadows, begging Ki-taek to let him stay. But the lumpenproletariat knows no solidarity and no class consciousness. At least not until the remarkable climax of the film. Ki-taek gags Geun Se, ties him up, and leaves him (and his wife, who is apparently dead) to rot in the bunker. The next day, during an impromptu birthday party, the blood-smeared Geun Se manages to get away, intent on hurting the Kims. In the crucial scene of the film, taking place in the garden, Geun Se is in a frenzy. The Kims and the Parks clearly see him as an impostor to be stopped. However, when Ki-taek observes Dong-ik's expression of disgust at Geun Se's odor, something is triggered in him, and he kills Dong-ik.

In Althusserian terms, Ki-taek—instead of being interpellated by the Subject, that is, by Donk-ik as the bearer of social authority—is interpellated by the abject (the smell, the stigma) undermining his recognition in the Subject. The scene hinges on the move from *ideological to psychoanalytic interpellation*, resolving Ki-taek's relation to the truth.[68] But what is this truth? Though incentivized by Geun Se's killing spree to form a provisional alliance with Dong-ik (an alliance that is ultimately but an extension of their existing social contract), the latter's olfactory disgust reminds Ki-taek that *there is no social relation*. Against the backdrop of this truth, for one fatal moment, the two lumpenproletarians are *untied together*.

The *Communist Manifesto* describes capitalist reality as a perpetually expanding smellscape, an age of perpetual dissipation, a new world odor. Within the capitalist system of desolidification, all "fixed, fast frozen relations, with their train of ancient and venerable prejudices and opinions, are swept away, all new-formed ones become antiquated before they can ossify. All that is solid melts into air."[69] In the midst of capitalist desolidification, its uninterrupted liquidation of all social conditions, the ephemeral smell-crumb abruptly, and provisionally, becomes something solid, a vehicle of an impossible solidarity. Ultimately, we can only hope to remove that classified smell by first grabbing on to it.

ACKNOWLEDGMENTS

I have written this book twice. The first version appeared in 2016 in the Slovenian book series Analecta, published by the Society for Theoretical Psychoanalysis in Ljubljana. The initial idea was to simply translate the work into English. However, it proved impossible to step into the same book twice. Not least because, strictly speaking, one cannot do it even once. In the course of writing the book anew, bits and pieces of the English manuscript appeared in journals *Problemi*, *Filozofski vestnik*, and *Cultural Critique*. I thank their respective editors for understanding the character of philosophical work, unfolding only in fits and starts, and hence for readily allowing me to rehash some of the ideas first presented in the pages of their journals.

Two books, two funding sources. The research presented here was made possible by the generous financial support by the Slovenian Research Agency and the Fulbright Program. Two funding sources, two institutions. I began working on the English manuscript during my four-year research stay at the University of Chicago and had finished it upon my return to the University of Ljubljana. The book bears marks of these distinctive intellectual environments, without which it would surely not have smelled the same.

I would like to express my thanks to everyone at Chicago's Department of Germanic Studies for so kindly welcoming me into their midst. I am particularly indebted to Eric Santner, who has supported me even when he had not yet had any real reason to. I consider this a mark of a true and lasting friendship. This book benefited greatly from several other scholars at Chicago, though I will limit myself to only mentioning two. A year after leaving Chicago, William Mazzarella invited me back to co-teach a graduate seminar on Walter Benjamin with him. William's attentiveness to new conceptual possibilities is only matched by the generosity of his inquisitive spirit. While at Chicago, I had the unique opportunity of auditing Moishe Postone's lectures on Marx. The Moses of political economy, Moishe stuttered when he first spoke my name

ACKNOWLEDGMENTS

(it's Hai-DEE-nee, by the way). His course influenced the analyses of political economy presented here, though we found ourselves in friendly and, at least for me, productive disagreements over the possibilities of a structuralist reading of Marx's *Capital*. It saddens me to think that, due to his death, I should now be granted the final word in the matter.

I owe a debt of gratitude to the People's Commissariat of Internal Affairs, that is, to Slavoj, Mladen, and Alenka, for their continuous support, now going back more than twenty years to my time as an undergraduate student. I'd also like to thank everyone at the MIT Press who had anything to do with making this book a reality, but especially to Thomas Weaver, Gabriela Bueno Gibbs, and Judy Feldmann for making sure, by an alchemy mysterious to me, that the process unfolded without leaving a single crease.

I have many more to thank, and if I am confining myself to merely listing their names, it is because their influence exceeds the limits of this book. In no particular order, I thank: Eric Powell, Jernej Habjan, Yuval Kremnitzer, Andrew Cutrofello, Eric Reinhart, Jean-Claude Milner, Daniel Chen, Hank Scotch, Joan Copjec, David Wellbery, Božena Shallcross, Katie Tucker Sorenson, Jean-Michel Rabaté, and Pam Pascoe. Finally, I owe everything, and everything else, to Lidija Šumah. Without her, nothing would have been possible. So as an obscenely inadequate token of my gratitude, I dedicate this book to her.

CHAPTER 1

1. The terms "proper name" and *nomen proprium* are used here in a loose sense of signifying correctness rather than the unique identity of a referent.

2. Our ability to name odors may depend on the language we speak. Some studies suggest that the problem of odor-naming is not universal. See, for instance, Constance Classen, David Howes, and Anthony Synnott, *Aroma: The Cultural History of Smell* (London: Routledge, 1994). Recent cross-cultural research shows odors play a significant role for the Jahai of the Malay Peninsula. Jahai speakers reportedly find it easy to name odors and have a variety of quality-specific words for them, consequently not having to rely on roundabout names. See Asifa Majid and Niclas Burenhult, "Odors Are Expressible in Language, as Long as You Speak the Right Language," *Cognition* 130 (2014): 266–270.

3. I am borrowing the term "signifying stress" from Eric Santner: "Thinking becomes a mode of attentiveness to a peculiar sort of address or apostrophe—to a *signifying stress*— immanent to our creaturely life. To use a Heideggerian locution, our *thrownness* into the world . . . means . . . that this social formation in which we find ourselves immersed . . . is itself haunted by a lack by which we are, in some peculiar way, addressed, 'excited,' to which we are in some fashion answerable." Eric L. Santner, "Miracles Happen: Benjamin, Rosenzweig, Freud, and the Matter of the Neighbor," in Slavoj Žižek, Eric L. Santner, and Kenneth Reinhard, *The Neighbor: Three Inquiries in Political Theology* (Chicago: University of Chicago Press, 2005), 86.

4. Two possible exceptions to this deadlock of linguistic coding of smells may come to mind: "stinky" and "fragrant." These, however, are not names for perceptual qualities, but rather hedonic values denoting the two extremes of the economic polarity of pleasure/unpleasure.

5. To compensate for the lack of proper names for smells, clumsy artificial terminologies were developed. See A. A. Brill, "The Sense of Smell in the Neuroses and Psychoses," *Psychoanalytic Quarterly* 1, no. 1 (1932): 41–42.

6. See chapter 15 of Carl Darling Buck, *A Dictionary of Selected Synonyms in the Principal Indo-European Languages: A Contribution to the History of Ideas* (Chicago: University of Chicago Press, 1949).

7. De anim. 2.9. All subsequent quotes reference the revised Oxford translation of Aristotle's *Complete Works* (Aristotle, *The Complete Works of Aristotle* [Princeton, NJ: Princeton University Press, 1995]).

8. Roman Jakobson, *On Language* (Cambridge, MA: Harvard University Press, 1990).

9. Jacques Lacan, "The Instance of the Letter in the Unconscious or Reason since Freud," in *Écrits*, trans. Bruce Fink (New York: W. W. Norton, 2006), 428–429.

10. Jakobson, *On Language*, 122. In *Texts for Nothing*, Samuel Beckett precisely captures this aphasic resistence to signification: "It's for ever the same murmur, flowing unbroken, like a single endless word and therefore meaningless, for it's the end that gives meaning to words." Samuel Beckett, *Texts for Nothing* (London: John Calder), 40.

11. Jakobson, *On Language*, 123.

12. The abundance of articles, published in major American newspapers, remembering this "unforgettable amnesiac" (as the *New York Times* described him) only days after his death in 2008, give us a good sense of H.M.'s notoriety. Unless lending their name to a disorder, a patient's fame very rarely exceeds that of those who treat them. Perhaps, though, Henry just hasn't found a doctor who would cast a long enough shadow for him to comfortably disappear in.

13. See Howard Eichenbaum, Thomas H. Morton, Harry Potter, and Suzanne Corkin, "Selective Olfactory Deficits in Case H.M.," *Brain* 106 (1983): 459–472. Suzanne Corkin treated or was involved in the treatment of H.M. for fifty years. See her extensive account of the case in Suzanne Corkin, *Permanent Present Tense: The Man with No Memory, and What He Taught the World* (London: Penguin Books, 2013).

14. The testing of H.M.'s olfactory perception was a "neuroscientific revelation": "The revelation for neuroscientists was that the brain circuit that is responsible for odor detection—*this bottle contains an odor*—and odor intensity discrimination—*this odor is stronger*—is separate from the circuit that supports odor discrimination—*this smells like cloves*. . . . Thanks to Henry, we now know that odor discrimination takes place in the front part of the parahippocampal gyrus, the amygdala, and the cortex around the amygdala. This ability to discriminate one odor from another and to recognize specific odors depended on these areas removed from Henry's brain, whereas the more elementary processes of detection, adaptation, and intensity discrimination relied on separate networks that were undisturbed." Corkin, *Permanent Present Tense*, 88.

15. Eichenbaum et al., "Selective Olfactory Deficits in Case H.M.," 467. See also Corkin, *Permanent Present Tense*, 87–89.

16. Claire Sulmont-Rossé, Sylvie Issanchou, and E. P. Köster, "Odor Naming Methodology: Correct Identification with Multiple-Choice versus Repeatable Identification in a Free Task," *Chemical Senses* 30, no. 1 (2005): 23. For a neurological account, see Benjamin D. Young, "Smell's Puzzling Discrepancy: Gifted Discrimination, Yet Pitiful Identification," *Mind & Language* 35, no. 1 (2020): 90–114. If the sense of smell is the lousiest of identifiers, we might be surprised to learn that it is an astoundingly accurate predictor of impending death. Scientists from the University of Chicago have shown that as an indicator of death in the next five years anosmia, that is, the loss of the sense of smell, only comes second to severe liver damage. See Jayant M. Pinto, Kristen E. Wroblewski, David W. Kern, L. Philip Schumm, and Martha K. McClintock, "Olfactory Dysfunction Predicts 5-Year Mortality in Older Adults," *PLOS ONE* 9, no. 10 (2014). Early in the COVID-19 pandemic, empirical studies revealed that the loss of smell is also the best predictor and indicator of COVID-19 infections. See Cristina Menni et al., "Real-Time Tracking of Self-Reported Symptoms to Predict Potential COVID-19," *Nature Medicine* 26 (2020): 1037–1040.

17. Eichenbaum et al., "Selective Olfactory Deficits in Case H.M.," 469.

18. Jakobson, *On Language*, 123. In his research into the forgetting of names, Freud highlights an analogous three-stage process. In place of the (1) forgotten name, (2) substitutes pop up, which the subject immediately recognizes as incorrect. However, (3) once the forgotten name is finally discovered, the subject recognizes it at once and is puzzled why she could not retrieve it before. See Sigmund Freud, *The Psychopathology of Everyday Life*, in *The Standard Edition of the Complete Psychological Works of Sigmund Freud*, vol. 6, trans. James Strachey (London: The Hogarth Press and The Institute of Psycho-Analysis, 2001), 2; henceforth cited as *SE*, followed by volume and page number.

19. I am borrowing Hegel's famous rendition of *Hic Rhodus, hic saltus* as "Here is the rose, dance here." G. W. F. Hegel, *Outlines of the Philosophy of Right*, trans. T. M. Knox (Oxford: Oxford University Press, 2008), 15.

20. That is, in none of the cases except for one: water, which is characteristically odorless. In the case of "water," the veridical label relates not to odor-identification but to odor-detection.

21. G. W. F. Hegel, *Phenomenology of Spirit*, trans. A. V. Miller (Oxford: Oxford University Press, 1977), 10.

22. *Crat.* 386e. Quoted from Plato's *Complete Works* (Indianapolis: Hackett, 1997). The *Cratylus* is translated by C. D. C. Reeve.

23. One must wonder what Platonic etymologies would say about the names of Plato's teachers. Do the names Cratylus and Socrates reflect the same essential being, possibly reducible to *kratos* ("power" or "strength")? And is "Plato" the name of the "distance" or "width" (from *platús*, "broad, wide") that spans between the two—their interface? In the *Cratylus*, at least, Plato's views in fact span both Cratylus's linguistic naturalism and the Socratic philosophy of the ultimately extralinguistic Forms.

24. Søren Kierkegaard, *Fear and Trembling*, in *Kierkegaard's Writings*, vol. 6, ed. and trans. Howard V. Hong and Edna H. Hong (Princeton, NJ: Princeton University Press, 1983), 123.

25. Jacques Lacan, *The Seminar of Jacques Lacan, Book II: The Ego in Freud's Theory and in the Technique of Psychoanalysis, 1954–1955*, trans. Sylvana Tomaselli, ed. Jacques-Alain Miller (New York: W. W. Norton, 1988), 71. As I attempt to show, defending Cratylus against Kierkegaard, Cratylus didn't really "go further instead of remaining standing there." His slogan was not "Don't just stand there, do something (move beyond your teacher's stance)," but rather "Don't just do something, stand there (push your teacher's stance to its extreme without abandoning it)!"

26. Søren Kierkegaard, *Repetition*, in *Repetition and Philosophical Crumbs*, trans. M. G. Piety (Oxford: Oxford University Press, 2009), 18. Incidentally, the book's epigraph by Flavius Philostratus makes mention of smell: "On wild trees the flowers are fragrant, on cultivated trees, the fruits." The motto relies on the opposition between wildflowers and cultivated fruits, ultimately between the nose and the mouth, smelling and eating. An earlier subtitle of Kierkegaard's *Repetition* read "A Fruitless Venture," hence a study of smelling rather than eating. Repetition, the narrator finds, is fruitless, impossible, yet it is precisely its fruitlessness that bears fruit (that is unconsumable). Repetition is barren in the sense of "not reproducing," of being incommensurable with reproduction, which is always a reproduction of the self-identical: we only ever repeat that which cannot be reproduced. As such, repetition is neither hope nor recollection. The latter are all too fruity: "Hope is an enticing fruit that fails to satisfy, recollection sorrowful sustenance that fails to satisfy." To will the fruitless flowers of repetition requires the courage of hopelessness: "It requires

youthfulness to hope and youthfulness to recollect, but it requires courage to will repetition. He who will only hope is cowardly." Kierkegaard, *Repetition*, 4.

27. By way of an example, think of the idiom "It is what it is," indicating the immutable nature of something. In Martin Scorsese's *The Irishman* (2019), the phrase is used at a crucial moment in the film to indicate that Jimmy Hoffa (Al Pacino) has run out of options and has no other choice but to yield to the demands of the heads of the crime families, surrendering to the immutable order of things. The phrase, repeated several times, is taken by Hoffa to mean that he is to make peace with his fellow union leader Anthony "Tony Pro" Provenzano (Stephen Graham), who has become the mafia's new favorite. However, despite the repetitive insistence that "it is what it is," the scheduled meeting is not at all what it is: instead of a meeting with Provenzano, the crime families have arranged for Hoffa's meeting with his executioner, his collaborator and friend Frank Sheeran (Robert De Niro). In his assessment of the phrase "It is what it is," Hoffa, a Union leader, represents the Eleatic Unity of Being, while Sheeran, knowing that "it" is never what "it" is, stands for the Cratylic splitting of the One. No wonder that Hoffa's end was brought about by the movement of a finger, that is, by Sheeran's pulling of the trigger at point-blank range.

28. Louis Althusser, *Philosophy of the Encounter: Later Writings, 1978–1987*, trans. G. M. Goshgarian (London: Verso, 2006), 265.

29. Paolo Virno, *An Essay on Negation: Towards a Linguistic Anthropology*, trans. Lorenzo Chiesa (Calcutta, London, and New York: Seagull Books, 2018), 182–183.

30. Althusser, *Philosophy of the Encounter*, 265. Singular words denoting singular entities, writes Althusser. If we define the singularity of smells as something inherently volatile and unstable, animated from one moment to the next by a different fleeting identity, thus resisting perceptual as well as linguistic containment, then, accordingly, this inherent instability of olfactory essences would immediately pass into an utter instability of language itself. Strictly speaking, such a language would be unspeakable.

31. For indication and designation, see Michel Foucault, *The Order of Things: An Archaeology of Human Sciences* (London: Routledge, 2002), 114–115.

32. Mary Ann Doane, "The Indexical and the Concept of Medium Specificity," *Differences* 18, no. 1 (2007): 136.

33. Charles S. Peirce, *Selected Philosophical Writings*, vol. 2: 1893–1913 (Bloomington: Indiana University Press, 1998), 9.

34. Jacques Lacan, *The Seminar of Jacques Lacan, Book III: The Psychoses, 1955–1956*, trans. Russell Grigg, ed. Jacques-Alain Miller (New York: W. W. Norton, 1993), 167.

35. Lacan, *The Seminar of Jacques Lacan, Book III*, 167.

36. Hegel, *Phenomenology of Spirit*, 64.

37. My critique of extralinguistic materialism does not posit the matter of language as the sole basis for materialism (or a materialism that *matters*). To anticipate: rather than situating matter in an extralinguistic realm, I first understand the extralinguistic matter as inherent to language—more precisely, as its subjectivizing effect—and, second, bring this divisive and divided subject-matter of language in relation to its indivisible excreta, or its excremental increments.

38. "Giving a fixed list of labels and verifying only whether participants choose the 'correct' one presupposes that everybody agrees on the same name for a given odor. In the case of odors, this assumption is not warranted. Indeed, while there is a strong social

pressure early in childhood to identify objects, colors or even sounds by consensual names, learning odor names occurs haphazardly in the course of olfactory experience. . . . Consequently, the language used to name odors is often idiosyncratic and lacks social agreement." Sulmont-Rossé, Issanchou, and Köster, "Odor Naming Methodology," 23.

39. Incidentally, Plato's discussion of names in the *Cratylus* already combines the two paradigms: adequation in relation to naturalism, and intersubjectivity in relation to conventionalism of the name, in turn opting for a kind of unconventional conventionalism of intersubjectivity and unnatural naturalism of adequation.

40. Richard L. Doty, Avron Marcus, and W. William Lee, "Development of the 12-Item Cross-Cultural Smell Identification Test (CC-SIT)," *Laryngoscope* 106, no. 3 (1996): 354.

41. One of Bette Howland's short stories begins with the words: "Aronesti disliked the smell of the house. It flagged a cue card at him: Nostalgia; but when he sniffed—'What is it? What is this smell? What do I remember?'—his imagination dived and skidded, like a false start in a dream." Nostalgia's rosy retrospection ultimately hinges on our failure to remember. See Bette Howland, "Aronesti," in *Calm Sea and Prosperous Voyage* (Brooklyn: A Public Space Books, 2019), 167.

42. Hans J. Rindisbacher, *The Smell of Books: A Cultural-Historical Study of Olfactory Perception in Literature* (Ann Arbor: University of Michigan Press, 1992), 212. The term "excarnation" was deployed by Eric Santner to account for the seismic shift in the functioning of sovereign power: "We will, in other words, be tracking in the domain of political economy what I have characterized as a surplus of immanence released into the social body by the ostensible 'excarnation' of sovereignty." Eric L. Santner, *The Weight of All Flesh: On the Subject-Matter of Political Economy* (Oxford and New York: Oxford University Press, 2016), 30. Also see Eric L. Santner, *The Royal Remains: The People's Two Bodies and the Endgames of Sovereignty* (Chicago: University of Chicago Press, 2011), 55, 96, 99.

43. The "Prefaces" to Proust's posthumously published *Against Sainte-Beuve*, containing early drafts of the first volume of *In Search of Lost Time*, initially mention "smell" (later crossed out and replaced with "taste") as triggering the "involuntary memory." Marcel Proust, *Against Sainte-Beuve and Other Essays*, trans. John Sturrock (London: Penguin Books, 1994), 3; see also chapter VII of "Autres manuscrits de Marcel Proust," in Marcel Proust, *Les soixante-quinze feuillets et autre manuscrits inédits* (Paris: Gallimard, 2021), e-book edition.

44. "But when from a long-distant past nothing subsists, after the people are dead, after the things are broken and scattered, taste and smell alone, more fragile but more enduring, more immaterial, more persistent, more faithful, remain poised a long time, like souls, remembering, waiting, hoping, amid the ruins of all the rest; and bear unflinchingly, in the tiny and almost impalpable drop of their essence, the vast structure of recollection." Marcel Proust, *In Search of Lost Time: The Complete Masterpiece*, trans. C. K. Scott Moncrieff (The Modern Library, 2012), e-book edition.

45. Proust, *In Search of Lost Time*.

46. Samuel Beckett, *Proust* (New York: Grove Press, 1957), 17.

47. In *Against Sainte-Beuve*, we read: "I soaked the toast in the cup of tea . . ." Proust, *Against Sainte-Beuve and Other Essays*, 3.

48. See Angelique Chrisafis, "Proust's Memory-Laden Madeleine Cakes Started Life as Toast, Manuscripts Reveal," *The Guardian*, October 19, 2015.

49. Josef Breuer and Sigmund Freud, *Studies on Hysteria*, SE 2: 7.

50. Freud, *The Interpretation of Dreams*, SE 5: 608.

51. Freud's first published history of a parapraxis, the analysis of the forgetting of the name Signorelli, appeared in the 1898 paper on "The Psychical Mechanism of Forgetfulness," which later became the opening chapter of *The Psychopathology of Everyday Life* (1901).

52. "I forgot *the one thing against my will* [the name Signorelli], while I wanted to forget *the other thing intentionally* [the repressed topic of death and sexuality]. The disinclination to remember was aimed against one content; the inability to remember emerged in another." Freud, *The Psychopathology of Everyday Life*, SE 6: 4. The parapraxis occurs on Freud's travels through my own Balkan neck of the woods, that is, during his trip from Ragusa (Dubrovnik in today's Croatia) to a place in Herzegovina. Illuminating the "other thing" intentionally forgotten, he recounts: "These Turks place a higher value on sexual enjoyment than on anything else, and in the event of sexual disorders they are plunged in a despair which contrasts strangely with their resignation towards the threat of death. One of my colleague's patients once said to him: '*Herr*, you must know that if *that* comes to an end then life is of no value.'" Freud, *The Psychopathology of Everyday Life*, SE 6: 3.

53. In *Proust and Signs*, Deleuze rightly points out apropos of *In Search of Lost Time* that "however important its role, memory intervenes only as the means of an apprenticeship that transcends recollection both by its goals and by its principles. The Search is oriented to the future, not to the past." Gilles Deleuze, *Proust and Signs*, trans. Richard Howard (London and New York: Continuum, 2008), 3–4.

54. Jakobson, *On Language*, 123.

55. For the *Nachdrängen*—*Urverdrängung* (after-pressure—primal repression) distinction, see, for instance, Freud's 1915 paper on "Repression." SE 14: 147.

56. "Repetition and recollection are the same movement, just in opposite directions, because what is recollected has already been and is thus repeated backwards, whereas genuine repetition is recollected forwards." Kierkegaard, *Repetition*, 3.

57. "The *Vorstellungsrepräsentanz* is the binary signifier. / This signifier constitutes the central point of *Urverdrängung*— . . . the point of *Anziehung*, the point of attraction, through which all the other repressions will be possible." Jacques Lacan, *The Seminar of Jacques Lacan, Book XI: The Four Fundamental Concepts of Psychoanalysis*, trans. Alan Sheridan, ed. Jacques-Alain Miller (New York: W. W. Norton, 1998), 218.

58. Is there such a thing as one's real name? And is one's real name something given to us, or something taken by us? Names given and names taken: Robert Zimmerman and Bob Dylan, Cassius Clay and Muhammad Ali, Saloth Sâr and Pol Pot, Saul and Paul . . . and finally, Aristocles and Plato. Would Platonism by the name Aristocleianism smell the same? And what was it that triggered Plato's rebranding in the first place? Did Cratylus, his teacher, inform him that "Aristocles" wasn't his real name? And doesn't any teacher worthy of their name effect a rebranding of their pupils that befits their non-identity-with-themselves, that is, their new subjectivization?

59. See Jacques-Alain Miller, "Matrix," trans. D. G. Collins, *Lacanian Ink* 12 (1997): 45–51.

60. "A and A are the same, with Nothing between them [*avec un Rien de difference*]. One can say, an entity including N is split, that is to say, at a distance from itself, constrained to repeat itself. Its N unceasingly separates from it, and it unceasingly reabsorbs its N." Miller, "Matrix," 45.

61. G. W. F. Hegel, *Science of Logic*, trans. A. V. Miller (New York: Routledge, 2010), 82–83. For a detailed reading of this passage, see Mladen Dolar, "Being and MacGuffin," *Crisis and Critique* 4, no. 1 (2017): 83–101.

62. Eric L. Santner, *Untying Things Together: Philosophy, Literature, and a Life in Theory* (Chicago: University of Chicago Press, 2022).

63. According to Heine, in 1831, on his deathbed, Hegel uttered these last words: "only one man ever understood me, and he didn't understand me." The only one who understood him while misunderstanding him was, of course, Hegel himself. Thus, his last words spell out the coda of his philosophy: reflexive opposition. See Heinrich Heine, *Zur Geschichte der Religion und Philosophie in Deutschland*, in *Historisch-kritische Gesamtausgabe der Werke*, vol. 8/1 (Hamburg: Hoffmann und Campe, 1979), 92. It was Bertolt Brecht who first fleshed out the idea of reflexive opposition from within Hegel's dialectic by noting that Hegel "contested the idea that one equals one, not only because everything that exists changes inexorably and relentlessly into something else—namely its opposite—but because *nothing is identical with itself*." Bertolt Brecht, *Refugee Conversations*, trans. Romy Fursland (London: Methuen, 2019), 62.

64. Jean-Claude Milner, *Le périple structural* (Paris: Éditions du Seuil, 2002), 164–165. Hans J. Rindisbacher noticed the connection between Saussurian ontology and modernist "surfacing of the olfactory": "The epoch of taming by naming is thus coming to its end, historically as well as ontologically. The naming authority, the subject, has organized the world along lines still adhered to on the day-to-day basis of a realism that has become our reality, and of the adult linguistic curtailment of sensory experience that has turned into our everyday iron cage of perception. It has set things and itself in relation to one another, but now begins to lose its identity. De Saussure's name stands for the first linguistic thrust in this direction, probing the margins of language and the object world; and Rilke is the first author in German to compose this new subject in prose." Rindisbacher, *The Smell of Books*, 206.

65. See Jacques Lacan, *The Seminar of Jacques Lacan, Book I: Freud's Papers on Technique, 1953–1954*, trans. John Forrester, ed. Jacques-Alain Miller (New York: W. W. Norton, 1991), 178, 219.

66. Slavoj Žižek, *The Indivisible Remainder: On Schelling and Related Matters* (London: Verso, 1996).

67. I borrow this turn of phrase from Santner: "we never cease becoming unconscious of what has no part in the field of knowledge." Eric L. Santner, "The Rebranding of Sovereignty in the Age of Trump," in William Mazzarella, Eric L. Santner, and Aaron Schuster, *Sovereignty, Inc.: Three Inquiries in Politics and Enjoyment* (Chicago: University of Chicago Press, 2020), 65.

68. "The gap of the unconscious may be said to be *pre-ontological*. . . . Indeed, what became at first apparent to Freud . . . is that it is neither being, nor non-being, but the unrealized." Lacan, *The Seminar of Jacques Lacan, Book XI*, 29–30.

69. Georges Didi-Huberman, "The Index of the Absent Wound (Monograph on a Stain)," *October* 29 (1984): 68. Also cited in Doane, "The Indexical and the Concept of Medium Specificity," 135.

70. "In the realm of perfumes, the odors . . . are not attributable to identifiable objects. Odors are in some way separated from their primary referents and therefore lose their informative-cognitive potential. They become *pure sensory qualities*." André Holley, "Cognitive Aspects of Olfaction in Perfumery," in *Olfaction, Taste, and Cognition*, ed. Catherine Rouby et al. (Cambridge: Cambridge University Press, 2002), 16–17; my emphasis.

71. Karl Marx, *Capital: A Critique of Political Economy*, vol. 1, trans. Ben Fowkes (London and New York: Penguin Books in association with New Left Review, 1976), 128.

72. Compare the German word for "odorant," *Geruchsstoff*, literally "smell-stuff."

73. For the concept of scientific literalization, see Jean-Claude Milner, "Back and Forth from Letter to Homophony," *Problemi International* 1 (2017): 93–94, 96–97.

74. Jacques-Alain Miller, "Elements of Epistemology," trans. Leonardo S. Rodriguez, *Analysis* 1 (1989): 33–34.

75. Gilles Deleuze, *The Logic of Sense*, trans. Mark Lester with Charles Stivale (New York: Columbia University Press, 1990), 23.

76. Gilles Deleuze and Félix Guattari, *Kafka. Pour une littérature mineure* (Paris: Minuit, 1975), 35.

77. "What is it precisely which I find intolerable? That which I cannot deal with alone, which makes me choke and faint? Bad air! Bad air! That something foul comes near me; that I must inhale the putrid odour of the entrails of a rotten soul!" Friedrich Nietzsche, *On the Genealogy of Morals*, trans. Michael A. Scarpitti (London: Penguin, 2013), "First Essay," §12. Nietzsche attributed the greatest value to the nose's prophylactic capacity for sniffing out the bullshit of Socratic philosophy, Christianity, and the German spirit alike, giving vent to his destructive love so as to air out the oppressively suffocating history of the West. As opposed to *Nächstenliebe*, the charitable "love of the neighbor," or literally "love of the proximate, the adjacent, the nearby," Nietzsche's tough love is *Fernstenliebe*, meaning "love of the farthest," a love requiring air and distance, an open-air love. With Nietzsche, smell becomes the philosophical sense par excellence. The nose knows, and to get to the truth, one must follow one's nose: "I was the first to *discover* the truth by being the first to experience lies as lies—smelling them out.—My genius is in my nostrils." Friedrich Nietzsche, *Ecce Homo*, trans. Walter Kaufmann (New York: Vintage Books, 1989), 326.

78. See Saul Kripke, *Naming and Necessity* (Cambridge, MA: Harvard University Press, 1980).

79. See Slavoj Žižek, *On Belief* (London: Routledge, 2001); Slavoj Žižek, *The Puppet and the Dwarf: The Perverse Core of Christianity* (Cambridge, MA: MIT Press, 2003).

CHAPTER 2

1. See Élisabeth Roudinesco, *Freud in His Time and Ours*, trans. Catherine Porter (Cambridge, MA: Harvard University Press, 2016), 230.

2. Recall Freud's thesis on the timelessness of the unconscious. In Kantian terms, the unconscious escapes the a priori forms of sensible experience.

3. "The pre-scientific view of dreams adopted by the peoples of antiquity was certainly in complete harmony with their view of the universe in general, which led them to project into the external world as though they were realities things which in fact enjoyed reality only within their own minds. Moreover, their view of dreams took into account the principal impression . . . of something alien, arising from another world and contrasting with the remaining contents of the mind. Incidentally, it would be a mistake to suppose that the theory of the supernatural origin of dreams is without its supporters in our own days." Freud, *The Interpretation of Dreams*, SE 5: 4.

4. At the beginning of his text, Freud strings together a series of dictionary definitions of this enigmatic German word, addressing the juncture of the ordinary and the occult: "*Heimlich*; adj. and adv. *vernaculus, occultus*; MHG. heimelîch, heimlîch. . . . *Heimlich*, as used of knowledge—mystic, allegorical; a *heimlich* meaning, *mysticus, divinus, occultus, figuratus*." Freud, "The Uncanny," SE 17: 225–226.

5. Freud, "The Future of an Illusion," SE 21: 27–28.

6. "Occultism is the metaphysics of dunces." Theodor W. Adorno, *Minima Moralia: Reflections from Damaged Life*, trans. E. F. N. Jephcott (London: Verso Books, 2005), 241.

7. See Jason Josephson-Storm, *The Myth of Disenchantment: Magic, Modernity, and the Birth of the Human Sciences* (Chicago: University of Chicago Press, 2017).

8. Roudinesco inscribes psychoanalysis into the history of the "dark Enlightenment" (see Roudinesco, *Freud in His Time and Ours*, 215–232).

9. John Maynard Keynes, "Newton, the Man," in *The Collected Writings of John Maynard Keynes*, vol. 10 (Cambridge: Cambridge University Press, 2013), 363–364.

10. See Jean Starobinski, *Words upon Words: The Anagrams of Ferdinand de Saussure* (New Haven, CT: Yale University Press, 1979).

11. See Emanuel Swedenborg, *Heaven and Hell*, trans. George F. Dole (West Chester: The Swedenborg Foundation, 2010).

12. André Breton, *Communicating Vessels*, trans. Mary Ann Caws and Geoffrey T. Harris (Lincoln: University of Nebraska Press, 1990), 152.

13. I am referring to Freud's infamous reply to Marie Bonaparte: "The great question that has never been answered and which I have not yet been able to answer, despite my thirty years of research into the feminine soul, is 'What does a woman want?'" Cited in Ernest Jones, *The Life and Work of Sigmund Freud*, vol. 2 (New York: Basic Books, 1955), 421. For a study of occultist surrealism, see Tessel M. Bauduin, *Surrealism and the Occult: Occultism and Western Esotericism in the Work and Movement of André Breton* (Amsterdam: Amsterdam University Press, 2014).

14. "This mysterious power (which is even now often described popularly as 'animal magnetism') must be the same power that is looked upon by primitive people as the source of taboo, the same that emanates from kings and chieftains and makes it dangerous to approach them (*mana*)." Freud, "Group Psychology and the Analysis of the Ego," SE 18: 125.

15. Freud, "New Introductory Lectures on Psycho-Analysis," SE 18: 34.

16. "The ideal condition of things would of course be a community of men who had subordinated their instinctual life to the dictatorship of reason. Nothing else could unite men so completely and so tenaciously, even if there were no emotional ties between them. But in all probability that is a Utopian expectation." Freud, "Why War?" SE 22: 213. Elsewhere, Freud opposes the dictatorship of reason to the religious prohibition against thought: "Our best hope for the future is that intellect—the scientific spirit, reason—may in process of time establish a dictatorship in the mental life of man." Freud, "New Introductory Lectures on Psycho-Analysis," SE 18: 171.

17. Adorno, *Minima Moralia*, 283–239. Adorno's thesis is analogous to Eric Santner's genealogical project of the psychotheology of everyday life, deriving the modern processes of democratization and secularization of power from the doctrine of the royal two bodies. Santner's central thesis is that with the onset of modernity, the king's second, sublime body as the bearer of his power is not simply eliminated but rather dispersed across the body of the population. The localized spirit of the One is dissociated into a multitude of spirits henceforth haunting the modern world; monotheism is supplanted by manatheism. See Santner, *The Royal Remains*; Ernst H. Kantorowicz, *The King's Two Bodies: A Study in Mediaeval Political Theology* (Princeton, NJ: Princeton University Press, 2016). For the term "manatheism," see Eric L. Santner, "Marx and Manatheism," *Problemi International* 3 (2019): 27–38.

18. Ernest Jones, *The Life and Work of Sigmund Freud*, vol. 3 (New York: Basic Books, 1957), 379.

19. Octave Mannoni, "I Know Well, but All the Same . . . ," trans. G. M. Goshgarian, in *Perversion and the Social Relation*, ed. Molly Anne Rothenberg, Dennis Foster, and Slavoj Žižek (Durham, NC: Duke University Press, 2003), 68–92.

20. Jones, *The Life and Work of Sigmund Freud*, vol. 3, 376–377. Flournoy, Myers, and James greatly influenced the surrealist concept of the "creative unconscious." See Claudie Massicotte, "Spiritual Surrealists: Séances, Automatism, and the Creative Unconscious," in *Surrealism, Occultism and Politics: In Search of the Marvellous*, ed. Tessel M. Bauduin et al. (New York: Routledge, 2018).

21. Adorno, *Minima Moralia*, 242.

22. Ernest Jones, *The Life and Work of Sigmund Freud. Edited and Abridged in One Volume by Lionel Trilling and Steven Marcus* (New York: Basic Books, 1961), 190–191.

23. See Jones, *The Life and Work of Sigmund Freud. Edited and Abridged in One Volume*, 205. Marie Bonaparte reports: "The friendship with Fliess began to decline as early as 1900, . . . when Freud published the book on dreams. Freud had not realized this! I taught it to him. His friendship with Fliess made him reluctant to impute envy to Fliess. Fliess could not bear the superiority of his friend. Nor could he tolerate, this time according to Freud, Freud's scientific criticisms . . . Ida Fliess, moreover, . . . out of jealousy, did everything possible to sow discord between the two friends, whereas Martha Freud understood very well that Fliess was able to give her husband something beyond what she could." Bonaparte interprets the declining friendship as follows: "As for bisexuality, if Fliess was the first to talk about it to Freud, he could not pretend to priority in this idea of biology. 'And if he gave me bisexuality, I gave him sexuality before that.' That is what Freud told me." Cited in Sigmund Freud, *The Complete Letters of Sigmund Freud to Wilhelm Fliess: 1887–1904*, trans. Jeffrey Moussaieff Masson (Cambridge, MA: The Belknap Press of Harvard University Press, 1985), 3, 4.

24. Jones, *The Life and Work of Sigmund Freud. Edited and Abridged in One Volume*, 188.

25. See Wilhelm Fliess, *Die Nasale Reflexneurose* (Wisbaden: JF Bergman, 1893).

26. Jones, *The Life and Work of Sigmund Freud. Edited and Abridged in One Volume*, 189.

27. Jones, *The Life and Work of Sigmund Freud*, vol. 3, 382–383. It is no coincidence that Freud should numerologize in correspondence with Jung (whose penchant for the occult is well known) and Ferenczi (who entertained a strong interest in spiritism, devoting to this topic his first paper, published in 1899).

28. Freud, "Notes Upon a Case of Obsessional Neurosis," *SE* 10: 247–248.

29. Lacan, "The Freudian Thing, or the Meaning of the Return to Freud in Psychoanalysis," in *Écrits*, 342.

30. Patrick Süskind, *Perfume: The Story of a Murderer*, trans. John E. Woods (London: Penguin Books, 2006), 3.

31. When referring to the original text, I am using the 2012 e-book edition of Patrick Süskind, *Das Parfum: Die Geschichte eines Mörders* (Zürich: Diogenes Verlag, 1985).

32. Süskind, *Perfume*, 185.

33. Süskind, *Perfume*, 145.

34. Süskind, *Perfume*, 30.

35. Süskind, *Perfume*, 30.

36. Süskind, *Perfume*, 27.

37. Süskind, Perfume, 27.

38. Süskind, Perfume, 28–29.

39. Süskind, Perfume, 29.

40. Like smells themselves, Grenouille is an *orphaned bastard*, his father unknown, his mother decapitated almost immediately after his birth when found guilty of "multiple infanticide." Süskind, Perfume, 6. Perhaps a recent study can help link his infanticide-driven mother to the fact of Grenouille being odorless: a newborn's *odorless* smell called hexadecanal makes mothers *more aggressive*. See Eva Mishor et al., "Sniffing the Human Body Volatile Hexadecanal Blocks Aggression in Men but Triggers Aggression in Women," *Science Advances* 7, no. 47 (2021): 1–13.

41. Süskind, Perfume, 48.

42. Süskind, Perfume, 173.

43. Süskind, Perfume, 156.

44. Apart from the nose gaining renewed prominence as the predictor of COVID-19 infections, the elbow too has acquired new relevance during the pandemic. The new etiquette entailed replacing the handshake with the elbow bump and, when coughing or sneezing, replacing the tissue with the crook of the elbow.

45. "The crook of your elbow is not just a plain patch of skin. It is a piece of highly coveted real estate, a special ecosystem, a bountiful home to no fewer than six tribes of bacteria. Even after you have washed the skin clean, there are still one million bacteria in every square centimeter." Nicholas Wade, "Bacteria Thrive in Inner Elbow; No Harm Done," *New York Times*, May 23, 2008.

46. Gilles Deleuze, Foucault, trans. Seán Hand (Minneapolis: University of Minnesota Press, 2006), 96–97, 100.

47. For the notion of "the extimate," see Jacques Lacan, *The Seminar of Jacques Lacan, Book VII: The Ethics of Psychoanalysis, 1959–1960*, trans. Dennis Porter, ed. Jacques-Alain Miller (London: Routledge, 1992), 139.

48. Süskind, Perfume, 173–174.

49. For the triumph of the gaze over the eye, see Lacan, *The Seminar of Jacques Lacan, Book XI*, 103.

50. Freud, Civilization and Its Discontents, SE 21: 91–92.

51. Süskind, Perfume, 46. Proust, too, takes his crumbs soaked, though in tea rather than milk. Before settling on the definitive source-name, Proust's crumbs, too, were associated with honey in the form of honey-mixed toast.

52. Süskind, Perfume, 44.

53. Süskind, Perfume, 30.

54. The smell-crumb fits Jean-Luc Nancy's notion of bodily discharge as "almost nothing, only an accent, a wrinkle, an irreplaceable feature. . . . It's not the body's soul, but its *spirit*: its point, its signature, its smell." Jean-Luc Nancy, *Corpus*, trans. Richard A. Rand (New York: Fordham University Press, 2008), 155.

55. See Michel Serres, *The Birth of Physics* (Manchester: Clinamen Press, 2000).

56. Süskind has perfumers pray to St. Joseph, their patron saint. Süskind, Perfume, 258. St. Joseph happens to also be the patron saint of expectant mothers and hence of the unborn.

57. Süskind, Perfume, 46.

58. Jacques Lacan, The Seminar of Jacques Lacan, Book XX: On Feminine Sexuality: The Limits of Love and Knowledge, 1972–1973, trans. Bruce Fink, ed. Jacques-Alain Miller (New York: W. W. Norton, 1998), 59–60.

59. Philip Roth, Portnoy's Complaint (New York: Vintage, 1994), 5.

60. Jean-Jacques Rousseau, Emile or On Education, trans. Allan Bloom (New York: Basic Books, 1979), 156.

61. Süskind, Perfume, 46, 45.

62. Süskind, Perfume, 47.

63. Jacques Lacan, The Seminar of Jacques Lacan, Book X: Anxiety, trans. A. R. Price, ed. Jacques-Alain Miller (Cambridge: Polity Press, 2014), 76. To briefly return to Eve again, Kierkegaard ascribes to her a "presentiment of a disposition" for sin. As a woman, she is also closer to anxiety. See Søren Kierkegaard, The Concept of Anxiety, in Kierkegaard's Writings, vol. 8, ed. and trans. Reidar Thomte in collaboration with Albert B. Anderson (Princeton, NJ: Princeton University Press, 1980), 47. In Paradise Lost, Milton relates the Christian doctrine of the Fall to Eve's olfactory temptation: "Fixt on the Fruit she gaz'd, which to behold / Might tempt alone, and in her ears the sound / Yet rung of his perswasive words, impregn'd / With Reason, to her seeming, and with Truth; / Mean while the hour of Noon drew on, and wak'd / An eager appetite, rais'd by the smell / So savorie of that Fruit, which with desire, / Inclinable now grown to touch or taste, / Sollicited her longing eye; yet first / Pausing a while, thus to her self she mus'd." John Milton, Paradise Lost (Malden: Blackwell, 2007), 237.

64. Süskind, Perfume, 44–45.

65. Süskind, Perfume, 139, 250.

66. Rainer Maria Rilke, The Notebooks of Malte Laurids Brigge, trans. Michael Hulse (London: Penguin Books, 2009), 42.

67. Descartes writes that endeavoring to use one's imagination to understand the ideas about God and the soul is tantamount to smelling with one's eyes. René Descartes, A Discourse on the Method, trans. Ian Maclean (Oxford: Oxford University Press, 2006), 32.

68. "We are driven to conclude," Freud writes, "that the death drives are by their nature mute [stumm] and that the clamour of life proceeds for the most part from Eros." Freud, "The Ego and the Id," SE 19: 46; translation amended.

69. Rilke, The Notebooks of Malte Laurids Brigge, 42.

70. Rilke, The Notebooks of Malte Laurids Brigge, 42.

71. From the atomic laminar flow via the clinamen to Democritus's den: "It required a clinamen, an inclination, at some point. When Democritus tried to designate it, presenting himself as already the adversary of a pure function of negativity in order to introduce thought into it, he says, It is not the $\mu\eta\delta\acute{\epsilon}\nu$ that is essential, and adds—it is not an $\mu\eta\delta\acute{\epsilon}\nu$, but a $\delta\epsilon\nu$, which in Greek, is a coined word. . . . What, then, did he say? He said . . . not perhaps nothing, but not nothing." Lacan, The Seminar of Jacques Lacan, Book XI, 63–64. Logically speaking, "not no-thing" is not "some-thing," meaning that the theorem $\neg\neg p \equiv p$ does not apply. See Simon Hajdini, "Varieties of Negation: From Drizzle and Decaf to the Anti-Semitic Figure of the Jew," Lacanian Ink 51 (2018): 108–127. For an illuminating Lacanian reading of ancient atomism, see Mladen Dolar, "The Atom and the Void—from Democritus to Lacan," Filozofski vestnik 34, no. 2 (2013): 11–26.

72. Jones, The Life and Work of Sigmund Freud, vol. 3, 376.

73. Süskind, *Perfume*, 48.

74. Süskind, *Perfume*, 48.

75. Kaja Silverman claims that Adam "understands that she is flesh of his flesh, but not that he is flesh of hers." Silverman's analysis focuses on Adam's self-understanding, disregarding the question of how Eve might have related to him. See Kaja Silverman, *Flesh of My Flesh* (Stanford: Stanford University Press, 2009), 40.

76. Süskind, *Perfume*, 49.

77. Süskind, *Perfume*, 49–50.

78. Süskind, *Perfume*, 248.

79. Süskind, *Perfume*, 255; my emphasis. We can imagine Grenouille agreeing with Kierkegaard: "I like lettuce, but I only eat the heart; the leaves, it seems to me, are for pigs." Kierkegaard, *Repetition*, 12.

80. Süskind, *Perfume*, 213.

81. Süskind, *Perfume*, 111.

82. Süskind, *Perfume*, 228.

83. The murderous pitting of the virgin is her *deflowering*. Curiously, flower is euphemistic of the vulva: "my virgin-flower was yet uncrop'd." John Cleland, *Fanny Hill: Memoirs of a Woman of Pleasure* (Ware: Wordsworth Classics, [1749] 1993), 43. In line with Kierkegaard's epigraph to *Repetition*, the act of deflowering is an act of cultivation, whereby the "sweet smell of virginity" is replaced by the *cloaca* of sexuality. See, for instance, the traditional duality between the "sweet smell of virginity" (παρθενικὴ εὐωδία) and the "foul smell of fornication" (πορνικὴ δυσωδία). Dirk Krausmüller, "Smell of Sweat, Smell of Semen: The Divinisation of the Body Fluids in Patriarch Methodius's Life of Theophanes of Agros," *Parekbolai* 11 (2021): 9–33.

84. G. W. F. Hegel, *Vorlesungen über die Ästhetik I*, in *Werke*, vol. 13 (Frankfurt am Main: Fischer Verlag, 1970), 184; *Aesthetics: Lectures on Fine Art*, trans. T. M. Knox (Oxford: Clarendon Press, 1975), 138. Only volatile substances, soluble in mucus, can reach and interact with the receptors, producing olfactory sensations. Until the very recent, and strikingly belated, discovery of odorant receptors and the ways in which they organize the olfactory system, we had no real understanding of olfactory perception. In 2004, the Nobel Prize in Physiology was awarded to Richard Axel and Linda Buck for this discovery (first made in 1991).

85. Franz Kafka, "A Hunger Artist," in *The Complete Stories*, trans. Willa and Edwin Muir (New York: Schocken Books, 1971), 268–277.

86. Michel de Montaigne, *The Complete Essays of Montaigne*, trans. Donald M. Frame (Stanford: Stanford University Press, 1958), 228.

87. Proust, *In Search of Lost Time*.

88. Max Horkheimer and Theodor W. Adorno, *Dialektik der Aufklärung. Philosophische Fragmente* (Frankfurt am Main: Fischer Verlag, 2006), 193; *Dialectic of Enlightenment: Philosophical Fragments*, trans. Edmund Jephcott (Stanford: Stanford University Press, 2007), 151.

89. The duality can be developed further via the distinction between hole and surface. Nancy writes apropos of visual perception: "But slits, holes, and zones do not present things to be seen . . . vision does not penetrate, but glides. . . . It is a touching that does not absorb." Nancy, *Corpus*, 45.

90. Süskind, *Perfume*, 28.

91. Süskind, Perfume, 50–51.

92. Henry T. Fincks, "The Gastronomic Value of Odours," Contemporary Review 50 (1886): 680.

93. See Meredith L. Blankenship et al., "Retronasal Odor Perception Requires Taste Cortex but Orthonasal Does Not," Current Biology 29, no. 1 (2019): 62–69.

94. Süskind, Perfume, 296.

95. Freud, Totem and Taboo, SE 13: 82.

96. Freud, Totem and Taboo, SE 13: 142.

97. Kierkegaard, Repetition, 6.

98. Kierkegaard, Repetition, 7.

99. Kierkegaard, Repetition, 8.

100. Kierkegaard, Repetition, 7, 9.

101. "He did not really love her, but only longed for her. . . . The young girl was not his beloved, she was simply the cause that awakened the poetic in him and thus transformed him into a poet. . . . She had permeated every aspect of his being. . . . She had made him into a poet, and with this signed her own death-sentence." Kierkegaard, Repetition, 9.

102. Lacan, The Seminar of Jacques Lacan, Book XI, 273.

103. Süskind, Perfume, 295.

104. Lacan, The Seminar of Jacques Lacan, Book XI, 194.

105. "This is what Freud tells us. Let us look at what he says—As far as the object in the drive is concerned, let it be clear that it is, strictly speaking, of no importance. It is a matter of total indifference." Lacan, The Seminar of Jacques Lacan, Book XI, 168.

106. For Freud, the initial murder of the primal father establishes the bond of kinship between the murderous sons. The subsequent totemic meals recapitulate this kinship: "But why is this binding force attributed to eating and drinking together? In primitive societies there was only one kind of bond which was absolute and inviolable—that of kinship. The solidarity of such a fellowship was complete. . . . Thus kinship implies participation in a common substance. It is therefore natural that it is not merely based on the fact that a man is a part of his mother's substance, having been born of her and having been nourished by her milk, but that it can be acquired and strengthened by food which a man eats later and with which his body is renewed. If a man shared a meal with his god he was expressing a conviction that they were of one substance; and he would never share a meal with one whom he regarded as a stranger." Freud, Totem and Taboo, SE 13: 134–135.

107. Freud, Three Essays on the Theory of Sexuality, SE 7: 182.

108. Freud, Three Essays on the Theory of Sexuality, SE 7: 222.

109. Freud, Three Essays on the Theory of Sexuality, SE 7: 179–180, 182.

110. H. Varendi, R. H. Porter, and J. Winberg, "Does the Newborn Baby Find the Nipple by Smell?" The Lancet 344, no. 8928 (1994): 989–990. Another experiment excluded other maternal stimuli as possible causes of the attraction. H. Varendi and R. H. Porter, "Breast Odor as the Only Maternal Stimulus Elicits Crawling Towards the Odor Source," Acta Paediatrica 90, no. 4 (2001): 372–375. The infant's olfactory attraction to the breast is considered inborn and spontaneous, but the odor cues remain unidentified. They may be similar to the odor of amniotic fluid surrounding the growing fetus in the womb, significantly marking its intrauterine "experience." See Maryse Delaunay-El Allam, Luc Marlier, and Benoist Schaal, "Learning at the Breast: Preference Formation for an Artificial Scent and

Its Attraction Against the Odor of Maternal Milk," *Infant Behavior and Development* 29, no. 3 (2006): 308–321; Julie A. Mennella, Catherine A. Forestell, and M. Yanina Pepino, "The Flavor World of Infants," *Dysphagia* 12, no. 4 (2003): 13. Additionally, studies indicate that breast-fed neonates recognize their mother's unique olfactory signature. R. H. Porter and J. Winberg, "Unique Salience of Maternal Breast Odors for Newborn Infants," *Neuroscience and Biobehavioral Review* 23, no. 3 (1999): 439. Freud could be right in more ways than one: their finding of the breast truly is a re-finding of the object lost at birth, though they may no longer bathe in it, only get a whiff of it: "Whenever the membranes of the egg in which the foetus emerges on its way to becoming a new-born are broken, imagine for a moment that something flies off." Lacan, *The Seminar of Jacques Lacan, Book XI*, 197.

111. "The breast is also something superimposed, who sucks what?—the organism of the mother." Lacan, *The Seminar of Jacques Lacan, Book XI*, 195.

112. Jacques-Alain Miller succinctly distinguishes between the object of satisfaction and satisfaction qua object: "That is what I would like to propose today, as a definition of Lacan's object *a*: object *a* is satisfaction as an object. Just as we distinguish between instinct and drive, we have to distinguish between the chosen object and the libido object, the latter being *satisfaction qua object*." Jacques-Alain Miller, "On Perversion," in *Reading Seminars I and II: Lacan's Return to Freud*, ed. Richard Feldstein et al. (Albany: SUNY Press, 1996), 313.

113. Mennella, Forestell, and Pepino, "The Flavor World of Infants," 13.

114. Lacan establishes a relation of equivalence between prenatal and postpartum states: the infant's parasitical relation to the breast is prefigured by the fetus's parasitical relation to the placenta. See Lacan, "Position of the Unconscious," in *Écrits*, 719.

115. Lacan, *The Seminar of Jacques Lacan, Book XI*, 268.

116. Immanuel Kant, *The Metaphysics of Morals*, trans. and ed. Mary Gregor (Cambridge: Cambridge University Press, 1996), 127.

117. See Jean-Claude Milner, "Reflections on the Me Too Movement and Its Philosophy," *Problemi International* 3 (2019): 65–87.

118. Milner, "Reflections on the Me Too Movement and Its Philosophy," 69.

119. Lucretius, *On the Nature of the Universe*, trans. Ronald Melville (New York: Oxford University Press, 1997), §§1091–1120.

120. By circumventing the pitfalls of the two paradigms, the contractual form promises to realize Lucretius's vision of sexual union: "By two hearts breathing as one in mutual passion, and neither masters the other nor is mastered." Lucretius, *On the Nature of the Universe*, §§1217–1218.

121. Marx, *Capital*, vol. 1, 126.

122. Marx, *Capital*, vol. 1, 128.

123. Marx quotes Boisguillebert: "'Money . . . has become the executioner of everything.' Finance is 'the alembic in which a frightful quantity of goods and commodities has been distilled in order to extract that unholy essence.'" Marx, *Capital*, vol. 1, 239, n. 56.

124. Hegel, *Aesthetics*, 37; translation corrected.

125. Theodor W. Adorno, *Negative Dialectics*, trans. E. B. Ashton (New York: Continuum, 2007), 139.

126. The English word "taste" is derived from *tangere* (to touch).

127. "What comes between in the case of sounds is air; the corresponding medium in the case of smell has no name." Aristotle, "On the Soul," 419a. Is the excarnated flesh the true medium of smell? In accordance with his *sarxism* (from *sarx*, "flesh"), Eric Santner posits

the flesh as the "*medium in which* our precious subject-matter circulates and in which our fundamental social bonds are sealed." Santner, *The Royal Remains*, 30.

128. Immanuel Kant, *Anthropology from a Pragmatic Point of View*, trans. Robert B. Louden (Cambridge: Cambridge University Press, 2006), 46.

129. Kant, *Anthropology from a Pragmatic Point of View*, 50; Immanuel Kant, *Anthropologie in pragmatischer Hinsicht*, in *Werkausgabe*, vol. 12 (Frankfurt am Main: Suhrkamp Verlag, 1977), 452.

130. Kant, *Anthropology from a Pragmatic Point of View*, 50; Kant, *Anthropologie in pragmatischer Hinsicht*, 452.

131. "The untouchable is the fact that it touches," writes Nancy, signaling the fact that touching only ever touches on the untouchable. Nancy, *Corpus*, 135.

132. The olfactory nerve's direct exposure to the environment makes it a handy pathway for viral infections, though the "mechanisms of transport via the olfactory nerve and subsequent spread through the CNS [central nervous system] are poorly understood." One possible transport is by *microfusion*. Debby Van Riel, Rob Verdijk, and Thijs Kuiken, "The Olfactory Nerve: A Shortcut for Influenza and Other Viral Diseases into the Central Nervous System," *Journal of Pathology* 235, no. 2 (2015): 277–287. COVID-19 infection frequently results in anosmia. Up until recently, the scientists struggled to determine whether the virus damages the nose, the brain, or both. The most current research suggests that the ongoing loss of smell is the result of nasal cell destruction triggered by an abnormal immune response. See John B. Finlay et al., "Persistent Post-COVID-19 Smell Loss Is Associated with Immune Cell Infiltration and Altered Gene Expression in Olfactory Epithelium," *Science Translational Medicine* 14, no. 676 (2022).

133. I am referring to Quentin Meillassoux's famous criticism of "correlationism": "For it could be that contemporary philosophers have lost the *great outdoors*, the *absolute* outside of pre-critical thinkers: that outside which was not relative to us, and which was given as indifferent to its own givenness to be what it is, existing in itself regardless of whether we are thinking of it or not; that outside which thought could explore with the legitimate feeling of being on foreign territory—of being entirely elsewhere." Quentin Meillassoux, *After Finitude: An Essay on the Necessity of Contingency*, trans. Ray Brassier (London: Continuum, 2008), 7.

134. Robert Mandrou, *Introduction to Modern France, 1500–1640: An Essay in Historical Psychology* (New York: Holmes & Meier, 1976), 54.

135. Moreover, there is no lip-kiss without a sniff-kiss: "Then his father Isaac said to him [that is, to Jacob posing as his brother Esau]: 'Come near and kiss me, my son.' So he came near and kissed him. And Isaac smelled the smell of his garments and blessed him and said, 'See, the smell of my son is as the smell of a field that the LORD has blessed!'" Gen. 27: 26–27.

136. E. Washburn Hopkins, "The Sniff-Kiss in Ancient India," *Journal of the American Oriental Society* 28 (1907): 120–121. Incidentally, Proust's *petites madeleines* episode, centered on smell, immediately follows the descriptions of the childhood drama of Mamma's goodnight kiss.

137. Horkheimer and Adorno, *Dialectic of Enlightenment*, 151.

138. Lucretius, *On the Nature of the Universe*, §1120. "Trauma" comes from Ancient Greek τραῦμα, "wound."

139. Søren Kierkegaard, *Either/Or: Part I*, trans. Howard V. Hong and Edna H. Hong (Princeton, NJ: Princeton University Press, 1988), 119–120.

140. Claude Lévi-Strauss, *The Naked Man: Introduction to a Science of Mythology: 4*, trans. John and Doreen Weightman (New York: Harper & Row, 1981), 656.

141. See Etienne Bonnot de Condillac, *Condillac's Treatise on the Sensations* (Los Angeles: School of Philosophy, University of Southern California, 1930).

142. For Kierkegaard, music is encircled by two silences. It is only "where language leaves off [that] I find the musical." Kierkegaard, *Either/Or: Part I*, 69. The silencing of language (its negation) is the beginning of the musical. This beginning is then followed by a second silencing (negation of negation): music finds its full realization only in the silencing of the musical, that is, in the silencing of the silencing of language.

143. "Language addresses itself to the ear. No other medium does this. The ear, in turn, is the most spiritually qualified sense. Most people, I believe, will agree with me on this point. . . . Apart from language, music is the only medium that is addressed to the ear." Kierkegaard, *Either/Or: Part I*, 68.

144. See Mladen Dolar, *A Voice and Nothing More* (Cambridge, MA: MIT Press, 2006), 171.

145. Franz Kafka, "Investigations of a Dog," in *The Complete Stories*, 282. The final part of the quote ("so near that they seemed far away") repeats the point made by Kierkegaard: "I . . . am close enough to hear and yet so infinitely far away." Kierkegaard, *Either/Or: Part I*, 120.

146. Kafka, "Investigations of a Dog," 284.

147. Kafka, "Investigations of a Dog," 280.

148. Kafka, "Investigations of a Dog," 281.

149. Kafka, "Investigations of a Dog," 291.

150. Kafka, "Investigations of a Dog," 291.

151. Kafka, "Investigations of a Dog," 280.

152. Kafka, "Investigations of a Dog," 282.

153. Kafka, "Investigations of a Dog," 281.

154. Kafka, "Investigations of a Dog," 279.

155. My analysis of Kafka's story is inspired by Dolar's illuminating reading of it. Dolar, *A Voice and Nothing More*, 161, 180–188.

156. "Besides, although what struck me most deeply at first about these dogs was their music, their silence seemed to me still more significant." Kafka, "Investigations of a Dog," 315.

157. Kafka, "Investigations of a Dog," 280.

158. Kafka, "Investigations of a Dog," 281.

159. Kafka, "Investigations of a Dog," 283.

160. Kafka, "Investigations of a Dog," 283.

161. Kafka, "Investigations of a Dog," 288.

162. Kafka, "Investigations of a Dog," 309.

163. Kafka, "Investigations of a Dog," 281.

164. Kafka, "Investigations of a Dog," 309.

165. Kafka, "Investigations of a Dog," 310–311.

166. Kafka, "Investigations of a Dog," 311.

167. Horkheimer and Adorno, *Dialectic of Enlightenment*, 151.

168. Kafka, "Investigations of a Dog," 315.

169. Kafka, "Investigations of a Dog," 287.

170. Kafka, "Investigations of a Dog," 287.

171. Kafka, "Investigations of a Dog," 304.

172. Friedrich Engels, *Dialectics of Nature*, trans. Clemens Dutt (London: Lawrence and Wishart, 1946), 285.

173. Kafka, "Investigations of a Dog," 287.

174. J. G. Fichte, *Foundations of Natural Right According to the Principles of Wissenschaftslehre*, trans. Michael Baur, ed. Frederick Neuhouser (Cambridge: Cambridge University Press, 2000), 77.

175. Fichte, *Foundations of Natural Right*, 77.

176. Kafka, "Investigations of a Dog," 282.

177. Kafka, "Investigations of a Dog," 283–284.

178. Kafka's *canis erectus* is distinguished from its ancestor, the *canis ferus*, by the three key characteristics attributed by Carl Linné (in the 1758 edition of the *Systema Naturae*) to Homo ferus, the "feral man," the supposed missing link in human evolution. Like Linné's *Homo ferus*, the *canis ferus* is *tetrapus* (four-legged), *mutus* (mute, or, in Kafka's case, unmusical), and *hirsutus* (hairy).

179. Kafka, "Investigations of a Dog," 282.

180. Kafka, "Investigations of a Dog," 284.

181. Kafka, "Investigations of a Dog," 283, 285.

182. Kafka, "Investigations of a Dog," 304.

183. Kafka, "Investigations of a Dog," 316.

184. Johann Gottfried Herder, *Outlines of a Philosophy of the History of Man*, trans. T. Churchill (New York: Bergman Publishers, 1966[?]), 92.

185. Fichte, *Foundations of Natural Right*, 77.

186. See Lacan, "Presentation on Psychical Causality," in *Écrits*, 152; Lacan, "Position of the Unconscious," in *Écrits*, 719.

187. Kafka, "Investigations of a Dog," 312.

188. See M. M. Fichter, "Franz Kafkas Magersucht," *Fortschritte der Neurologie-Psychiatrie* 56, no. 7 (1988): 231–238.

189. Kafka, "A Hunger Artist," 277.

190. Kafka, "A Hunger Artist," 277.

CHAPTER 3

1. The latter endeavor is reminiscent of the esoteric ideas of biodynamic agriculture developed in 1924 by Rudolf Steiner.

2. Süskind, *Perfume*, 162.

3. Süskind, *Perfume*, 160.

4. Süskind, *Perfume*, 162.

5. Süskind, *Perfume*, 163.

6. Süskind, *Perfume*, 167.

7. Alain Corbin, *The Foul and the Fragrant: Odor and the French Social Imagination* (Leamington Spa: Berg Publishers, 1986), 16.

8. Freud, *The Complete Letters of Sigmund Freud to Wilhelm Fliess*, 278; letter dated November 14, 1897.

9. Freud was mistaken. On November 12, 1897, Mercury was not in conjunction with Venus but with Mars. A makeshift analysis of the error proves salient: the feminine symbol (Venus) is substituted for the masculine one (Mars).

10. Freud, *The Complete Letters of Sigmund Freud to Wilhelm Fliess*, 278.

11. "The question of the erect gait of the anthropoid apes became a very important issue in the eighteenth century. Indeed, the erect posture of *humans themselves* came into dispute. In 1771 the Italian Pietro Moscati argued that humans were by nature quadrupeds; their original constitution entailed walking on all fours. Hence, it was a *cultural deviation*—and one with significant costs in human health—to assume an upright gait." John H. Zammito, *The Gestation of German Biology: Philosophy and Physiology from Stahl to Schelling* (Chicago: University of Chicago Press, 2018), 195. In the osmological narrative, the advent of bipedalism effects a loss as its negative determinant. Same holds for Plato's famous definition of the human as a *featherless biped* (Stm. 266): with man's assumption of the erect posture, something is shed, and no feather is left to tickle man's nose.

12. Entry "Odorat" of the *Encyclopédie* (supplement, 1777). Cited in Corbin, *The Foul and the Fragrant*, 6.

13. Herder, *Outlines of a Philosophy of the History of Man*, 85–86. If man, Freud dixit, is a prosthetic God, then the hands are his first prostheses, the first instruments of his "second nature." To think is to "incessantly *feel after* new and clear ideas." Etymologically, "to conceive" (*con-capio, begreifen*) is "to take in," "to grasp," "to take a hold of." With smell losing its sway, sight, (conceptual) touch, and language gain the upper hand: "But Nature has constructed man for the use of language: for this he is framed erect, and his vaulted breast is placed on a column. . . . There may, there must be superior creatures, whose reason looks through the eye, a visible character being sufficient for them to form and discriminate ideas: but the man of this world is a pupil of the ear, which first teaches him gradually to understand the language of the eye." Herder, *Outlines of a Philosophy of the History of Man*, 89. Thus the philosophical salience of the senses of sight, touch, and hearing is thought to result from a denigration of smell.

14. Immanuel Kant, "Reviews of Herder's Ideas on the Philosophy of the History of Mankind," in *Political Writings*, ed. H. S. Reis (Cambridge: Cambridge University Press, 2013), 204–205.

15. Fichte, *Foundations of Natural Right*, 77. Retracing the entire early history of this, for all intents and purposes, homogeneous narrative concerning hominization would require us to write a separate book. But let us haphazardly add one final reference. In the already cited chapter IX of his *Dialectics of Nature*, titled "The Part Played by Labour in the Transition from Ape to Man," Engels recounts a whopping narrative, deriving all key events in the history of the human species from bipedalism as "*the decisive step in the transition from ape to man*." By this process, "*the hand became free* and could henceforth attain ever greater dexterity and skill. . . . No simian hand has ever fashioned even the crudest stone knife," let alone "conjure into being the pictures of Raphael, the statues of Thorwaldsen, the music of Paganini." This "development of labour necessarily helped to bring the members of society closer together," and so "men in the making arrived at the point where *they had something to say* to one another. . . . First comes labour, after it, and then side by side with it, articulate speech." And so on. (Engels, *Dialectics of Nature*, 279–284.)

16. Immediately preceding this sentence, Freud inserts a curiously lengthy description of Bellevue's smellscape: "Otherwise life at Bellevue is turning out to be very pleasant for

everyone. The evenings and mornings are enchanting; the scent of lilac and laburnum has been succeeded by that of acacia and jasmine; the wild roses are in bloom and everything, as I too notice, happens suddenly." Was the famous dream triggered by a smell-crumb? (Freud, *The Complete Letters of Sigmund Freud to Wilhelm Fliess*, 417; letter dated June 12, 1900.)

17. Freud, *The Interpretation of Dreams*, SE 5: 107.

18. "The scabs on the turbinal bones recalled a worry about my own state of health. I was making frequent use of cocaine at that time to reduce some troublesome nasal swellings, and I had heard a few days earlier that one of my women patients who had followed my example had developed an extensive necrosis of the nasal mucous membrane. I had been the first to recommend the use of cocaine, in 1885, and this recommendation had brought serious reproaches down on me. The misuse of that drug had hastened the death of a dear friend of mine. This had been before 1895 [the date of the dream]." Freud, *The Interpretation of Dreams*, SE 5: 111.

19. Max Schur, *Freud: Living and Dying* (New York: International Universities Press, 1972), 79–87.

20. Freud, *The Interpretation of Dreams*, SE 5: 116.

21. Freud, *The Interpretation of Dreams*, SE 5: 116.

22. Lacan, *The Seminar of Jacques Lacan, Book II*, 158.

23. Lacan, *The Seminar of Jacques Lacan, Book II*, 159.

24. Lacan, *The Seminar of Jacques Lacan, Book II*, 158.

25. J. M. Brand and R. P. Galask, "Trimethylamine: The Substance Mainly Responsible for the Fishy Odor Often Associated with Bacterial Vaginosis," *Obstetrics & Gynecology* 68, no. 5 (1986): 682–685.

26. Grenouille's mother was a fish seller, delivering her baby in her fish booth, amid "fish guts that lay there already," and cutting the umbilical cord with her fish knife. The scene takes place at the Cimetière des Innocents, "the most putrid spot in the whole kingdom." But the malodor comes from rotten fish rather than rotting corpses: "The fish . . . stank so vilely that the smell masked the odour of corpses." Süskind, *Perfume*, 5. Grenouille is born and dies in this same spot. Is the formula of trimethylamine the hermetic, enigmatic answer to the question of the meaning of Süskind's novel?

27. William Shakespeare, *The Tempest*, act 2, scene 2, lines 26–29.

28. Stephen C. Mitchell and Robert L. Smith, "Trimethylamine—The Extracorporeal Envoy," *Chemical Senses* 41 (2016): 275–279.

29. Lacan, *The Seminar of Jacques Lacan, Book II*, 160.

30. "The libido is the essential organ in understanding the nature of the drive. This organ is unreal [*irréel*]. Unreal is not imaginary. The unreal is defined by articulating itself on the real in a way that eludes us, and it is precisely this that requires that its representation should be mythical." Lacan, *The Seminar of Jacques Lacan, Book XI*, 205.

31. Freud, "New Introductory Lectures on Psycho-Analysis," SE 18: 95.

32. Lacan, *The Seminar of Jacques Lacan, Book XI*, 197–198. Lacan's lamella is clearly inspired by Freud's zoological analogy to the processes of libidinal investment: "Thus we form the idea of there being an original libidinal cathexis of the ego, from which some is later given off to objects, but which fundamentally persists and is related to the object-cathexes much as the body of an amoeba [*Protoplasmatierchen*] is related to the pseudopodia which it puts out." Freud, "On Narcissism: An Introduction," SE 14: 75.

33. I am referring to Derrida's rendering of pure auto-affection: hearing oneself speak is the minimal mark of consciousness. See Jacques Derrida, *Voice and Phenomenon: Introduction to the Problem of the Sign in Husserl's Phenomenology*, trans. Leonard Lawlor (Evanston: Northwestern University Press, 2011).

34. Jacques-Alain Miller, "Suture (Elements of the Logic of the Signifier)," *Screen* 18, no. 4 (1977–1978): 28–29.

35. Jean-Claude Milner, *L'Œuvre claire: Lacan, la science, la philosophie* (Paris: Éditions du Seuil, 2015), 129.

36. Milner, *Le périple structural*, 165.

37. Lacan, "The Freudian Thing," in *Écrits*, 341.

38. Lacan, "The Freudian Thing," in *Écrits*, 340.

39. Lacan, "The Freudian Thing," in *Écrits*, 340.

40. Lacan, "The Freudian Thing," in *Écrits*, 342.

41. Hegel, *Aesthetics*, 361.

42. "Adequation" comes from the Latin *ad-aequre* (to make equal). Claiming that what is at stake in an *inadequate* thought is a relation of non-equivalence, is to some degree true but inaccurate. Inadequation is not a mere absence of equivalence, let alone an absence of a relation. Standing for the relation of opposition rather than that of equivalence, inadequation refers solely to entities that are reflexively opposed, that is, self-differing.

43. This paradigm is, once again, best exemplified by Nietzsche who had a good nose for the truth—that is, a good nose for the stinking mirage-like truth, as well as for the truth secreted by the mirage-like truth in the process of establishing itself as the truth of the mirage: "I hear and smell it." Friedrich Nietzsche, *Thus Spoke Zarathustra*, trans. Graham Parkes (Oxford: Oxford University Press, 2005), 156. On the very first page of *Dawn*, Nietzsche identifies with the mole. Visually impaired, the mole isn't relying on eyesight, but for this very reason sees farther, all the way to the new dawn. Friedrich Nietzsche, *Dawn: Thoughts on the Presumptions of Morality*, trans. Brittain Smith (Stanford: Stanford University Press, 2011), 1. In the *Eighteenth Brumaire*, Marx equated this visually impaired creature with the revolution, quoting Shakespeare's *Hamlet*: "But the revolution is thoroughgoing. . . . And when it has done this second half of its preliminary work, Europe will leap from its seat and exultantly exclaim: Well grubbed, old mole!" Karl Marx, *The Eighteenth Brumaire of Louis Bonaparte* (New York: International Publishers, 1975), 121.

44. Lacan, *The Seminar of Jacques Lacan, Book XI*, 49.

45. Claude Lévi-Strauss, *Introduction to the Work of Marcel Mauss*, trans. Felicity Baker (London: Routledge & Kegan Paul, 1987), 62.

46. Lacan, *The Seminar of Jacques Lacan, Book XI*, 36.

47. Lacan, "Presentation on Psychical Causality," in *Écrits*, 125.

48. The unconscious knows no time, Freud tells us. The thesis regarding the timelessness of the unconscious entails a reflexive loop: on the one hand, it radically desubstantializes the unconscious, which lacks support in time as the substance of things; on the other hand, it desubstantializes time itself by confronting us with a temporal mode that is at odds with the Kantian identity of time and substance.

49. Lacan, *The Seminar of Jacques Lacan, Book XI*, 51.

50. "Our experience then presents us with a problem, which derives from the fact that, at the very heart of the primary processes, we see preserved the insistence of the trauma in making us aware of its existence." Lacan, *The Seminar of Jacques Lacan, Book XI*, 55.

51. Robert Pfaller, *On the Pleasure Principle in Culture: Illusions Without Owners*, trans. Lisa Rosenblatt, with Charlotte Eckler and Camilla Nielsen (London: Verso, 2014).

52. Catherine Malabou, *The New Wounded: From Neurosis to Brain Damage*, trans. Steven Miller (New York: Fordham University Press, 2012), xv.

53. Malabou, *The New Wounded*, xiv.

54. Malabou, *The New Wounded*, 9.

55. Louis Crocq, *Les traumatismes psychiques de guerre* (Paris: Odile Jacob, 1999), 270. Cited in Malabou, *The New Wounded*, 153.

56. Lacan, "The Instance of the Letter in the Unconscious or Reason since Freud," in *Écrits*, 430. Lacan returns to Descartes's cogito on various occasions, which are best presented in Mladen Dolar, "Cogito as the Subject of the Unconscious," in *Cogito and the Unconscious*, ed. Slavoj Žižek (Durham, NC: Duke University Press, 1998), 11–40.

57. "At this point, there springs up a misunderstood form of the un, the Un of the *Unbewusste*. Let us say that the limit of the *Unbewusste* is the *Unbegriff*—not the non-concept, but the concept that is lacking." Lacan, *The Seminar of Jacques Lacan, Book XI*, 26; translation amended.

58. Lacan makes use of the concept of anamorphosis within the context of subverting traditional metaphysical notions of seeing and the gaze as relating to the cognitive process. Here, the gaze is not on the side of the Spirit gazing at and contemplating the external object from a distance. Rather, the gaze is the crack of exteriority or the anamorphic stain of objectivity. Smell presents us with the anamorphic mechanism in its pure form. The stain of objectivity is not dependent on the perspective that the subject assumes in relation to it: in this precise sense, the olfactory stain cannot be destained or deanamorphosized. For an insightful reading of the concept of anamorphosis, see Mladen Dolar, "Anamorphosis," *S: Journal of the Circle for Lacanian Ideology Critique* 8 (2015): 125–140.

59. Lacan, "The Freudian Thing," in *Écrits*, 342.

60. Blaise Pascal, *Pensées*, trans. Roger Ariew (Indianapolis: Hackett Publishing, 2004), 6.

61. Mladen Dolar, *Prozopopeja* (Ljubljana: Society for Theoretical Psychoanalysis, 2006), 125.

62. Freud, "On the Universal Tendency to Debasement in the Sphere of Love," *SE* 11: 189.

63. Pascal, *Pensées*, 16.

64. J. W. Goethe, *Autobiographische Schriften* 2, in *Werke*, vol. 10 (Hamburg: Beck, 2002), 546. Reportedly, Napoleon placed great emphasis on odors: "Napoleon was very sensitive to odors and always masked unpleasant ones with large quantities of Cologne water. Mereschowskij quotes him as saying about Corsica: 'I would recognize my land of birth with my eyes closed, solely and alone by its odor.'" Brill, "The Sense of Smell in the Neuroses and Psychoses," 30–31.

65. The episode ended with Napoleon's retreat. There was no getting rid of the nose. Perhaps it was precisely as missing that the nose began deciding the fate of Napoleon's army.

66. Lacan, "The Freudian Thing," in *Écrits*, 342.

67. "Essential for the Greek concept of fate and its historical change is the relation to the concept of Necessity (Ananke). From Homer to Aeschylus, Moira has the character of Ananke. The archaic connection of destiny and necessity is later supplanted by the conceptual connection of chance and necessity." Dieter Bremer, "Der Begriff des Schicksals bei Hegel und seine griechische Ursprünge," *Antike und Abendland* 35 (1989): 26.

68. Lacan, *The Seminar of Jacques Lacan, Book XI*, 53.

69. Lacan, "The Freudian Thing," in Écrits, 342.

70. "The most extraordinary case seemed to me to be one in which a young man had exalted a certain sort of 'shine on the nose' into a fetishistic precondition. The surprising explanation of this was that the patient had been brought up in an English nursery but had later come to Germany, where he forgot his mother-tongue almost completely. The fetish, which originated from his earliest childhood, had to be understood in English, not German. The 'shine [Glanz] on the nose'—was in reality a 'glance at the nose'. The nose was thus the fetish, which, incidentally, he endowed at will with the luminous shine which was not perceptible to others." Freud, "Fetishism," SE 21: 152.

71. Lacan, "The Freudian Thing," in Écrits, 342.

72. Freud first published his case study of the Rat Man in 1909. After his death, the original notes on the case were discovered among Freud's papers, escaping his habit of destroying any analysis-related materials upon its publication. In these notes, the capacity to identify people based on their odor is described in more detail: "He turns out to be a renifleur. In his youth he was able to recognize people by the smell of their clothes; he could distinguish family smells, and he got positive pleasure from the smell of women's hair." Freud, "Addendum: Original Record of the Case," SE 10: 295.

73. In "Dreams and Telepathy," for instance, Freud quotes a letter from his female patient: "I have extraordinarily keen powers of observation, and quite exceptionally sharp hearing, also a very keen sense of smell. With my eyes bandaged I can pick out by smell people I know from among a number of others." Freud, "Dreams and Telepathy," SE 18: 212.

74. Freud, "Notes Upon a Case of Obsessional Neurosis," SE 10: 247–248.

75. Freud, "On the Universal Tendency to Debasement in the Sphere of Love," SE 11: 189.

76. Kafka, "Investigations of a Dog," 304.

77. Freud, Civilization and Its Discontents, SE 21: 98.

78. Freud, Civilization and Its Discontents, SE 21: 99, note. Shame is the negative of modesty and decency. Prior to Freud, Herder had already established a link between the advent of bipedalism and the birth of decency or "modesty, which, in consequence of the erect posture, cannot fail to be developed at an early period." Herder, Outlines of a Philosophy of the History of Man, 95.

79. Freud, Civilization and Its Discontents, SE 21: 100, note.

80. Samo Tomšič defines this duality in precise terms: "The inner moments of every concrete act of repression are originary repression (the constitution of the repressed) and the labour of repression (the satisfaction of the repressed tendency)." Samo Tomšič, The Capitalist Unconscious: Marx and Lacan (London: Verso, 2015), 140.

81. To avoid translating Freud's term triebhaft with "instinctual," the adjective "libidinous" is used.

82. Nancy concisely sums up such prohibitive disgust: "The body's exteriority and alterity include the unbearable: dejection, filth, the ignoble waste that is still part of it, still belongs to its substance and especially its activity, since it has to expel it, which is not one of its lesser functions. From excrement to the outgrowth of nails, hairs, or every kind of wart or purulent malignity, it has to put outside, and separate from itself, the residue or excess of its assimilatory processes, the excess of its own life. The body doesn't want to say, see, or smell this. It feels shame about it, and all kinds of daily distress and embarrassment. The soul enjoins itself to silence concerning a whole part of the body whose own form it is." Nancy, Corpus, 157.

83. Horkheimer and Adorno, *Dialectic of Enlightenment*, 151.

84. "Two hundred fifty-four subjects responded. Ninety-one percent were current nose pickers although only 75% felt 'almost everyone does it'; 1.2% picked at least every hour. For 2 subjects (0.8%), nose picking caused moderate to marked interferences with daily functioning. Two subjects spent between 15 and 30 minutes and 1 over 2 hours a day picking their nose. For 2 others, perforation of the nasal septum was a complication." J. W. Jefferson and T. D. Thompson, "Rhinotillexomania: Psychiatric Disorder or Habit?" *Journal of Clinical Psychiatry* 56, no. 2 (1995): 56–59.

85. Sylvia Plath, *The Unabridged Journals of Sylvia Plath, 1950–1962* (New York: Anchor Books, 2000), e-book edition. Let us briefly return to the Theosophical Society. Rudolf Steiner, perhaps the most famous Austrian occultist (born in Donji Kraljevac in today's Croatia), was one of the Theosophical Society's most notorious members. In 1911, Steiner gave a series of lectures in Prague. At least one of these lectures was attended by Kafka, who reports on visiting Steiner in his room at hotel Victoria. Kafka's visit was prompted by his personal experiences of clairvoyance that echo his job as an insurance agent, that is, a professional clairvoyant. Of interest to us here is the curious concluding section of Kafka's report that focuses on Steiner's nose-picking: "He listened very attentively without apparently looking at me at all, entirely devoted to my words. He nodded from time to time, which he seems to consider an aid to strict concentration. At first a quiet head cold disturbed him, his nose ran, he kept working his handkerchief deep into his nose, one finger at each nostril." Franz Kafka, *The Diaries 1910–1923*, trans. Joseph Kresh and Martin Greenberg (New York: Schocken Books, 1976), e-book edition. Following this report, Kafka indicatively adds a short passage on the Jewish question. The poisonous connection between Judaism and the physiognomy of the nose is well known, and so is Steiner's poisonous anti-Semitism. Does Steiner's nose-picking not betray his libidinally displaced desire of expunging the Jew in front of him, flicking him to the floor like a booger?

86. Freud, "On the Universal Tendency to Debasement in the Sphere of Love," *SE* 11: 188–189.

87. Freud, *Civilization and Its Discontents*, *SE* 21: 105.

88. Freud, *Civilization and Its Discontents*, *SE* 21: 106, note.

89. With the emergence of the erect posture, the genitals are not only revealed but move to the coronal plane. And so do the perennially enlarged breasts in women—a characteristic singular among primates.

90. As early as 1905, Freud notes in his analysis of "Dora": "Such feelings of [disgust] seem originally to be a reaction to the smell (and afterwards also to the sight) of excrement." Freud, "Fragment of an Analysis of a Case of Hysteria," *SE* 7: 31. Here again it is necessary to oppose the idea of maturation, development or progress, supposedly beginning with the "less developed" organ of smell, which (to paraphrase Marx) shows to the "more developed" eye its own future. There is no "natural metamorphosis" of the drives; their gradation is a matter of logical priority, not natural generation: "There is no relation of production between one of the partial drives and the next." Lacan, *The Seminar of Jacques Lacan, Book XI*, 180.

91. The Slovenian word for "swear word" (*psovka*) is etymologically related to "dog" (*pes*). Freud, *Civilization and Its Discontents*, *SE* 21: 101, note; Sigmund Freud, *Das Unbehagen in der Kultur*, in *Gesammelte Werke*, vol. 14 (Frankfurt am Main: Suhrkamp Verlag, 1999), 459, note.

92. Toilet culture is the minimal mark of culture. Early in the COVID-19 pandemic, prior to the first lockdowns, we witnessed the deranged spectacle of people panic-buying toilet paper, causing its subsequent shortages. But given the fundamental role played by the

norm of hiding one's excreta in human societies, the panic-buying of toilet paper must be understood as a desperate defense of culture and civilized life in the moment of their perceived disintegration.

93. Kant, *Anthropology from a Pragmatic Point of View*, 50; Kant, *Anthropologie in pragmatischer Hinsicht*, 452.

94. Similarly, Freud claims in 1893, referencing "an English writer," that "the man who first flung a word of abuse at his enemy instead of a spear was the founder of civilization." Freud, "On the Psychical Mechanism of Hysterical Phenomena: A Lecture," SE 3: 36. The etymology of "touch" confirms the link: "to touch" is "to strike, offend" (from Vulgar Latin *tuccō*). For a long time, Freud's reference remained obscure. In 1962, Ola Andersson traced the witticism back to a Hughlings-Jackson paper Freud was familiar with, having quoted it in his aphasia-book: "It has been said that he who was the first to abuse his fellow-man instead of knocking out his brains without a word, laid thereby the basis of civilization." The reference does not help in tracking down the source, for Hughlings-Jackson, too, is quoting. The search was impossible to begin with: no authorship can be ascribed to such a feat. Ola Andersson, *Studies in the Prehistory of Psychoanalysis. The Etiology of Psychoneuroses and Some Related Themes in Sigmund Freud's Scientific Writings and Letters, 1886–1896* (Uppsala: Norstedt, 1962), 109–110; John Hughlings-Jackson, "On Affections of Speech from Disease of the Brain," *Brain* 2, no. 3 (1879): 216, note.

95. Freud, *Totem and Taboo*, SE 13: 29; translation amended. In Strachey's translation, the first sentence reads: "the patient shows a strong *desire* to touch," though Freud is not discussing a particular case here: "Zu allem Anfang, in ganz früher Kinderzeit, äußerte sich eine starke Berührungslust, deren Ziel weit spezialisierter was, als man geneigt wäre zu erwarten." Sigmund Freud, *Totem und Tabu*, in *Gesammelte Werke*, vol. 9 (Frankfurt am Main: Suhrkamp Verlag, 1999), 39.

96. Freud, *Totem and Taboo*, SE 13: 29, note 1.

97. In a generalized sense, Freud ascribes to *tasten* a key role in the process of sense-perception, understanding it as ego's palpating sampling of external stimuli (not limited to tactile perception in the strict sense). As such, palpating is a function of the pleasure principle and not a vehicle of enjoyment. See Freud, "Negation," SE 19: 238–239.

98. As already noted, in his *Outlines of a Philosophy of the History of Man*, Herder ascribes great importance to the evolutionary emergence of "free and skillful hands," directly relating it to the advent of bipedalism. Hands, and particularly the fingers, are organs of the *sense of feeling*, not of touch: "the hands have fingers endued with the sense of feeling," "an den Händen sein fühlende Finger." Herder, *Outlines of a Philosophy of the History of Man*, 68; Johann Gottfried Herder, *Ideen zur Philosophie der Geschichte der Menschheit* (Frankfurt am Main: Deutscher Klassiker Verlag, 1989), 112.

99. Freud, *Three Essays on the Theory of Sexuality*, SE 7: 209–210; Sigmund Freud, *Drei Abhandlungen zur Sexualtheorie*, in *Gesammelte Werke*, vol. 5 (Frankfurt am Main: Suhrkamp Verlag, 1999), 111.

100. Freud, *Three Essays on the Theory of Sexuality*, SE 7: 156; Freud, *Drei Abhandlungen zur Sexualtheorie*, 55.

101. Returning to all things "incompatible with our aesthetic standards of culture," as Freud understands it, we can observe how *tastelessness* as a negative measure of public decorum, or *sensus decori*, is distributed among the physical senses. Take, for instance, the role ascribed by Kant to the policing power of the state: "The police look after public security, convenience and also propriety; for it makes it much easier for the government to perform its business of governing the people by laws if the public sense of propriety (*sensus*

decori—a negative taste) is not dulled by affronts to the moral sense such as begging, uproar in the streets, offensive smells [*Gestank*] and public prostitution [*öffentliche Wollust*] (*venus volgivaga*)." Kant, *The Metaphysics of Morals*, 149. Note the sensorial distribution of the offensively tasteless or the publicly untouchable (*to touch is to offend*): *the eye* (offended by begging), *the ear* (offended by the uproar in the streets), *the nose* (offended by stench), *the sense of touch* (offended by public displays of sexual impropriety). Smell, however, displays a logical priority: the enumerated public affronts to the moral sense force us to co-enjoy.

102. Dolar, *A Voice and Nothing More*, 78–79.

103. Freud, *Jokes and Their Relation to the Unconscious*, SE 8: 97.

104. Freud, *Jokes and Their Relation to the Unconscious*, SE 8: 97.

105. Freud, *Jokes and Their Relation to the Unconscious*, SE 8: 98.

106. In the passage from the jokes-book, Freud is a bit more reserved, speaking of "a hypothetical primary desire to touch." Freud, *Jokes and Their Relation to the Unconscious*, SE 8: 98.

107. Freud, *Jokes and Their Relation to the Unconscious*, SE 8: 97.

108. Freud, *Civilization and Its Discontents*, SE 21: 106, note.

109. "*Mulier tum bene olet, ubi nihil olet*," writes Plautus in *Mostellaria*, which fortuitously translates as "The Ghost (Play)."

110. Montaigne, *The Complete Essays of Montaigne*, 228. The use of perfumes is deemed inherently suspicious and figures as an olfactory marker of exclusion, or social othering. The second marker is inodorousness (exemplified by Grenouille), while the third relates to foul smells of lower social classes (addressed in the final section of this book): "The primary negative olfactory characteristics ascribed to the other," Constance Classen writes, "are: (a) foul, (b) dangerously fragrant, and (c) inodorate." Constance Classen, "The Odor of the Other: Olfactory Symbolism and Cultural Categories," *Ethos* 20, no. 2 (1992): 158.

111. Sándor Ferenczi, "The Ontogenesis of the Interest in Money," in *First Contributions to Psycho-Analysis*, trans. Ernest Jones (London: Karnac, 2002), 327.

112. "Limitation in the possibility of an enjoyment raises the value of the enjoyment." Freud, "On Transience," SE 14: 305. In several of his works, and fully in line with the claim just quoted, Freud argues that, compared to our social systems, the sexual morality of primitive societies was actually more restrictive: "It is true that, on particular occasion, primitive man's sexuality will override all inhibitions; but for the most part it seems to be more strongly held in check by prohibitions than it is at higher levels of civilization." Freud, "The Taboo of Virginity," SE 11: 198.

113. The term "surplus scarcity" was coined by Eric Santner. In my mind, it elegantly solves the specific conceptual problem of how to reconcile the Lacanian concept of lack, on the one hand, and surplus-enjoyment, on the other: the surplus is lack qua object, that is, a surplus scarcity. See Santner, *Untying Things Together*, 143.

114. See, for instance, Ana Lilia Cerda-Molina et al., "Changes in Men's Salivary Testosterone and Cortisol Levels, and In Sexual Desire After Smelling Female Axillary and Vulvar Scents," *Frontiers in Endocrinology* 4 (2013): 1–9. In one study of the effects of pleasant non-bodily odors on human male sexual response a combined odor of lavender and pumpkin pie produced the greatest result. Alan R. Hirsch and Jason J. Gruss, "Human Male Sexual Response to Olfactory Stimuli," *Journal of Neurological and Orthopaedic Medicine and Surgery* 3 (March 2014).

115. Cited in Brill, "The Sense of Smell in the Neuroses and Psychoses," 31.

116. Alenka Zupančič, *The Odd One In: On Comedy* (Cambridge, MA: MIT Press, 2008), 206–207.

117. See, for instance, Charmaine Borg et al., "The Influence of Olfactory Disgust on (Genital) Sexual Arousal in Men," *PLOS One* 14, no. 2 (2019): 2.

118. I am borrowing the term "too-muchness" from Eric Santner (see Santner, *The Royal Remains*, 30, 70, 105, 109, 158, 201, 207).

119. George Orwell, *The Road to Wigan Pier* (Clarendon: Oxford University Press, 2021), 88. See Brill's comment: "Like many other physicians I have seen many a marital disruption as a result of oezenas and halitoses." Brill, "The Sense of Smell in the Neuroses and Psychoses," 7. In the study I previously referenced, the "aversive odor used . . . was a mixture containing multiple disgust elicitors. One of the elements used had some similarities to skunk odor, while other parts were associated with rotten garlic and the odor of smelly feet. The elements combined created a new type of odor that is considered highly disgusting, easily perceivable and yet low in toxicity." Borg et al., "The Influence of Olfactory Disgust on (Genital) Sexual Arousal in Men," 4–5.

120. Orwell, *The Road to Wigan Pier*, 88.

121. "We know, too, that anyone who violates a taboo by coming into contact with something that is taboo becomes taboo himself and that then no one may come into contact with him." Freud, *Totem and Taboo*, SE 13: 27.

122. As already mentioned, unlike visual traces, smell-traces are considered much less indicative of the existence of objects. The issue is related to the US legal polemic concerning the question whether odor alone is sufficient for a finding of probable cause. Whereas no warrant is typically needed for items in "plain view," the doctrine does not commonly include "plain smell" items. For the principal arguments guiding the polemic, see Michael A. Sprow, "Wake Up and Smell the Contraband: Why Courts That Do Not Find Probable Cause Based on Odor Alone Are Wrong," *William and Mary Law Review* 42 (2000): 289–318.

123. Cited from https://rabüro.de/kuendigung-eines-wohnraummietverhaeltnisses-wegen-mutwilligen-verspritzenvon-surstroemming-im-treppenhaus/ (last accessed February 8, 2023).

124. Friedrich S. Krauss, ed., *Anthropophyteia: Jahrbücher für Folkloristische Erhebungen und Forschungen zur Entwicklungsgeschichte der geschlechtlichen Moral*, vol. 1 (Leipzig: Deutsche Verlag-Aktien-Gesellschaft, 1904), 224.

125. Lacan, *The Seminar of Jacques Lacan, Book XI*, 103.

126. Ontogenetically, the first instance of this excremental object is the smell of an unwashed breast: "We studied the involvement of naturally occurring odours in guiding the baby to the nipple. One breast of each participating mother was washed immediately after delivery. The newborn infant was placed prone between the breasts. Of 30 infants, 22 spontaneously selected the unwashed breast. The washing procedure had no effect on breast temperature. We concluded that the infants responded to olfactory differences between the washed and unwashed breasts." Varendi, Porter, and Winberg, "Does the Newborn Baby Find the Nipple by Smell?," 989.

127. Freud, "On the Universal Tendency to Debasement in the Sphere of Love," SE 11: 189.

128. A study found that "merely sniffing negative-emotion-related odorless tears obtained from women donors induced reductions in sexual appeal attributed by men to pictures of women's faces. Moreover, after sniffing such tears, men experienced reduced self-rated sexual arousal, reduced physiological measures of arousal, and reduced levels of testosterone. Finally, functional magnetic resonance imaging revealed that sniffing women's tears

selectively reduced activity in brain substrates of sexual arousal in men." Shani Gelstein et al., "Human Tears Contain a Chemosignal," *Science* 331, no. 6014 (2011): 226–230. To my knowledge, dacryphilia—a form of paraphilia characterized by the subject's arousal by tears or sobbing—is very poorly studied. One (very limited) study suggested that the arousal is prompted not by tears but rather by their alternative sensorial representations, such as the sight of crying or curled lips.

129. Freud, "Preface to Bourke's *Scatalogic Rites of All Nations*," SE 12: 335.

130. Freud, "Preface to Bourke's *Scatalogic Rites of All Nations*," SE 12: 336.

131. Lacan, "The Subversion of the Subject and the Dialectic of Desire in the Freudian Unconscious," in *Écrits*, 696.

132. Freud, *Three Essays on the Theory of Sexuality*, SE 7: 187, note.

133. Freud, *Three Essays on the Theory of Sexuality*, SE 7: 187, note.

134. Lou Andreas-Salomé, "'Anal' und 'Sexual,'" in *Imago: Zeitschrift für Anwendung der Psychoanalyse auf die Geisteswissenschaften*, vol. 4 (Vienna: Internationaler Psychoanalytischer Verlag, 1916), 249.

135. Andreas-Salomé, "'Anal' und 'Sexual,'" 249.

136. Freud, *Totem and Taboo*, SE 13: 27.

137. "Character and Anal Erotism," SE 9: 172–173.

138. Or maybe not. James seems to be misquoting Lord Palmerston, the British statesman and two-time prime minister of the United Kingdom, whose statement is found in the English illustrated weekly *Once a Week*: "'Well,' said Lord Palmerston, 'dirt is only matter in a wrong place.' That which is dirt in London," adds the author, "becomes sugar in the tropics." The statement is not metaphorical. The dirt in question are the dried excreta that the English exported to the colonies as fertilizer for sugar cane cultivation. Profitably employed, dirt loses its toxicity—*pecunia non olet*. William Bridges Adams, "The Refuse of Towns and Cities," *Once a Week* 2, no. 32 (1860): 130. Often, the phrase in question is mistakenly attributed to Mary Douglas's 1966 book *Purity and Danger*: "If we abstract pathogenicity and hygiene from our notion of dirt, we are left with the old definition of dirt as matter out of place." Mary Douglas, *Purity and Danger: An Analysis of Concepts of Pollution and Taboo* (London: Routledge, 2008), 44.

139. William James, *Varieties of Religious Experience: A Study in Human Nature* (London: Routledge, [1902] 2002), 107–108.

140. I am borrowing the term "part of no part," *part des sans-part*, from Rancière. See Jacques Rancière, *Disagreement: Politics and Philosophy*, trans. Julie Rose (Minneapolis: University of Minnesota Press, 1999), 9.

141. Freud, *The Interpretation of Dreams*, SE 4: 48.

142. "The anal level is the locus of metaphor—one object for another, give the faeces in place of the phallus. This shows you why the anal drive is the domain of oblativity, of the gift." Lacan, *The Seminar of Jacques Lacan, Book XI*, 104.

143. Freud, "Character and Anal Erotism," SE 9: 174. The duality of the most precious and the worthless pertains to cultural waste-management as such. Culture separates waste from utility, yet what is truly cultural is the utilizing of the futile, the putting to use of all things useless: "The telltale sign of culture resides in the fact that what is useless is at the same time most highly valued." Mladen Dolar, "Of Drives and Culture," *Problemi International* 1 (2017): 63.

144. Ferenczi, "The Ontogenesis of the Interest in Money," 321.

145. Ferenczi, "The Ontogenesis of the Interest in Money," 322; Sándor Ferenczi, "Zur Ontogenie des Geldinteresses," in *Schriften zur Psychoanalyse*, vol. 1 (Frankfurt am Main: Fischer Verlag, 1970), 200.

146. Ferenczi, "The Ontogenesis of the Interest in Money," 327.

147. René Descartes, *Meditations on First Philosophy*, trans. Elizabeth S. Haldane and G. R. T. Ross (London: Routledge, 1993), 55.

148. In 1975, during his visit to MIT, Lacan was famously asked (by none other than Noam Chomsky) a question regarding thought, and provided a puzzling response: "We think we think with our brains; personally, I think with my feet. That's the only way I really come into contact with anything solid." Cited in Élisabeth Roudinesco, *Jacques Lacan*, trans. Barbara Bray (New York: Columbia University Press, 1997), 378–379. The osmological narrative may elucidate the cryptic response, for where do human feet come from if not from the advent of bipedalism, instituting the *orthopedia* of the cogito?

149. Adriana Cavarero, *Inclinations: A Critique of Rectitude*, trans. Amanda Minervini (Stanford: Stanford University Press, 2016), 11.

150. Cavarero, *Inclinations*, 11.

151. "But looking closer, . . . we see two postural paradigms . . . : the first relates to individualistic ontology, the second to a relational ontology." Cavarero, *Inclinations*, 10. Looking even closer, a third postural paradigm is revealed.

152. Cavarero, *Inclinations*, 104.

153. Referring back to the idea of our birth *inter urinas et faeces*, we can further distinguish our position from Cavarero's powerful reinterpretation of (Arendtian) natality as a surrendering to another. Cavarero, *Inclinations*, 122. What characterizes the birth of the subject *inter urinas et faeces* is not a relation to the (m)Other but an enjoyment in and of the excreta of (m)Otherness.

154. Lacan, *The Seminar of Jacques Lacan, Book XX*, 14–15.

155. Jacques-Alain Miller, "Théorie de lalangue (rudiment)," *Ornicar?* 1 (1975): 32.

156. "This scent was a blend of both, of evanescence and substance, not a blend, but a unity, although slight and frail as well, and yet solid and sustaining, like a piece of thin, shimmering silk . . . and yet again not like silk, but like pastry soaked in honey-sweet milk—and try as he would he couldn't fit those two together: milk and silk!" Süskind, *Perfume*, 46.

157. In my native language, Slovenian, "Spirit" (*duh*) and "smell" (*duh*) are homophones, homonyms, and homographs, while, moreover, sharing the same etymology. This book was born of their homophony.

158. Kant takes note of the connection between babbling and kissing: "Furthermore, when the child tries to speak, the mangling of words is so charming for the mother and nurse, and this inclines them to hug and kiss him constantly, and they thoroughly spoil the tiny dictator by fulfilling his every wish and desire." Kant, *Anthropology from a Pragmatic Point of View*, 16.

159. For the smell of burnt pudding, see the case study of Miss Lucy R. in Breuer and Freud, *Studies on Hysteria*, SE 2: 107.

160. Milner, "Back and Forth from Letter to Homophony," 89.

161. The same argument could also be applied to the status of communication that, according to Lacan, is essentially a miscommunication (see Lacan, *The Seminar of Jacques Lacan, Book III*, 163). This does not mean that we can never understand each other, but

rather that the only ones understood are the misunderstood. Accordingly, all communication is a managing of the excrements of communication. In our time, this structural diarrhea of communication is amplified by new possibilities of instant publication. Thus, social media and networking companies, like Twitter, are essentially in the waste-management business.

162. Alenka Zupančič, *What IS Sex?* (Cambridge, MA: MIT Press, 2017), 50.

163. Zupančič, *What IS Sex?*, 47.

164. Milner, "Back and Forth from Letter to Homophony," 88.

165. Alain Badiou and Barbara Cassin, *There's No Such Thing as a Sexual Relationship: Two Lessons in Lacan*, trans. Susan Spitzer and Kenneth Reinhard (New York: Columbia University Press), 2017.

CHAPTER 4

1. Freud, *Three Essays on the Theory of Sexuality*, SE 7: 186; Freud, *Drei Abhandlungen zur Sexualtheorie*, 87.

2. "The capital-relation presupposes a complete separation between the workers and the ownership of the conditions for the realization of their labor." Marx, *Capital*, vol. 1, 874.

3. Marx, *Capital*, vol. 1, 873.

4. Marx, *Capital*, vol. 1, 873.

5. "In actual history, it is a notorious fact that conquest, enslavement, robbery, murder, in short, force, play the greatest part. In the tender annals of political economy, the idyllic reigns from time immemorial. . . . As a matter of fact, the methods of primitive accumulation are anything but idyllic." Marx, *Capital*, vol. 1, 874. Short of actual enslavement and murder, the process of primitive defecation also entails conquest, robbery, in short: the use of force.

6. Marx, *Capital*, vol. 1, 871.

7. Marx, *Capital*, vol. 1, 874.

8. Karl Marx, *Grundrisse: Foundations of the Critique of Political Economy (Rough Draft)*, trans. Martin Nicolaus (Harmondsworth: Penguin, 1973), 460. For an excellent reading of the relationship between primitive and capitalist accumulation, see Werner Bonefeld, "Primitive Accumulation and Capitalist Accumulation: Notes on Social Constitution and Expropriation," *Science & Society* 75, no. 3 (2011): 379–399. The same duality of presupposition and result was observed in the two waste-management practices of potty- and language-training. There, too, we were faced with the same question: Is the excrement the precondition of toilet-culture or is it its result? Does language presuppose llanguage or does the latter result from the former? In all three cases, the solution to the problem is provided by the concept of the *resulting presupposition*.

9. Marx, *Capital*, vol. 1, 873.

10. Marx, *Capital*, vol. 1, 876; Karl Marx, *Das Kapital: Kritik der politischen Ökonomie*, in *Werke*, vol. 23 (Berlin: Dietz Verlag, 1962), 744.

11. Marx, *Capital*, vol. 1, 874.

12. The new contiguity presupposes the emergence of a new commodity, namely the commodity of labor-power, sold by its owner (the worker) to the capitalist. In this context, Marx refers to the tactile organ and uses tactile metaphors: the impoverished proletarians "had nothing to sell except their own skins." This contiguity, the "selling of their own skins," reproduces the initial division, for "someone who has brought his own hide

[*Haut*] to market . . . now has nothing else to expect but—a tanning [*Gerberei*]." Marx, *Capital*, vol. 1, 873, 280; Marx, *Das Kapital*, 191.

13. Marx, *Capital*, vol. 1, 875.

14. Marx, *Capital*, vol. 1, 926.

15. Suetonius, *The Lives of the Caesars* (G. Bell, 1914), 319.

16. Rajesh Nair and Seshadri Sriprasad, "'Pecunia non olet!' Money That Does Not Smell and the Birth of Public Lavatories," *Journal of Urology* 183, no. 4, supplement (2010): e438.

17. Incidentally, this famous anecdote reported by Suetonius is not the only source attesting to Vespasian's "anal character": "Outlandish devices won Vespasian his reputation for 'avarice.' . . . The numerous anecdotes on avarice that have made their contribution to Vespasian's 'character', masquerading as factual, show how hard pressed the Empire was to pay its way." Barbara Levick, *Vespasian* (London: Routledge, 1999), 103.

18. Nair and Sriprasad, "'Pecunia non olet!,'" e439.

19. Marx, *Capital*, vol. 1, 205.

20. Marx, *Capital*, vol. 1, 142.

21. Marx, *Capital*, vol. 1, 202; my emphasis.

22. Marx, *Capital*, vol. 1, 132; Marx, *Das Kapital*, 56. This key point was made by the authors of the *Neue Marx-Lektüre*, dating back to the 1960s and proposing a new reading of Marx's economic theories. Today, Michael Heinrich is one of the school's best-known and most prolific representatives. See Michael Heinrich, *An Introduction to the Three Volumes of Karl Marx's Capital*, trans. Alexander Locascio (New York: Monthly Review Press, 2012).

23. "It is clear that the concept which operates in the system, formed solely through the determination of subsumption, is a redoubled concept: *the concept of identity to a concept.* / This redoubling, induced in the concept by identity, engenders the logical dimension, because in effecting the disappearance of the thing it gives rise to the emergence of the numerable." Miller, "Suture," 27–28.

24. Marx, *Capital*, vol. 1, 205.

25. Strictly speaking, this thesis requires a corollary. The translation of the movement of exchange in simple commodity circulation into Lacanian terms signals that what is at stake in it remains irreducible to simple satisfaction of needs, to a leveled-out calculus of needs and their satisfaction. The intervention of the monetary signifier introduces into this movement the instance of desire, thus essentially transforming it. Here, we encounter the problem that Wolfgang Fritz Haug developed in his famous *Critique of Commodity Aesthetics* (1971). Haug adds to Marx's couple of natural and value form of the commodity (its use- and its exchange-value) the category of aesthetic form, which is irreducibly attached to commodities as use-values. Commodities never satisfy bare needs: that which lures us into consumption is precisely the surplus of (signifying) demand over need, the surplus that opens up the space of desire. See Wolfgang Fritz Haug, *Kritik der Warenästhetik: Gefolgt von Warenästhetik im High-Tech-Kapitalismus* (Frankfurt am Main: Suhrkamp, 2009).

26. I have addressed this issue briefly in Simon Hajdini, "Marx and Spinoza? On Kordela's *Epistemontology* as the Latest Systematic Program of Spinozist Marxism," *Cultural Critique* 112 (2021): 103–128.

27. "Therefore," A. Kiarina Kordela writes, "Lacan's 'the unconscious is structured like language' . . . also means that the unconscious is structured as the network of exchange-values." A. Kiarina Kordela, *Epistemontology in Spinoza-Marx-Freud-Lacan: The (Bio)Power of Structure* (New York: Routledge, 2018), 160. See also Samo Tomšič's remark in his influential

book *The Capitalist Unconscious* (2015): "Just as political economy handles the difference between exchange-value and use-value, Saussure introduces an analogical difference between linguistic value and meaning." Tomšič, *The Capitalist Unconscious*, 31.

28. Marx, *Capital*, vol. 1, 125.

29. Marx, *Capital*, vol. 1, 126.

30. Marx, *Capital*, vol. 1, 126.

31. Marx, *Capital*, vol. 1, 125.

32. I am relying on Milner's analysis of Saussure's analogy. See Milner, *Le périple structural*, 33–34.

33. Ferdinand de Saussure, *Course in General Linguistics*, trans. Wade Baskin (New York: Columbia University Press, 2011), 112.

34. "Here we witness a decisive shift: Saussure constructs a model of the sign that is separate from any theory of representation." Milner, *Le périple structural*, 28.

35. Marx, *Capital*, vol. 1, 139.

36. Marx, *Capital*, vol. 1, 125.

37. "Hence it is clear that with the phrase 'origin' (*Genesis*) he [Marx] does not mean the historical emergence of money, but rather a conceptual relationship of development. He is not concerned with the historical development of money (not even in a completely abstract sense) but with a conceptual reconstruction of the connection between the 'simple form of value' (a commodity expressing its value through another commodity) and the 'money form.'" Heinrich, *An Introduction to the Three Volumes of Karl Marx's Capital*, 56. Marx: "The simple commodity form is therefore the germ of the money-form." Marx, *Capital*, vol. 1, 163.

38. Marx, *Capital*, vol. 1, 162.

39. The only, albeit key, point of my disagreement with Michael Heinrich's otherwise consistently enlightening readings of Marx's *Capital* concerns the reflexivity of the relation of equivalence. For Heinrich, the relation of equivalence is not merely symmetrical and transitive but also reflexive. See Michael Heinrich, *Die Wissenschaft vom Wert. Die Marxsche Kritik der Politischen Ökonomie zwischen wissenschaftlicher Revolution und klassischer Tradition* (Münster: Westfälisches Dampfboot, 2014), 199 and 5n.

40. See Freud, *Three Essays on the Theory of Sexuality*, SE 7: 182.

41. Saussure, *Course in General Linguistics*, 121.

42. Karl Marx, *Capital: A Critique of Political Economy*, vol. 2, trans. Ben Fowkes (London and New York: Penguin Books in association with New Left Review, 1992), 137.

43. Marx, *Capital*, vol. 1, 166.

44. Kordela, *Epistemontology in Spinoza-Marx-Freud-Lacan*.

45. Moishe Postone, *Time, Labor, and Social Domination: A Reinterpretation of Marx's Critical Theory* (Cambridge: Cambridge University Press, 1993), 156.

46. Postone, *Time, Labor, and Social Domination*, 151.

47. Kordela, *Epistemontology in Spinoza-Marx-Freud-Lacan*, 4, 10.

48. Marx, *Capital*, vol. 1, 165.

49. Milner, *L'Œuvre claire*, 129.

50. Moreover: "The prolongation of the working day beyond the limits of the natural day, into the night, only . . . slightly quenches the vampiric thirst for the living blood of labor."

And "the vampire will not let go 'while there remains a single muscle, sinew or drop of blood to be exploited.'" Marx, *Capital*, vol. 1, 342, 367, 416.

51. Daniel De Leon, "The Hookworm," *Daily People* 10 (1909): 142.

52. Heinrich, *An Introduction to the Three Volumes of Karl Marx's Capital*, 14.

53. Robert L. Bussard, "The 'Dangerous Class' of Marx and Engels: The Rise of the Idea of the Lumpenproletariat," *History of European Ideas* 8, no. 6 (2012): 677.

54. "In another sense . . . the extra-economic or social no longer lies outside capital and economics but has been absorbed into it: so that being unemployed or without economic function is no longer to be expelled from capital but to remain within it. Where everything has been subsumed under capitalism, there is no longer anything outside it; and the unemployed—or here the destitute, the paupers—are as it were employed by capital to be unemployed; they fulfil an economic function by way of their very non-functioning (even if they are not paid to do so)." Fredric Jameson, *Representing Capital: A Reading of Volume One* (London: Verso, 2011), 71. Not everything is consumed (employed) by capital, yet there is nothing (the unemployed included) not consumed by it. The totality of capital is the totality of the non-All, that is: ubiquitous.

55. Karl Marx and Friedrich Engels, *Manifesto of the Communist Party* (1848), in *The Cambridge Companion to* The Communist Manifesto, trans. Terrell Carver (New York: Cambridge University Press, 2015), 244; Karl Marx and Friedrich Engels, *Manifesto of the Communist Party* (1848), in *The Portable Karl Marx*, ed. Eugene Kamenka (London: Penguin Books, 1983), 215.

56. Montaigne, *The Complete Essays of Montaigne*, 228.

57. Instead, it is socialism that requires a thorough deodorization: "Socialism . . . does not smell any longer of revolution and the overthrow of tyrants; it smells of crankishness, machine-worship, and the stupid cult of Russia. Unless you can remove that smell, and very rapidly, Fascism may win." Orwell, *The Road to Wigan Pier*, 13.

58. Orwell, *The Road to Wigan Pier*, 87.

59. Orwell, *The Road to Wigan Pier*, 88.

60. Orwell, *The Road to Wigan Pier*, 88; my emphasis.

61. Marx and Engels, *Manifesto of the Communist Party* (1848), in *The Cambridge Companion to* The Communist Manifesto, 244.

62. Documenting the bleak living and working conditions of the working class is England's industrial north, Orwell comments on the nonexistence of the working class and our olfactory duty to it: "It is a kind of duty to see and smell such places now and again, especially smell them, lest you should forget that they exist; though perhaps it is better not to stay there too long." Orwell, *The Road to Wigan Pier*, 11. Today, obscene sensorial tours of poor neighborhoods are being offered to politically enlightened tourists. See Rivke Jaffa et al., "What Does Poverty Feel Like? Urban Inequality and the Politics of Sensation," *Urban Studies* 57, no. 5 (2020): 1015–1031.

63. J. E. Caerwyn Williams, "Posidonius's Celtic Parasites," *Studia Celtica* 14 (1979): 313–343.

64. Ernst H. Kantorowicz, *Laudes Regiae: A Study in Liturgical Acclamations and Medieval Ruler Worship* (Berkeley: University of California Press, 1946), 83. Santner directly relates the king-instituting acclamations to the spectral substance of Value, which "keeps the economy humming." Santner, *The Weight of All Flesh*, 239.

65. Santner, "The Rebranding of Sovereignty in the Age of Trump," 76.

66. Cited in Santner, *The Weight of All Flesh*, 26.

67. For the term "idle worship," see Santner, *The Weight of All Flesh*, 237–282.

68. "In the little writing I gave you of analytic discourse, *a* is written in the upper left-hand corner, and is supported by S$_2$, in other words, by knowledge insofar as it is in the place of truth. It is from that point that it interpellates [*l'interpelle*] $, which must lead to the production of S$_1$, that is, of the signifier by which can be resolved what? Its relation to truth." Lacan, *The Seminar of Jacques Lacan, Book XX*, 91; translation corrected. For a detailed discussion of the differences between ideological and psychoanalytical interpellation, see Simon Hajdini, "Comedy from *a* to Z," *Problemi International* 1 (2017): 129–158.

69. Marx and Engels, *Manifesto of the Communist Party* (1848), in *The Portable Karl Marx*, 207.

BIBLIOGRAPHY

Adorno, Theodor W. *Minima Moralia: Reflections from Damaged Life*. Translated by E. F. N. Jeph-cott. London: Verso Books, 2005.

Adorno, Theodor W. *Negative Dialectics*. Translated by E. B. Ashton. New York: Continuum, 2007.

Althusser, Louis. *Philosophy of the Encounter: Later Writings, 1978–1987*. Translated by G. M. Gosh-garian. London: Verso, 2006.

Andersson, Ola. *Studies in the Prehistory of Psychoanalysis: The Etiology of Psychoneuroses and Some Related Themes in Sigmund Freud's Scientific Writings and Letters, 1886–1896*. Uppsala: Norstedt, 1962.

Andreas-Salomé, Lou. "'Anal' und 'Sexual.'" *Imago: Zeitschrift für Anwendung der Psychoanalyse auf die Geisteswissenschaften* 4, no. 5 (1916): 249–273.

Aristotle. *The Complete Works of Aristotle*. Princeton, NJ: Princeton University Press, 1995.

Badiou, Alain, and Barbara Cassin. *There's No Such Thing as a Sexual Relationship: Two Lessons in Lacan*. Translated by Susan Spitzer and Kenneth Reinhard. New York: Columbia University Press, 2017.

Bauduin, Tessel M. *Surrealism and the Occult: Occultism and Western Esotericism in the Work and Movement of André Breton*. Amsterdam: Amsterdam University Press, 2014.

Beckett, Samuel. *Proust*. New York: Grove Press, 1957.

Beckett, Samuel. *Texts for Nothing*. London: John Calder, 1999.

Blankenship, Meredith L., et al. "Retronasal Odor Perception Requires Taste Cortex but Orthonasal Does Not." *Current Biology* 29, no. 1 (2019): 62–69.

Bonefeld, Werner. "Primitive Accumulation and Capitalist Accumulation: Notes on Social Constitution and Expropriation." *Science & Society* 75, no. 3 (2011): 379–399.

Borg, Charmaine, et al. "The Influence of Olfactory Disgust on (Genital) Sexual Arousal in Men." *PLOS One* 14, no. 2 (2019).

Brand, J. M., and R. P. Galask. "Trimethylamine: The Substance Mainly Responsible for the Fishy Odor Often Associated with Bacterial Vaginosis." *Obstetrics & Gynecology* 68, no. 5 (1986): 682–685.

Brecht, Bertolt. *Refugee Conversations*. Translated by Romy Fursland. London: Methuen, 2019.

Bremer, Dieter. "Der Begriff des Schicksals bei Hegel und seine griechische Ursprünge." *Antike und Abendland* 35 (1989): 24–38.

Breton, André. *Communicating Vessels*. Translated by Mary Ann Caws and Geoffrey T. Harris. Lincoln: University of Nebraska Press, 1990.

Breuer, Josef, and Sigmund Freud. *Studies on Hysteria*. In *The Standard Edition of the Complete Psychological Works of Sigmund Freud*. Vol. 2. Translated by James Strachey. London: The Hogarth Press and the Institute of Psycho-Analysis, 2001.

Bridges Adams, William. "The Refuse of Towns and Cities." *Once a Week* 2, no. 32 (1860): 128–131.

Brill, A. A. "The Sense of Smell in the Neuroses and Psychoses." *Psychoanalytic Quarterly* 1, no. 1 (1932): 7–42.

Buck, Carl Darling. *A Dictionary of Selected Synonyms in the Principal Indo-European Languages: A Contribution to the History of Ideas*. Chicago: University of Chicago Press, 1949.

Bussard, Robert L. "The 'Dangerous Class' of Marx and Engels: The Rise of the Idea of the Lumpenproletariat." *History of European Ideas* 8, no. 6 (2012): 675–692.

Cavarero, Adriana. *Inclinations: A Critique of Rectitude*. Translated by Amanda Minervini. Stanford: Stanford University Press, 2016.

Cerda-Molina, Ana Lilia, et al. "Changes in Men's Salivary Testosterone and Cortisol Levels, and in Sexual Desire after Smelling Female Axillary and Vulvar Scents." *Frontiers in Endocrinology* 4 (2013): 1–9.

Chrisafis, Angelique. "Proust's Memory-Laden Madeleine Cakes Started Life as Toast, Manuscripts Reveal." *The Guardian*, October 19, 2015. www.theguardian.com/books/2015/oct/19/proust-madeleine-cakes-started-as-toast-in-search-of-lost-time-manuscripts-reveal.

Classen, Constance. "The Odor of the Other: Olfactory Symbolism and Cutural Categories." *Ethos* 20, no. 2 (1992): 133–166.

Classen, Constance, David Howes, and Anthony Synnott. *Aroma: The Cultural History of Smell*. London: Routledge, 1994.

Cleland, John. *Fanny Hill: Memoirs of a Woman of Pleasure*. Ware: Wordsworth Classics, [1749] 1993.

Condillac, Etienne Bonnot de. *Condillac's Treatise on the Sensations*. Los Angeles: School of Philosophy, University of Southern California, 1930.

Corbin, Alain. *The Foul and the Fragrant: Odor and the French Social Imagination*. Leamington Spa: Berg Publishers, 1986.

Corkin, Suzanne. *Permanent Present Tense: The Man with No Memory, and What He Taught the World*. London: Penguin Books, 2013.

Delaunay-El Allam, Maryse, Luc Marlier, and Benoist Schaal. "Learning at the Breast: Preference Formation for an Artificial Scent and Its Attraction Against the Odor of Maternal Milk." *Infant Behavior and Development* 29, no. 3 (2006): 308–321.

De Leon, Daniel. "The Hookworm." *Daily People* 10 (1909): 142.

Deleuze, Gilles. *The Logic of Sense*. Translated by Mark Lester with Charles Stivale. New York: Columbia University Press, 1990.

Deleuze, Gilles. *Foucault*. Translated by Seán Hand. Minneapolis: University of Minnesota Press, 2006.

Deleuze, Gilles. *Proust and Signs*. Translated by Richard Howard. London and New York: Continuum, 2008.

Deleuze, Gilles, and Félix Guattari. *Kafka. Pour une littérature mineure*. Paris: Minuit, 1975.

Derrida, Jacques. *Voice and Phenomenon: Introduction to the Problem of the Sign in Husserl's Phenomenology*. Translated by Leonard Lawlor. Evanston: Northwestern University Press, 2011.

Descartes, René. *Meditations on First Philosophy*. Translated by Elizabeth S. Haldane and G. R. T. Ross. London: Routledge, 1993.

Descartes, René. *A Discourse on the Method*. Translated by Ian Maclean. Oxford: Oxford University Press, 2006.

Didi-Huberman, Georges. "The Index of the Absent Wound (Monograph on a Stain)." *October* 29 (1984): 63–82.

Doane, Mary Ann. "The Indexical and the Concept of Medium Specificity." *Differences* 18, no. 1 (2007): 128–152.

Dolar, Mladen. "Cogito as the Subject of the Unconscious." In *Cogito and the Unconscious*, edited by Slavoj Žižek, 11–40. Durham, NC: Duke University Press, 1998.

Dolar, Mladen. *Prozopopeja*. Ljubljana: Society for Theoretical Psychoanalysis, 2006.

Dolar, Mladen. *A Voice and Nothing More*. Cambridge, MA: MIT Press, 2006.

Dolar, Mladen. "The Atom and the Void—from Democritus to Lacan." *Filozofski vestnik* 34, no. 2 (2013): 11–26.

Dolar, Mladen. "Anamorphosis." *S: Journal of the Circle for Lacanian Ideology Critique* 8 (2015): 125–140.

Dolar, Mladen. "Being and MacGuffin." *Crisis and Critique* 4, no. 1 (2017): 83–101.

Dolar, Mladen. "Of Drives and Culture." *Problemi International* 1 (2017): 55–79.

Doty, Richard L., Avron Marcus, and W. William Lee. "Development of the 12-Item Cross-Cultural Smell Identification Test (CC-SIT)." *Laryngoscope* 106, no. 3 (1996): 353–356.

Douglas, Mary. *Purity and Danger: An Analysis of Concepts of Pollution and Taboo*. London: Routledge, 2008.

Eichenbaum, Howard, Thomas H. Morton, Harry Potter, and Suzanne Corkin. "Selective Olfactory Deficits in Case H.M." *Brain* 106 (1983): 459–472.

Engels, Friedrich. *Dialectics of Nature*. Translated by Clemens Dutt. London: Lawrence and Wishart, 1946.

Ferenczi, Sándor. "Zur Ontogenie des Geldinteresses." In *Schriften zur Psychoanalyse*, vol. 1, 198–205. Frankfurt am Main: Fischer Verlag, 1970.

Ferenczi, Sándor. "The Ontogenesis of the Interest in Money." In *First Contributions to Psycho-Analysis*. Translated by Ernest Jones, 319–331. London: Karnac, 2002.

Fichte, J. G. *Foundations of Natural Right According to the Principles of Wissenschaftslehre*. Translated by Michael Baur. Edited by Frederick Neuhouser. Cambridge: Cambridge University Press, 2000.

Fichter, M. M. "Franz Kafkas Magersucht." *Fortschritte der Neurologie-Psychiatrie* 56, no. 7 (1988): 231–238.

Fincks, Henry T. "The Gastronomic Value of Odours." *Contemporary Review* 50 (1886): 680–695.

Finlay, John B., et al. "Persistent Post-COVID-19 Smell Loss Is Associated with Immune Cell Infiltration and Altered Gene Expression in Olfactory Epithelium." *Science Translational Medicine* 14, no. 676 (2022): eaddo484.

Fliess, Wilhelm. *Die Nasale Reflexneurose*. Wiesbaden: JF Bergman, 1893.

Foucault, Michel. *The Order of Things: An Archaeology of Human Sciences.* London: Routledge, 2002.

Freud, Sigmund. *The Complete Letters of Sigmund Freud to Wilhelm Fliess: 1887–1904.* Translated by Jeffrey Moussaieff Masson. Cambridge, MA: The Belknap Press of Harvard University Press, 1985.

Freud, Sigmund. *Das Unbehagen in der Kultur.* In *Gesammelte Werke*, vol. 14, 419–506. Frankfurt am Main: Suhrkamp Verlag, 1999.

Freud, Sigmund. *Drei Abhandlungen zur Sexualtheorie.* In *Gesammelte Werke*, vol. 5, 27–145. Frankfurt am Main: Suhrkamp Verlag, 1999.

Freud, Sigmund. *The Standard Edition of the Complete Psychological Works of Sigmund Freud.* Translated by James Strachey. London: The Hogarth Press and the Institute of Psycho-Analysis, 2001.

Freud, Sigmund. *Totem und Tabu.* In *Gesammelte Werke*, vol. 9. Frankfurt am Main: Suhrkamp Verlag, 1999.

Gelstein, Shani, et al. "Human Tears Contain a Chemosignal." *Science* 331, no. 6014 (2011): 226–230.

Goethe, J. W. *Autobiographische Schriften 2.* In *Werke*, vol. 10. Hamburg: Beck, 2002.

Hajdini, Simon. "Comedy from *a* to Z." *Problemi International* 1 (2017): 129–158.

Hajdini, Simon. "Varieties of Negation: From Drizzle and Decaf to the Anti-Semitic Figure of the Jew." *Lacanian Ink* 51 (2018): 108–127.

Hajdini, Simon. "Marx and Spinoza? On Kordela's *Epistemontology* as the Latest Systematic Program of Spinozist Marxism." *Cultural Critique* 112 (2021): 103–128.

Haug, Wolfgang Fritz. *Kritik der Warenästhetik: Gefolgt von Warenästhetik im High-Tech-Kapitalismus.* Frankfurt am Main: Suhrkamp, 2009.

Hegel, G. W. F. *Vorlesungen über die Ästhetik I.* In *Werke*, vol. 13. Frankfurt am Main: Fischer Verlag, 1970.

Hegel, G. W. F. *Aesthetics: Lectures on Fine Art.* Translated by T. M. Knox. Oxford: Clarendon Press, 1975.

Hegel, G. W. F. *Phenomenology of Spirit.* Translated by A. V. Miller. Oxford: Oxford University Press, 1977.

Hegel, G. W. F. *Outlines of the Philosophy of Right.* Translated by T. M. Knox. Oxford: Oxford University Press, 2008.

Hegel, G. W. F. *Science of Logic.* Translated by A. V. Miller. New York: Routledge, 2010.

Heine, Heinrich. *Zur Geschichte der Religion und Philosophie in Deutschland.* In *Historisch-kritische Gesamtausgabe der Werke*, vol. 8/1, 9–120. Hamburg: Hoffmann und Campe, 1979.

Heinrich, Michael. *An Introduction to the Three Volumes of Karl Marx's Capital.* Translated by Alexander Locascio. New York: Monthly Review Press, 2012.

Heinrich, Michael. *Die Wissenschaft vom Wert. Die Marxsche Kritik der Politischen Ökonomie zwischen wissenschaftlicher Revolution und klassischer Tradition.* Münster: Westfälisches Dampfboot, 2014.

Herder, Johann Gottfried. *Outlines of a Philosophy of the History of Man.* Translated by T. Churchill. New York: Bergman Publishers, 1966[?].

Herder, Johann Gottfried. *Ideen zur Philosophie der Geschichte der Menschheit.* Frankfurt am Main: Deutscher Klassiker Verlag, 1989.

Hirsch, Alan R., and Jason J. Gruss. "Human Male Sexual Response to Olfactory Stimuli." *Journal of Neurological and Orthopaedic Medicine and Surgery* 3 (March 2014) https://aanos.org/human-male-sexual-response-to-olfactory-stimuli/ (accessed February 10, 2023).

Holley, André. "Cognitive Aspects of Olfaction in Perfumery." In *Olfaction, Taste, and Cognition*, edited by Catherine Rouby et al., 16–26. Cambridge: Cambridge University Press, 2002.

Hopkins, E. Washburn. "The Sniff-Kiss in Ancient India." *Journal of the American Oriental Society* 28 (1907): 120–134.

Horkheimer, Max, and Theodor W. Adorno. *Dialektik der Aufklärung. Philosophische Fragmente.* Frankfurt am Main: Fischer Verlag, 2006.

Horkheimer, Max, and Theodor W. Adorno. *Dialectic of Enlightenment: Philosophical Fragments.* Translated by Edmund Jephcott. Stanford: Stanford University Press, 2007.

Howland, Bette. "Aronesti." In *Calm Sea and Prosperous Voyage*, 167–180. Brooklyn: A Public Space Books, 2019.

Hughlings-Jackson, John. "On Affections of Speech from Disease of the Brain." *Brain* 2, no. 3 (1879): 203–222.

Jaffa, Rivke, et al. "What Does Poverty Feel Like? Urban Inequality and the Politics of Sensation." *Urban Studies* 57, no. 5 (2020): 1015–1031.

Jakobson, Roman. *On Language.* Cambridge, MA: Harvard University Press, 1990.

James, William. *Varieties of Religious Experience: A Study in Human Nature.* London: Routledge, [1902] 2002.

Jameson, Fredric. *Representing Capital: A Reading of Volume One.* London: Verso, 2011.

Jefferson, J. W., and T. D. Thompson. "Rhinotillexomania: Psychiatric Disorder or Habit?" *Journal of Clinical Psychiatry* 56, no. 2 (1995): 56–59.

Jones, Ernest. *The Life and Work of Sigmund Freud.* Vol. 2. New York: Basic Books, 1955.

Jones, Ernest. *The Life and Work of Sigmund Freud.* Vol. 3. New York: Basic Books, 1957.

Jones, Ernest. *The Life and Work of Sigmund Freud. Edited and Abridged in One Volume by Lionel Trilling and Steven Marcus.* New York: Basic Books, 1961.

Josephson-Storm, Jason. *The Myth of Disenchantment: Magic, Modernity, and the Birth of the Human Sciences.* Chicago: University of Chicago Press, 2017.

Kafka, Franz. "A Hunger Artist." In *The Complete Stories*, 268–277. Translated by Willa and Edwin Muir. New York: Schocken Books, 1971.

Kafka, Franz. "Investigations of a Dog." In *The Complete Stories*, 278–316. Translated by Willa and Edwin Muir. New York: Schocken Books, 1971.

Kafka, Franz. *The Diaries 1910–1923.* Translated by Joseph Kresh and Martin Greenberg. New York: Schocken Books, 1976 (e-book edition).

Kant, Immanuel. *Anthropologie in pragmatischer Hinsicht.* In *Werkausgabe.* Vol. 12, 395–690. Frankfurt am Main: Suhrkamp Verlag, 1977.

Kant, Immanuel. *The Metaphysics of Morals.* Translated and edited by Mary Gregor. Cambridge: Cambridge University Press, 1996.

Kant, Immanuel. *Anthropology from a Pragmatic Point of View.* Translated by Robert B. Louden. Cambridge: Cambridge University Press, 2006.

Kant, Immanuel. "Reviews of Herder's Ideas on the Philosophy of the History of Mankind." In *Political Writings*, edited by H. S. Reis, 201–220. Cambridge: Cambridge University Press, 2013.

Kantorowicz, Ernst H. *Laudes Regiae: A Study in Liturgical Acclamations and Medieval Ruler Worship.* Berkeley: University of California Press, 1946.

Kantorowicz, Ernst H. *The King's Two Bodies: A Study in Mediaeval Political Theology.* Princeton, NJ: Princeton University Press, 2016.

Keynes, John Maynard. "Newton, the Man." In *The Collected Writings of John Maynard Keynes.* Vol. 10, 363–374. Cambridge: Cambridge University Press, 2013.

Kierkegaard, Søren. *The Concept of Anxiety.* In *Kierkegaard's Writings.* Vol. 8. Edited and translated by Reidar Thomte in collaboration with Albert B. Anderson. Princeton, NJ: Princeton University Press, 1980.

Kierkegaard, Søren. *Fear and Trembling.* In *Kierkegaard's Writings.* Vol. 6. Edited and translated by Howard V. Hong and Edna H. Hong, 1–123. Princeton, NJ: Princeton University Press, 1983.

Kierkegaard, Søren. *Either/Or: Part I.* Translated by Howard V. Hong and Edna H. Hong. Princeton, NJ: Princeton University Press, 1988.

Kierkegaard, Søren. *Repetition.* In *Repetition and Philosophical Crumbs,* 1–81. Translated by M. G. Piety. Oxford: Oxford University Press, 2009.

Kordela, A. Kiarina. *Epistemontology in Spinoza-Marx-Freud-Lacan: The (Bio)Power of Structure.* New York: Routledge, 2018.

Krausmüller, Dirk. "Smell of Sweat, Smell of Semen: The Divinisation of the Body Fluids in Patriarch Methodius's Life of Theophanes of Agros." *Parekbolai* 11 (2021): 9–33.

Krauss, Friedrich S., ed. *Anthropophyteia: Jahrbücher für Folkloristische Erhebungen und Forschungen zur Entwicklungsgeschichte der geschlechtlichen Moral.* Vol. 1. Leipzig: Deutsche Verlag-Aktien-Gesellschaft, 1904.

Kripke, Saul. *Naming and Necessity.* Cambridge, MA: Harvard University Press, 1980.

Lacan, Jacques. "Conférences et entretiens dans des universités nord-américaines." *Scilicet* 6–7 (1976): 5–63.

Lacan, Jacques. *The Seminar of Jacques Lacan, Book II: The Ego in Freud's Theory and in the Technique of Psychoanalysis, 1954–1955.* Translated by Sylvana Tomaselli. Edited by Jacques-Alain Miller. New York: W. W. Norton, 1988.

Lacan, Jacques. *The Seminar of Jacques Lacan, Book I: Freud's Papers on Technique, 1953–1954.* Translated by John Forrester. Edited by Jacques-Alain Miller. New York: W. W. Norton, 1991.

Lacan, Jacques. *The Seminar of Jacques Lacan, Book VII: The Ethics of Psychoanalysis, 1959–1960.* Translated by Dennis Porter. Edited by Jacques-Alain Miller. London: Routledge, 1992.

Lacan, Jacques. *The Seminar of Jacques Lacan, Book III: The Psychoses, 1955–1956.* Translated by Russell Grigg. Edited by Jacques-Alain Miller. New York: W. W. Norton, 1993.

Lacan, Jacques. *The Seminar of Jacques Lacan, Book XI: The Four Fundamental Concepts of Psychoanalysis.* Translated by Alan Sheridan. Edited by Jacques-Alain Miller. New York: W. W. Norton, 1998.

Lacan, Jacques. *The Seminar of Jacques Lacan, Book XX: On Feminine Sexuality: The Limits of Love and Knowledge, 1972–1973.* Translated by Bruce Fink. Edited by Jacques-Alain Miller. New York: W. W. Norton, 1998.

Lacan, Jacques. *Écrits.* Translated by Bruce Fink. New York: W. W. Norton, 2006.

Lacan, Jacques. *The Seminar of Jacques Lacan, Book X: Anxiety.* Translated by A. R. Price. Edited by Jacques-Alain Miller. Cambridge: Polity Press, 2014.

Levick, Barbara. *Vespasian*. London: Routledge, 1999.

Lévi-Strauss, Claude. *The Naked Man: Introduction to a Science of Mythology: 4*. Translated by John and Doreen Weightman. New York: Harper & Row, 1981.

Lévi-Strauss, Claude. *Introduction to the Work of Marcel Mauss*. Translated by Felicity Baker. London: Routledge & Kegan Paul, 1987.

Lucretius. *On the Nature of the Universe*. Translated by Ronald Melville. New York: Oxford University Press, 1997.

Majid, Asifa, and Niclas Burenhult. "Odors Are Expressible in Language, as Long as You Speak the Right Language." *Cognition* 130 (2014): 266–270.

Malabou, Catherine. *The New Wounded: From Neurosis to Brain Damage*. Translated by Steven Miller. New York: Fordham University Press, 2012.

Mandrou, Robert. *Introduction to Modern France, 1500–1640: An Essay in Historical Psychology*. New York: Holmes & Meier, 1976.

Mannoni, Octave. "I Know Well, but All the Same . . ." Translated by G. M. Goshgarian. In *Perversion and the Social Relation*, edited by Molly Anne Rothenberg, Dennis Foster, and Slavoj Žižek, 68–92. Durham, NC: Duke University Press, 2003.

Marx, Karl. *Das Kapital: Kritik der politischen Ökonomie*. In *Werke*. Vol. 23. Berlin: Dietz Verlag, 1962.

Marx, Karl. *Grundrisse: Foundations of the Critique of Political Economy (Rough Draft)*. Translated by Martin Nicolaus. Harmondsworth: Penguin, 1973.

Marx, Karl. *The Eighteenth Brumaire of Louis Bonaparte*. New York: International Publishers, 1975.

Marx, Karl. *Capital: A Critique of Political Economy*. Vol. 1. Translated by Ben Fowkes. London and New York: Penguin Books in association with New Left Review, 1976.

Marx, Karl. *Capital: A Critique of Political Economy*. Vol. 2. Translated by Ben Fowkes. London and New York: Penguin Books in association with New Left Review, 1992.

Marx, Karl, and Friedrich Engels. *Manifesto of the Communist Party* (1848). In *The Portable Karl Marx*, edited by Eugene Kamenka, 203–241. New York: Penguin Books, 1983.

Marx, Karl, and Friedrich Engels. *Manifesto of the Communist Party* (1848). In *The Cambridge Companion to The Communist Manifesto*, 237–260. Translated by Terrell Carver. New York: Cambridge University Press, 2015.

Massicotte, Claudie. "Spiritual Surrealists: Séances, Automatism, and the Creative Unconscious." In *Surrealism, Occultism and Politics: In Search of the Marvellous*, edited by Tessel M. Bauduin et al., 23–38. New York: Routledge, 2018.

Meillassoux, Quentin. *After Finitude: An Essay on the Necessity of Contingency*. Translated by Ray Brassier. London: Continuum, 2008.

Mennella, Julie A., Catherine A. Forestell, and M. Yanina Pepino. "The Flavor World of Infants." *Dysphagia* 12, no. 4 (2003): 10–20.

Menni, Cristina, et al. "Real-Time Tracking of Self-Reported Symptoms to Predict Potential COVID-19." *Nature Medicine* 26 (2020): 1037–1040.

Miller, Jacques-Alain. "Théorie de lalangue (rudiment)." In *Ornicar?* 1 (1975): 16–34.

Miller, Jacques-Alain. "Elements of Epistemology." Translated by Leonardo S. Rodriguez. *Analysis* 1 (1989): 27–42.

Miller, Jacques-Alain. "On Perversion." In *Reading Seminars I and II: Lacan's Return to Freud*, edited by Richard Feldstein et al., 306–320. Albany: SUNY Press, 1996.

Miller, Jacques-Alain. "Matrix." Translated by D. G. Collins. In *Lacanian Ink* 12 (1997): 45–51.

Miller, Jacques-Alain. "Suture (Elements of the Logic of the Signifier)." *Screen* 18, no. 4 (1977–1978): 24–34.

Milner, Jean-Claude. *Le périple structural*. Paris: Éditions du Seuil, 2002.

Milner, Jean-Claude. *L'Œuvre claire: Lacan, la science, la philosophie*. Paris: Éditions du Seuil, 2015.

Milner, Jean-Claude. "Back and Forth from Letter to Homophony." *Problemi International* 1 (2017): 81–98.

Milner, Jean-Claude. "Reflections on the Me Too Movement and Its Philosophy." *Problemi International* 3 (2019): 65–87.

Milton, John. *Paradise Lost*. Malden: Blackwell, 2007.

Mishor, Eva, Daniel Amir, Tali Weiss, Danielle Honigstein, Aharon Weissbrod, Ethan Livne, et al. "Sniffing the Human Body Volatile Hexadecanal Blocks Aggression in Men but Triggers Aggression in Women." *Science Advances* 7, no. 47 (2021): 1–13.

Mitchell, Stephen C., and Robert L. Smith. "Trimethylamine—The Extracorporeal Envoy." *Chemical Senses* 41 (2016): 275–279.

Montaigne, Michel de. *The Complete Essays of Montaigne*. Translated by Donald M. Frame. Stanford: Stanford University Press, 1958.

Nair, Rajesh, and Seshadri Sriprasad. "'Pecunia Non Olet! Money That Does Not Smell and the Birth of Public Lavatories." *Journal of Urology* 183, no. 4, supplement (2010): e438–e439.

Nancy, Jean-Luc. *Corpus*. Translated by Richard A. Rand. New York: Fordham University Press, 2008.

Nietzsche, Friedrich. *Ecce Homo*. Translated by Walter Kaufmann. New York: Vintage Books, 1989.

Nietzsche, Friedrich. *Thus Spoke Zarathustra*. Translated by Graham Parkes. Oxford: Oxford University Press, 2005.

Nietzsche, Friedrich. *Dawn: Thoughts on the Presumptions of Morality*. Translated by Brittain Smith. Stanford: Stanford University Press, 2011.

Nietzsche, Friedrich. *On the Genealogy of Morals*. Translated by Michael A. Scarpitti. London: Penguin, 2013.

Orwell, George. *The Road to Wigan Pier*. Clarendon: Oxford University Press, 2021.

Pascal, Blaise. *Pensées*. Translated by Roger Ariew. Indianapolis: Hackett, 2004.

Peirce, Charles S. *Selected Philosophical Writings*, vol. 2: *1893–1913*. Bloomington: Indiana University Press, 1998.

Pfaller, Robert. *On the Pleasure Principle in Culture: Illusions Without Owners*. Translated by Lisa Rosenblatt, with Charlotte Eckler and Camilla Nielsen. London: Verso, 2014.

Pinto, Jayant M., Kristen E. Wroblewski, David W. Kern, L. Philip Schumm, and Martha K. McClintock. "Olfactory Dysfunction Predicts 5-Year Mortality in Older Adults." *PLOS ONE* 9, no. 10 (2014): e107541.

Plath, Sylvia. *The Unabridged Journals of Sylvia Plath, 1950–1962*. New York: Anchor Books, 2000 (e-book edition).

Plato. *Complete Works*. Indianapolis: Hackett, 1997.

Porter, R. H., and J. Winberg. "Unique Salience of Maternal Breast Odors for Newborn Infants." *Neuroscience and Biobehavioral Review* 23, no. 3 (1999): 439–449.

Postone, Moishe. *Time, Labor, and Social Domination: A Reinterpretation of Marx's Critical Theory.* Cambridge: Cambridge University Press, 1993.

Proust, Marcel. *Against Sainte-Beuve and Other Essays.* Translated by John Sturrock. London: Penguin Books, 1994.

Proust, Marcel. *In Search of Lost Time: The Complete Masterpiece.* Translated by C. K. Scott Moncrieff. The Modern Library, 2012 (e-book edition).

Proust, Marcel. *Les soixante-quinze feuillets et autre manuscrits inédits.* Paris: Gallimard, 2021.

Rancière, Jacques. *Disagreement: Politics and Philosophy.* Translated by Julie Rose. Minneapolis: University of Minnesota Press, 1999.

Rilke, Rainer Maria. *The Notebooks of Malte Laurids Brigge.* Translated by Michael Hulse. London: Penguin Books, 2009.

Rindisbacher, Hans J. *The Smell of Books: A Cultural-Historical Study of Olfactory Perception in Literature.* Ann Arbor: University of Michigan Press, 1992.

Roth, Philip. *Portnoy's Complaint.* New York: Vintage, 1994.

Roudinesco, Élisabeth. *Freud in His Time and Ours.* Translated by Catherine Porter. Cambridge, MA: Harvard University Press, 2016.

Roudinesco, Élisabeth. *Jacques Lacan.* Translated by Barbara Bray. New York: Columbia University Press, 1997.

Rousseau, Jean-Jacques. *Emile or On Education.* Translated by Allan Bloom. New York: Basic Books, 1979.

Santner, Eric L. "Miracles Happen: Benjamin, Rosenzweig, Freud, and the Matter of the Neighbor." In Slavoj Žižek, Eric L. Santner, and Kenneth Reinhard, *The Neighbor: Three Inquiries in Political Theology,* 76–133. Chicago: University of Chicago Press, 2005.

Santner, Eric L. *The Royal Remains: The People's Two Bodies and the Endgames of Sovereignty.* Chicago: University of Chicago Press, 2011.

Santner, Eric L. *The Weight of All Flesh: On the Subject-Matter of Political Economy.* Oxford and New York: Oxford University Press, 2016.

Santner, Eric L. "Marx and Manatheism." *Problemi International* 3 (2019): 27–38.

Santner, Eric L. "The Rebranding of Sovereignty in the Age of Trump." In William Mazzarella, Eric L. Santner, and Aaron Schuster, *Sovereignty, Inc.: Three Inquiries in Politics and Enjoyment,* 19–112. Chicago: University of Chicago Press, 2020.

Santner, Eric L. *Untying Things Together: Philosophy, Literature, and a Life in Theory.* Chicago: University of Chicago Press, 2022.

Saussure, Ferdinand de. *Course in General Linguistics.* Translated by Wade Baskin. New York: Columbia University Press, 2011.

Schur, Max. *Freud: Living and Dying.* New York: International Universities Press, 1972.

Serres, Michel. *The Birth of Physics.* Manchester: Clinamen Press, 2000.

Silverman, Kaja. *Flesh of My Flesh.* Stanford: Stanford University Press, 2009.

Sprow, Michael A. "Wake Up and Smell the Contraband: Why Courts That Do Not Find Probable Cause Based on Odor Alone Are Wrong." *William and Mary Law Review* 42 (2000): 289–318.

Starobinski, Jean. *Words upon Words: The Anagrams of Ferdinand de Saussure.* New Haven, CT: Yale University Press, 1979.

Suetonius. *The Lives of the Caesars.* G. Bell, 1914.

Sulmont-Rossé, Claire, Sylvie Issanchou, and E. P. Köster. "Odor Naming Methodology: Correct Identification with Multiple-Choice versus Repeatable Identification in a Free Task." *Chemical Senses* 30, no. 1 (2005): 23–27.

Süskind, Patrick. *Das Parfum: Die Geschichte eines Mörders*. Zürich: Diogenes Verlag, 1985.

Süskind, Patrick. *Perfume: The Story of a Murderer*. Translated by John E. Woods. London: Penguin Books, 2006.

Swedenborg, Emanuel. *Heaven and Hell*. Translated by George F. Dole. West Chester: The Swedenborg Foundation, 2010.

Tomšič, Samo. *The Capitalist Unconscious: Marx and Lacan*. London: Verso, 2015.

Van Riel, Debby, Rob Verdijk, and Thijs Kuiken. "The Olfactory Nerve: A Shortcut for Influenza and Other Viral Diseases into the Central Nervous System." *Journal of Pathology* 235, no. 2 (2015): 277–287.

Varendi, H., and R. H. Porter. "Breast Odor as the Only Maternal Stimulus Elicits Crawling Towards the Odor Source." *Acta Paediatrica* 90, no. 4 (2001): 372–375.

Varendi, H., R. H. Porter, and J. Winberg. "Does the Newborn Baby Find the Nipple by Smell?" *The Lancet* 344, no. 8928 (1994): 989–990.

Virno, Paolo. *An Essay on Negation: Towards a Linguistic Anthropology*. Translated by Lorenzo Chiesa. Calcutta, London, and New York: Seagull Books, 2018.

Wade, Nicholas. "Bacteria Thrive in Inner Elbow; No Harm Done." *New York Times*, May 23, 2008.

Williams, J. E. Caerwyn. "Posidonius's Celtic Parasites." *Studia Celtica* 14 (1979): 313–343.

Young, Benjamin D. "Smell's Puzzling Discrepancy: Gifted Discrimination, Yet Pitiful Identification." *Mind & Language* 35, no. 1 (2020): 90–114.

Zammito, John H. *The Gestation of German Biology: Philosophy and Physiology from Stahl to Schelling*. Chicago: University of Chicago Press, 2018.

Zupančič, Alenka. *The Odd One In: On Comedy*. Cambridge, MA: MIT Press, 2008.

Zupančič, Alenka. *What IS Sex?* Cambridge, MA: MIT Press, 2017.

Žižek, Slavoj. *The Indivisible Remainder: On Schelling and Related Matters*. London: Verso, 1996.

Žižek, Slavoj. *On Belief*. London: Routledge, 2001.

Žižek, Slavoj. *The Puppet and the Dwarf: The Perverse Core of Christianity*. Cambridge, MA: MIT Press, 2003.

INDEX

Note: figures are indicated by an f.

Sichanderswerden, 6. *See also* Self-othering
Sichverzehren, 51, 75, 90. *See also*
Self-devouring
Signification, resistance to, 3
Signifying function, 3
Signifying stress, 1–2, 3
Signorelli, 16, 102, 154n51, 154n52
Silence, 65
Silencing of language, 165n142
Silverman, Kaja, 161n75
Similarity disorder, 3–5, 16–17. *See also*
Olfactory anomia
Slips of the tongue. *See* Parapraxes
Smell-crumbs, 44–45, 46–47, 49, 52
Smith, Adam, 123, 125, 128
Smut, 99–100
Sniff-kiss, 63, 68, 98, 136, 139
Socialism, 181n57
Socrates, 20, 107, 151n23
"Song of Quoodle, The" (Chesterton), ix
Source-naming, 1–2, 4–5, 14, 16, 17–18, 23–24, 26, 29–30. *See also* Step-naming
Sovereignty, 153n42
Species, 26–27
Spinoza, 83, 85
Spirit, 36, 49, 51, 75, 82–83, 91, 116, 126
Spiritualism, 34
Steiner, Rudolf, 166n1, 172n85
Step-naming, 2–3, 4–5, 14, 16, 25–26. *See also* Source-naming
St. Joseph, 159–160n56
Structuralist structure, 113. *See also*
Hyperstructuralism
Subjectivity, 21–22
Submission, 88, 89
Suetonius, 126
Superstition, 34
Surplus-enjoyment, 95, 101, 102, 116, 120
Surplus-scarcity 71, 100, 116, 174n113
Surplus-value 100, 120–121, 139
Surrealism, 35
Surströmming, 101–102
Süskind, Patrick, 40–47, 49–51, 52–53, 54, 55, 57, 58–59, 60–61, 73–74
Suspicion, 48–49, 100
Swear words, 96–97, 99–100, 106, 126
Swedenborg, Emanuel, 35
Synesthetic borrowing, 2–3
Synthetic odor-compositions, 23

Taboo, 35, 101, 104–105, 106, 157n14, 175n121
Talking cure, 16
Taste
loss of, 53–54
names from, 2
as practical sense, 60–61
Tastelessness, 173–174n101. *See also Sensus decori*
Theoretical senses, 59, 61
Theosophical Society, 35–36, 172n85
Three Essays on the Theory of Sexuality (Freud), 98, 99, 104, 105, 119–120
Thus Spoke Zarathustra (Nietzsche), 169n43
Tip-of-the-tongue phenomena, 3
Titus, 126
Toilet culture, 172–173n92
Toilet training, 111, 119, 121, 124, 178n8
Tomšič, Samo, 171n80, 179–180n27
Totem and Taboo (Freud), 54, 103–104
Touch, 2, 60–61, 62, 97–98, 102–104, 105–106, 108–109, 115–116
Traces, 10–12, 20–21
Traumatism, 86–87
Treatise on Sensations (Condillac), 64–65
Trimethylamine, 79–80
Trimethylaminuria (fish odor syndrome), 80
Truth
as *adequatio*, 6, 112
Cartesian notion of, 84–85, 87
Lacan and, 81–82, 84, 87–88, 89
naming and, 6
theory of, 81–82, 83, 84
Tyche, 89–90

Unary signifiers, 18
Unbegriff, 87
Unbewusste, 170n57
Unconscious
concept of, 35
Real and, 85–86
timelessness and, 169n48
truth of, 82
Unheimliche, Das (Freud), 34
Unity of Being, 9, 18–19, 31, 152n27
University of Pennsylvania Smell
Identification Test (UPSIT), 13